MALPRACTICE
Risk Management for Dentists

MALPRACTICE

Risk Management for Dentists

Louis A. Ebersold, DDS, JD

PennWell Books
DENTAL
ECONOMICS
PennWell Publishing Company
Tulsa, Oklahoma USA

Copyright © 1986 by
PennWell Publishing Company
1421 South Sheridan Road/P.O. Box 1260
Tulsa, OK 74101

Library of Congress cataloging in publication data

Ebersold, Louis A.
    Malpractice: risk management for dentists

    Includes index.
    1. Dentists—Malpractice—United States.
I. Title. [DNLM: 1. Financial Management. 2. Malpractice.
3. Practice Management, Dental WU 44.1 E16m]
KF2910.D33E24   1986   346.7303'32   86-15138
    ISBN 0-87814-309-2   347.306332

Printed in the United States of America

1 2 3 4 5   90 89 88 87 86

Contents

Preface

At some time we've all said, "Tomorrow I'm going to get organized." Today, however, is the tomorrow of yesterday, and many of us are still looking for the time or inspiration to address some of those thankless tasks. Tax reports, writing a will, and drafting an office manual all come to mind. This book will not help with your 1040 form, and you really need a lawyer for your will, but what you learn here *will* make a good chapter on risk management in your office manual.

It doesn't matter whether you are a new or an established practitioner. If you have questions about any of the legal aspects of dental practice and want to avoid the possibility of a negligence lawsuit, the time you spend reading these chapters will give you both reassurances and guidelines.

The text is designed to help you establish communication and record-keeping systems that will assist you in preventing dental malpractice claims. That is accomplished largely by taking some of the mysteries out of the law.

The legal world is unfamiliar territory to most dentists, but don't forget that the maxillofacial area is similarly incomprehensible to the average lawyer as well as to the general public. From our own practices, we know we can help patients overcome their uncertainties about dental work by explaining and preparing—by laying good foundations. Once informed, patients often choose the most comprehensive care obtainable.

In the same way, this book will introduce the dentist to happenings in the legal world that affect the practice of dentistry. Armed with information about current standards, legal theories, and defenses, the reader can easily grasp the importance of preoperative discussions with patients, detailed record-keeping procedures, and postoperative follow-ups. All these areas have an immediate bearing on an unhappy patient's decision to sue—*and* on a lawyer's decision to take the case.

Suggestions are made for revamping your record-keeping procedures, and checklists are provided for selected topics. This material is calculated to help you organize and reorganize and, even more important, to help you meet the better-educated, more assertive, and less complacent dental patient of the 80s and 90s.

Why is this particular text so important? The steadily rising trend in health-care litigation is reason enough. Insurance premiums have leaped dramatically in recent years. Old-line insurance companies are leaving the field, and the future is uncertain and ominous. Various groups of physicians and dentists have created their own "mutual" companies, and some practitioners have made the reckless decision to "go bare." The word "crisis," though overused, seems increasingly appropriate.

There's truth in the old adage, "Forewarned is forearmed." The health practitioner who is practicing under outdated notions of legal and medical/dental standards is a **sitting duck.** Whatever the cause—either unreasonable expectations by patients or substandard care by dentists—a tidal wave of litigation is approaching dental offices. Unprepared and vulnerable dental-health professionals will be swept under at least once, and perhaps several times, during their careers. Only conscientious and informed practitioners will remain high and dry—and they will have done so by *being prepared.*

MALPRACTICE
Risk Management for Dentists

1
What Is Dental Malpractice?

Let's face it. Professional negligence can occur—perhaps not as often as some insurance executives would have us believe, but malpractice can, and does, happen. Little mistakes are made, small problems are glossed over, careful explanations are postponed, or an instrument slips. Murphy's Law applies.

Separating innocent mishaps from culpable malpractice is the job of the legal system. Until recently, treatment failures were written off as mishaps, but not anymore. These days, judges and juries are swinging toward the other end of the scale.

Dental malpractice is the common term used to describe a particular type of negligence—professional negligence involving a dentist. Even though there are other terms that identify the basic subject quite accurately—"professional liability" and "professional responsibility," for instance—"malpractice" is the word that sticks in the public's mind in regard to dental claims for injuries.

Dental malpractice is a civil offense. Civil lawsuits take place between individuals, as distinguished from criminal cases, which involve the state (through the district attorney or the attorney general) on one side, and the accused individual or individuals on the other.

Civil cases can be heard in either state or federal trial courts. The federal courts are used only in those malpractice cases in which the parties live or practice in more than one state.

1

Defending against a claim of dental malpractice *after* the legal papers have been filed is a problem of "doing the best with what you've got." If you believe the claim against you is unjust, your best defense lies in your own dental records. Your recollection of the incident or incidents that gave rise to the allegations is second best; it is never a good substitute for accurate and complete records.

If you have inadequate records and can't remember the specifics of the incident, your legal defense becomes extremely difficult. The best defense is a good offense; that means you should have enough information about the claim almost to prove that the situation described was not born of negligence, let alone malice or willful misconduct.

All persons practicing a profession are subject to *claims* arising out of their work, when the work falls short of the patient's or client's expectations. But to *prove* malpractice, the plaintiff or claimant (the person who brings the charge in civil court) has to establish the existence of four major elements in the case. If the plaintiff can offer proof in each of the four so-called *prima facie* elements, then and only then will a judge give a case to the jury for a verdict.

Dental Standards and the Elements of Professional Negligence

Because a plaintiff has to prove there is ample reason to hold a professional responsible, professionals are best prepared by knowing what is expected if a court scrutinizes their practice. *Preparing to defend against a dental malpractice case before the fact is far superior to an after-the-fact reaction. Know what's expected, then conduct your practice accordingly.*

The elements of professional negligence are as follows:

1. Establish a standard of care for the procedure involved.
2. Demonstrate how the standard was breached.
3. Establish a causal link between the injury claimed and the breach of standard.
4. Prove actual and permanent injury in monetary terms.

Standard of Care

It's easy to prove that there's a standard way to care for patients in any number of service specialties. The professions are essentially self-contained entities with the power to grant licenses to certain individuals who go to school, graduate, and then take a licensing exam. Relying on the tested principles of the educational community, the public can presume that there are certain minimal levels of competence for each and every diagnostic and treatment modality in each and every field of health care.

Example: Standards are found just about everywhere. Textbooks and treatises can provide clues, if not hard proof, about commonly accepted *correct* dental practices. The trouble with books, however, is that they eventually become obsolete. Courts have tried not to accept references to "book facts" alone because the authors are often not available to verify the facts as currently timely, or to state whether or not other practices would also be acceptable in the situation being examined.

The best evidence of standard practice is to ask a person with good credentials to appear at the trial or hearing and to instruct the court on current practice. Then both sides have the opportunity to ask questions of this "expert." Expert witnesses may, of course, refer to treatises in their presentation to establish or support their opinions on the appropriate standard of care.

Breach of Standard

Performing at a level *below* those minimal or standard diagnostic and treatment levels is a breach of the implied promise that every practitioner makes to the public. By presenting themselves to the public as professionals, practitioners promise to perform at or above the standard expectations of their peers.

Example: Breach of duty is the heart of malpractice. To offer proof of a breach of a professional duty, the plaintiff must find an "expert," someone equally qualified in dentistry, who will state that the actions of the involved dentist fell below the standard of care. Evidence in cases such as mismanagement of periodontal disease would require either another general dentist or a periodontist to look at the evidence (X-rays, medical and dental records, and patient history) and to come to the conclusion that the dentist involved failed (1) to diagnose in a timely manner, (2) to treat in an appropriate manner, or (3) to refer the patient when his or her treatment appeared unsuccessful.

Causal Link or Proximate Cause

Proof must also be presented to the court that the breach of some duty led directly to the injury about which the plaintiff is complaining. The legal community uses the word "proximate" in order to limit the possibility that something or someone else intervened between the breach of duty and the infliction of the injury.

Example: If a dentist, in treating a patient over a ten-year period, fails to take any diagnostic dental radiographs on a willing and cooperative patient in spite of ample clinical evidence of developing periodontal disease, that dentist would be practicing below the standard of care and in breach of his or her duty to use all diagnostic tools available. On the other hand, if the patient alleges that the actual injury is a chronically infected maxillary sinus, there is no malpractice case because no evidence is available to link the failure to diagnose the periodontal disease with the sinusitis.

In a 1985 Louisiana case, the required elements of dental malpractice were tested by a plaintiff who accused an orthodontist of negligence.[1] After undergoing two unsuccessful sessions of treatment, the plaintiff sought out a second orthodontist and a lawyer. At trial, however, the plaintiff failed to produce any expert testimony that the treatment was not only unsuccessful but also negligent.

The court then outlined the issues to which an expert witness must testify in order to establish negligence. First, the expert must establish the degree of knowledge or skill or the degree of care ordinarily exercised by dentists performing the same procedures. Second, the expert must show that the dentist either lacked the degree of knowledge or failed to use reasonable care and diligence, along with his or her best judgment. Finally, the court said that the expert must determine that the plaintiff suffered injury as a direct or proximate result of this lack of knowlege or failure to exercise care.

In this case, the plaintiff had no expert. The court dismissed the claim because it had no evidence of a standard of care, no evidence that the standard was breached, and no one who could link the plaintiff's injury to the orthodontist's actions or inactions.

Actual and Permanent Injury

Finally, a plaintiff must be able to provide proof that an injury has occurred and to place a dollar figure on the damage. Courts commonly accept evidence of injury from plaintiffs themselves with proof of paid medical bills from practitioners who followed the injury after the fact. These damages are called *special damages*, as they can be proved by outside sources with some particularity. The courts will also accept evidence of *general damages*; these are less certain, such as pain and suffering caused by or aggravated by the mishap. It is these so-called general damages that are subject to so much adverse criticism. Some states have enacted legislation to place arbitrary caps, maximum amounts that individuals can receive in general damages.

In many cases, the injury is clearly evident, as in tooth or bone loss as seen on serial radiographs. Most soft-tissue injuries in the mouth, however, leave little or no scar. (In order to establish some kind of "permanency" from soft-tissue injuries, the plaintiff often alleges a fear of going to the dentist as a result of the trauma.) At trial, the plaintiff would have a hard time proving permanency of injury unless he or she had visited another practitioner to have the wounds treated. In such an instance, the second dentist would be called as a witness to prove the existence of the injury. The second dentist's records and/or photographic evidence would be enough to prove actual damages.

At this point we have set the stage for a dental malpractice suit. We know what *theoretical legal* hurdles the plaintiff must cross. Now let's consider some of the *practical realities* involved.

A Step-by-Step Guide to Litigation

The stranger in the waiting room won't tell your staff what his business is, except that it's personal to you. He doesn't have an appointment and his name is unfamiliar. *Enter the private process server.*

The uniformed officer looms large in the small waiting room, which is usually half filled with dental patients. He or she waits patiently until the good doctor comes out to find out what's going on. *Behold the sheriff's deputy.*

In either case, the conversation is cryptic and to the point. "Are you Dr. A. B. Smith? If so, these papers are for you. Oh, by the way, do you have the correct time?"

You have just been served with process in a dental malpractice case. The bundle of papers you have received is the opening step in what will probably be a lengthy battle of wits and endurance.

In almost every state, the papers will contain two common elements. One is a *complaint* or *claim*, which identifies in summary form the allegations of the case. The other is a *summons*, or an order requiring you to file an answer to the allegations.

After you have composed yourself, read the allegations carefully, make a copy of the papers, and notify your insurance carrier by phone for further instructions.

Do not make any other contacts until you have spoken to your carrier or his agent. *Do not* add anything to the patient's record, no matter how important or helpful you think it will be. Most likely, the carrier will ask for a copy of your records and a letter explaining the treatment sequence chronologically. In addition, the carrier will want to be advised of any special communications with the complaining party and/or any practitioners who also saw or treated the patient during the time in question.

The carrier will assign the case to an adjuster. The adjuster's job is to investigate the claim, make a preliminary determination as to liability and, if necessary, assign the case to a law firm. If the adjuster feels that there is a strong case in favor of the dentist, or if the claimant wants an unrealistic amount of money to settle the case, the adjuster will turn the file over to a lawyer both to answer the charges and otherwise to defend the dentist.

You'll meet your insurer-provided lawyer sometime after that initial appraisal. At that point, these subjects need to be addressed:

1. The dentistry involved in the alleged incident needs to be explained to the lawyer in lay terms.
2. The dental records must be examined to determine whether they confirm or deny the allegations of the complaint.

3. The usual or standard procedure regarding the treatment you provided or failed to provide needs to be established.
4. Witnesses to the alleged negligence need to be identified.
5. It must be established whether or not you or any of your staff said anything to the claimant patient at or about the time of the incident to suggest fault on your part.
6. It must be determined whether or not you have done anything since the incident that might be construed as an admission of fault.

Since the complaint is usually only a summary of the allegations, the lawyer will want to know as many details as possible—everything you know about the plaintiff patient.

Your lawyer is looking for some item in the four elements of malpractice (described earlier) that will block this case from ever reaching a jury. What was the standard of care (duty)? Did a breach of that duty really take place, or was the whole problem a simple failure of treatment? Was the breach directly related to the damages? What, if anything, were the actual monetary damages?

After the initial interview, your lawyer will file an *answer* to the complaint unless he or she has spotted a technical error in the complaint, such as improper jurisdiction. Such an error will allow him to argue against one or all of the counts of negligence on a legal technicality.

The answer may be general in its contents, admitting some parts of the complaint and denying others. In addition, the answer may also allege one or both of two common and important defenses in dental cases: (1) failure of the plaintiff to file the suit before a legally permissible deadline (*statute of limitations*), and (2) alleging that the plaintiff contributed to his or her own injuries (*contributory negligence*).

After an answer has been filed, the court will typically set a date for a hearing or trial on the case, sometime well in the future. Federal courts are usually faster at setting a trial date, but you may still expect to spend considerable time waiting for your day in court. For this kind of case, waits of a year or more are common throughout the judicial system. During that period your lawyer may be busy with many cases, while you stay focused on this one event. You must stay calm and deal with events as they occur.

All states now permit both sides to collect information from many sources, concerning the circumstances surrounding the incident and everything that has happened to the claimant since the incident. This process is called *discovery*. Both state and federal courts permit a great deal of latitude in securing this kind of information, not all of which will be brought up in the trial.

Months may pass with no apparent change in the status of the case, but you should expect to make at least one major appearance before any trial or hearing. This is called an oral *deposition*. The sessions can be lengthy and exhausting; the claimant's lawyer will come prepared to ask a long list of probing questions concerning your care of the claimant and your practice in general. Everything is transcribed verbatim for use in the trial.

Conversely, your lawyer will be able to take the plaintiff's deposition. You may wish to be present to hear that person's allegations so that you can gain an understanding of the plaintiff's credibility and have early notice of any possibly untruthful statement.

Another form of discovery is a series of written questions given to you to answer and sign, which will also be used by the other side in trial. These questions, called *interrogatories*, are very often boilerplate material—standard questions—with a few original questions added that pertain especially to your case. (See Appendices A and B for comprehensive interrogatories.)

Pure Boilerplate

Name each and every continuing educational course of study you have attended in the past fifteen (15) years, and name the sponsoring institution or entity, the name of the speaker, and whether or not you received any credit for such course to be applied to the requirement for relicensure in this state.

Partial Boilerplate

When did you first examine Mrs. X and what was your diagnosis and treatment plan at that time?

No Boilerplate

Did you ever have a conversation with plaintiff and her husband on or about Labor Day, 1986, concerning the incidents? What was the subject and outcome of that conversation?

At some point before trial, the claimant will be required to name any expert witnesses he or she intends to introduce at trial. After they have been identified, your lawyer may well take a separate deposition of each expert. The object is to find out what the person has determined, and on what he or she bases his or her opinion. You may be present while that kind of deposition is being taken. You may be able to show your own attorney that the plaintiff's expert has not reviewed the whole record, or is making statements contrary to common understanding in the profession.

Finally, after discovery is complete, and possibly after one trial date has been postponed for one reason or another, you will have your day in court. Whether it is a hearing, as under some states' mandatory arbitration rules, or a full trial before a judge and jury, the plaintiff will be allowed to make all the statements and present all the testimony focusing on the four elements of professional negligence, as discussed earlier.

When the plaintiff is finished testifying and all the witnesses have come and gone, your attorney will make a perfunctory request, called a *motion to dismiss*: that even without considering the dentist's defense, the claimant has not made a case in dental malpractice.

The judge will then consider all the evidence he or she has heard thus far in a light most favorable to the plaintiff. If the judge feels that there is not enough evidence to convince a reasonable person that all four elements of the case have been proved, he or she may dismiss the case in your favor.

If, however, there is some evidence in the claimant's case, the judge must dismiss the motion and call on you to present your side of the story.

Now it's your turn to explain what really happened on the day in question, what your understanding of the appropriate standards are, and how you feel the injuries really occurred. You will be assisted by your own experts, who have been identified earlier and possibly deposed. You will be expected to be present during the entire proceedings, which might be as short as part of one day or as long as a week or more. At the close of the presentation of your witnesses and your evidence, each attorney will summarize the case, emphasizing the testimony favorable to his or her own client.

In a jury trial, the judge will then spend an hour or so telling the jury how to conduct their deliberations and what they must and must not consider regarding the evidence. After that the jury retires to reach a verdict.

After a jury verdict, the losing party can ask the judge to change the verdict if it is clearly erroneous. Failing that, the losing party can ask for a new trial. If *that* fails, the losing party can appeal the verdict to a higher court on technical grounds. The higher court will not listen to testimony nor second-guess the trial court. They will overturn the verdict if one or more technical errors were made that prejudiced the case substantially in the favor of one party or the other.

After appeal, a losing defendant must pay the judgment. If the losing party was an unsuccessful plaintiff, he or she must forget the claim forever. You only have one shot at a trial on the merits of a matter. In summary fashion, then, your day in court comes to an end.

Three Case Studies

Throughout this book, references will be made to one or more of the following case studies. These three cases exemplify a wide range of the problems involving dentistry that have come to the attention of the American legal system.

Plaintiffs have been successful in a significant number of the cases represented here. On the theory that it's better to study cases where liability has attached than where dentists have prevailed, these cases should help you prepare for the unexpected.

Case Study 1.

Undiagnosed Periodontal Disease: Supervised Neglect

The first of these scenarios involves periodontal disease. Statistics show that the alleged failure to diagnose this disease makes the top of the charts in dental malpractice. To a lawyer, the script reads like something out of Perry Mason. The emotional "victim" comes into the law office with a sad tale of trust and confidence gone awry.

"For x number of years, I went to good old Dr. Trustee, and he never said anything about gum disease. He never told me I had a problem, and he never sent me to see anybody about it."

Fill in any large number for x. The so-called victim will go on to tell the lawyer about the circumstances that led to the "revelation"—the discovery of the periodontal disease. Two common versions go like this:

Version A: While Dr. Trustee was away on vacation, Mrs. V (for victim) chipped a tooth and sought out her neighbor's dentist for some fast and temporary service "till the doc gets back." Dr. Temporary, the man who is taking calls for Dr. Trustee, casually remarks, "I see you have periodontal disease." Or he might be a little more tactful and say, "You'd better get in to see Dr. Trustee to have a look at your gums." Or he might say, "I can put a temporary filling in, but this tooth is loose and you may have to have it extracted."

These, of course, are "revelations" to the patient. Dr. Trustee had never mentioned the problems that Dr. Temporary has found. Mrs. V will now either call Dr. Trustee when he gets back, or she will call her lawyer.

Version B: Mrs. V, a long-term patient of Dr. Trustee, moves out of town and consults a new dentist in her new community. Dr. Newtown examines her mouth and teeth. He makes enough initial findings to warrant a referral to a periodontist because of what he describes as "a relatively advanced case of periodontal disease," but he makes no critical remarks of anything or anyone. When she is seen in Dr. Gardner's periodontal office, Mrs. V asks a number of questions: "What needs to be done? How long will it take? How much will it cost? How much pain or time off from work am I likely to encounter?" The periodontist, Dr. Gardner, fields each question with ready information, describing the services and the prognosis in careful detail.

Then Mrs. V asks the hard questions: "How long have I had periodontal disease? Is it something that just springs up overnight?" Dr. Gardner gives the usual scientific answers about the chronicity and progression of the disease.

Finally, Mrs. V asks the big one: "Shouldn't my old dentist, Dr. Trustee, have said something about this to me a number of years ago?" Dr. Gardner may not be able to handle this question with grace and diplomacy. After all, he only has his new patient's word about her regularity at Dr. Trustee's office. Dr. Gardner doesn't know whether Dr. Trustee had said anything to Mrs. V about periodontal disease during that period of time.

Still, Dr. Gardner can, and often does, answer the question on the assumption that Mrs. V's version of the story is true, honest, and accurate. Basically, he will acknowledge that if Mrs. V visited Dr. Trustee's office every six months for the past ten years, never refused any diagnostic X-rays, and followed Dr. Trustee's advice about home care, and if Dr. Trustee never mentioned periodontal disease to her and never discussed a referral to a periodontist for further workup or diagnosis, then Dr. Trustee *failed to live up to dental standards*. He blew it. He failed to diagnose and/or refer Mrs. V for definitive periodontal treatment.

Dr. Gardner doesn't give in easily. He usually offers such an opinion only under pressure. In another climate and another society, his job would be one of pure service only. Today, however, in answer to questions posed by anxious patients, Dr. Gardner is becoming a source of opinion, and that generally means bad news for Dr. Trustee. Given another set of facts from Dr. Trustee, Dr. Gardner might come to an altogether different conclusion, but in this particular situation, he is limited to what he hears from the patient.

Case Study 2.

Premature Crown and Bridge Failure: Pathetic Prosthesis

The second scenario involves crown and bridge—lots and lots of crown and bridge. Mr. Newvo is an executive on the way up. He has a steady job, a new family, and bright prospects. It hasn't always been easy for Newvo, and he has accumulated a fair number of debts. His financial problems have forced him to postpone some health-care services, including work on his teeth.

Now, however, he sees his teeth as holding him back. He earnestly wants to advance in his career, and he blames his slow progress on his gap-toothed smile.

In consultation with Dr. Swifty, Newvo learns that it's possible to correct this unattractive smile and at the same time add years to the strength and utility of his tooth. "By golly," he says, "maybe the doctor is right. Maybe I should invest in myself and get a full set of new caps"—all with low, low monthly payments.

Newvo's company insurance plan helps, but after the deductible and the difference between Dr. Swifty's fee and the scheduled fee, the plan covers only 50% of the balance. Newvo still commits himself to a hefty bundle; he has seen the light and the word, and the word is "porcelain." With the treatment plan he has agreed to, Newvo has single-handedly created work for a whole platoon of dental technicians.

Work begins immediately. All twenty teeth are prepared and temporized one Monday morning. Things do not go smoothly, though. First Newvo loses one temporary while out of town. Then several of the teeth become extremely sensitive to cold. Swifty starts one root canal and then another until Newvo is relieved, but only for a short time.

After all the units are cemented, Newvo complains of continued sensitivity and a hard-to-explain feeling of discomfort with the new caps. Swifty makes innumerable occlusal adjustments (grinds the bite). Soon, and somewhat predictably, pieces of porcelain begin to crack away from the underlying metal of the bridgework.

Understandably, Newvo falls behind in his monthly payments, and Swifty's staff begins to stick little messages on the monthly bills. Newvo isn't happy, and neither is Swifty. Newvo doesn't have the new look and feel he expected, and Swifty doesn't have the cash *he* expected.

Newvo stays away from all dentists for a year or more before seeking a new dentist. When a number of units fall out at the company New Year's party, Dr. Secondhand agrees to see Newvo on an emergency basis.

Dr. Secondhand takes one look and knows there's trouble ahead. He sees grossly heavy crown margins and damage to the periodontal tissues. He sees peeled porcelain on units that are finally cemented. He sees an occlusal plane prepared and adjusted in consultation with the village smithy. It's not as if the work is twenty years old, either—it's more like twenty *months*.

Dr. Secondhand recommends that Newvo see a periodontist, and also mentions that the full series of crowns needs to be redone. Newvo is steamed! His insurance will not help on the second series, and Secondhand's fees are even higher than Swifty's.

When Swifty is contacted, he says, "I haven't seen the guy in over a year. How am I supposed to know what's happened to my work in that time? Newvo abandoned me. I told him I'd take care of everything, but he never came back. The gum problem is his fault, not mine. Also, I heard he got in a barroom fight. That accounts for the broken porcelain. Besides, he owes me big bucks."

A variation of this tale, on a slightly different scale, results from overzealous collection efforts. Swifty sends Newvo to Collection. Collection tries the standard procedures, then hires an attorney, who files suit. Newvo asks his company attorney to recommend a trial lawyer, and after talking to Dr. Secondhand, that lawyer files a counterclaim for negligence. Bingo!

Case Study 3.

Oral Surgery Mishaps:
"Oops, Wasn't That the Lingual Nerve?"

The third example involves surgical complications. Out-of-control pre- and postoperative infections are the most serious of the reported cases, but postoperative nerve damage is close behind.

The average case involves the ubiquitous "wisdom tooth." Here, a lower third molar is the subject of a number of bizarre complications that end up as causes of litigation.

Dr. Newon Block is a recent graduate with a hitch in the service or a residency under his belt. The setting could be a clinic, a private office, a storefront, or anywhere else. The patient, a slightly overweight female, comes in with pain in her face and jaw. She cannot open her mouth very wide and couldn't sleep last night. Ms. Totally Innocent is aided and comforted on her trip to the dentist by her live-in boyfriend, a night-school law student.

Dr. Block tries to take a periapical X-ray, but cannot because of the trismus and swelling. He elects to place the patient on antibiotics, and writes a prescription for 250 mg. generic penicillin V. He gives Totally an appointment to have the tooth X-rayed and removed three days later.

Two days later, Newon gets a phone call from the boy-friend. He's calling from Totally's hospital room, where she has just undergone an emergency tracheotomy. Apparently the antibiotics were either not taken, were not effective, or were too little, too late. Totally is diagnosed as suffering from a cellulitis resulting from tooth infection.

As a variation on this initial set of facts, Dr. Newon Block gets lucky and does see Totally three days later. At that appointment, he attempts to remove the offending tooth and the contralateral tooth (the same tooth on the opposite side of the mouth) "as a preventive measure." During the attempt to extract the nonsymptomatic tooth, the lingual nerve is stretched, separated, or severed. The patient is left with a sensory deficit on the portion of the tongue supplied by that nerve.

The dentist did not mention the possibility of any nerve damage. He relied on the extremely small possibility that this adverse side effect would ever occur.

The patient, however, makes her living as a wine taster, a fact known to Dr. Block because she had written it down on his new-patient registration form. She thinks she deserves some sort of special consideration because of the nature of her work, and because the possibility of lingual nerve damage during third-molar removal is well known to the dental profession. She may be right!

Purpose of the Case Studies

These three slightly bizarre fact patterns and the varia-tions in each case were scripted carefully, and contain the elements of negligence found in the majority of dental mal-practice claims. With the admonition that "forewarned is forearmed," we shall use these situations to see how minor problems and accidents can turn into major problems and malpractice awards. After studying several cases and learning how plaintiffs can use the legal system to their advantage, practitioners will know how to head off many problems before they arise.

Reference: Dental Malpractice

1. Gurdin v. Dongieux 468 So.2d 1241 (La. App. 4 Cir. 1985).

2
Legal Defenses to Dental Malpractice

The decision to defend or to settle a dental malpractice suit depends on many factors. Attorneys for both sides weigh the strengths and weaknesses of each individual case, and then a decision is made either to seek a settlement or to "fight all the way to the Supreme Court."

An attorney representing the defendant dentist may consider a number of *legal* defenses. The defense can be statutory, such as the *statute of limitations;* or it can simply be a common-law development, such as *contributory negligence.* The statute of limitations requires a plaintiff to file for redress within a designated period of time after the alleged incident. Contributory negligence is a way to shift the burden of fault partially back to the plaintiff.

Statutory rules come from the legislative process. Each state's statutes are developed during the annual legislative session, and these rules are subject to change or "tinkering" over the years. As each statute is tested in courtroom situations, exceptions arise, which then become the basis for subsequent legislative alteration.

Common-law rules, on the other hand, come strictly from court decisions. They do not usually become a part of the statutes unless, as in some states, the common-law rule is adopted by the state legislature and then included in the statutory code.

Contributory negligence and statute of limitations (failure to file a lawsuit before the statutory time period runs out) are the two most popular legal defenses available to defendants in a dental malpractice suit. Other legal defenses include failure to state a claim upon which relief can be granted, assumption of the risk of injury, and—most common of all—simple denial. Denial means that the defendant did not breach the standard of care as alleged.

In addition, there are dozens of procedural defenses that can be thrown up before a court will hear the case. These are the so-called "technicalities" of the law, the parts that gain all the notoriety. When you hear that a case was "thrown out on a technicality," it simply means that the judge felt the plaintiff had failed to cover one or more procedural points in the lawsuit.

If any procedural problems arise—such as naming the wrong defendant, failure to serve process on the correct defendant, or suing in the wrong court—and the plaintiff is unable to convince the court that the case is a permissible exception to the rule, the dental malpractice case can be dismissed, usually "without prejudice." This term means that the case is dismissed temporarily. Such cases may later be revived or refiled either in another court or in the same court; presumably they have been reworded to conform with correct procedure.

As a defendant in a case being dismissed because of procedural error, the dentist should ask his or her attorney if the case could be dismissed *with* prejudice. That wording acts to bar the plaintiff from refiling or going to another court on the same set of facts. This move, of course, will not bar the plaintiff from filing an appeal to a higher court in the same jurisdiction. Dismissal with prejudice prohibits the plaintiff from repeating the same charges at the trial level of the system.

Contributory Negligence

The rules for contributory negligence require a *patient* to use such care as the so-called "reasonable man" would ordinarily use in similar circumstances. If he or she has failed to do so, the plaintiff cannot hold the dentist responsible for the consequences of his or her own want of ordinary care.

It all boils down to this: if a patient is negligent, he or she cannot prevail. The patient's own negligence prevents him or her from blaming the dentist for the original negligence. That's the *theoretical* basis for contributory negligence—a total bar to recovery against patients whose behavior contributed to their own injuries. This rule can be a major benefit in allegations of failure to diagnose and treat periodontal disease, where some proof exists that the patient was contributing to the disease state by failing to maintain good oral health habits.

Some states have enacted statutes to eliminate the harshness of the contributory negligence penalty when a patient is *slightly* at fault and the dentist is *significantly* negligent. Those states operate under a system of *comparative* negligence. In such instances, the mere fact of evidence of contributory negligence on the plaintiff's part will not bar some recovery in a dental malpractice case.

As an example, suppose a dentist has a patient who requires an extraction. The dentist removes the tooth without taking an X-ray, dispenses a handful of antibiotic tablets without identifying the drug, and offers no further explanation to the patient as to follow-up care. The dentist then locks his office door and leaves town for a week's vacation, without having made any arrangements for emergency coverage.

Suppose further that the patient develops a postoperative soreness and progressive swelling in the first days after the extraction and tries, without success, to find the dentist. Believing that the problem is only temporary and self-limiting, the patient makes no attempt to find another dentist, preferring to await the return of the regular doctor. The patient's condition deteriorates, and concerned family members encourage him or her to seek help at a hospital emergency room. The patient goes to the ER, but not in time to avoid a tracheotomy and multiple intra- and extraoral incision and drainage sites, a multiday hospital confinement, and the administration of massive doses of sophisticated antibiotics.

The admission diagnosis? Cellulitis secondary to tooth extraction. Hospital dental and oral surgery staff find a raging head and neck infection, a retained root tip in the extraction site, and a fracture of the mandible.

On the other side of the coin, the patient took only a few of the antibiotic pills that were dispensed by the defendant dentist. The patient remembers and readily admits knowing that the pills were antibiotics, and that the instructions were to take them all.

Ultimately the facts will show that the dentist was potentially negligent on a number of counts: failure to take a preoperative dental X-ray; failure to note that a root tip remained in the extraction site (or, alternatively, knowledge of the retained root tip, but failure to tell the patient that it remained in the jaw); failure to refer the patient to someone to remove the root tip; failure to administer, dispense, or prescribe sufficient antibiotics and/or instructions for follow-up care; and finally, failure to make arrangements for emergency office coverage (abandonment).

Don't forget, however, that the patient was at fault for not taking all the medicine as advised by the dentist, and possibly for not contacting another dentist, a physician, or a hospital sooner.

Even though some contributory fault is present, the balance is clearly in favor of the patient in this hypothetical example.

In *comparative*-negligence states, the courts are free to find for the patient, but reduce the monetary award by the amount of comparative negligence they find on the plaintiff's part. That can be done on a percentage basis: if the jury finds the dentist liable and awards the plaintiff $10,000 but finds the patient ten percent (10%) negligent by comparison, they can reduce the damage award by 10% and award only $9,000.

States that still operate under strict contributory negligence are notorious for bending over backward to avoid the harsh result of dismissal in cases of negligence on the part of both parties. This is true especially when the defendant's original negligence was severe and the contributory negligence was minor. In those states, however, the jury must still be instructed that if they find any contributory negligence on the part of the patient, they may not award the plaintiff any damages.

The law makes a distinction between contributory negligence that occurs at the same time as the defendant's original negligence and that which follows the defendant's negligence. To constitute a complete bar to recovery, the contributory negligence must have been an *active* and *efficient* contributing cause of the injury. Further, it must have been simultaneous and cooperating with the negligence of the defendant.

Thus the contributory negligence of the patient which is *subsequent* to the negligence of the dentist and which serves *to aggravate* the injury inflicted by the dentist acts only to affect the amount of damages recoverable by the patient. In the example cited above, the contributing negligence followed the original negligence and aggravated the injury. In a pure test of this principle, the defendant would contend that the failure to take the medication as instructed was the *sole* cause of the developing cellulitis.

Acts or omissions by the patient *during* treatment have been distinguished from those occurring *after* treatment. Many dentists may wonder about the helpfulness of the defense that the patient moved during treatment and contributed thereby to the injury. Other dentists might like the answer to the question: "Isn't it possible that the patient's sudden and unexpected jerking during the procedure was actually the *original* negligence, and not just a contributing factor?"

On both counts the courts have been very tough on the dentist, ruling more often than not that the ultimate responsibility was the dentist's. In an early case, the court summarized as follows:

...the electrically operated revolving disk that a dentist was using to polish a bridge he was fitting to plaintiff's teeth slipped and cut the flesh at the base of the tongue, and defendant attempted to account for the infliction of the wound by testifying that plaintiff voluntarily jerked her head causing the disk to break and throwing the jagged revolving part against the tissues beneath the tongue, but plaintiff denied that she moved, and the jury found that the dentist's negligence caused the injury.[1]

The court allowed the jury to decide between the conflicting stories. The jury found for the plaintiff and that the plaintiff was free of any contributory negligence.

Another scenario that is familiar to a number of dentists, not all of whom have been sued, goes something like this:

> Doctor warns patient that there would be a slight pain as the needle was inserted and that the patient should stay still as possible. In spite of the warning, when the needle was inserted, the patient jerked his head in such a violent manner as to cause it to break...[2]

The "broken needle" and the "broken disk" cases are essentially the same: the dentist claims that the patient's movement was the sole cause of the injury in each case, and the plaintiff claims that he or she did not move. In both cases, juries believed the patient; therefore the injury occurred without any voluntary action on plantiff's part at the time. The behavior of the patient is a question of fact, and the jury is free to believe or disbelieve the patient's version.

Patient's Home Care as Contributory Negligence

In a 1958 New York case, the guidelines for contributory negligence were outlined in a decision involving ill-fitting crown and bridgework.[3] The court in that case felt that the plaintiff presented enough evidence of reasonable behavior to overcome the defense of contributory negligence. The judge pointed out in the decision that the plaintiff appeared to have done nothing to bring about the condition of her mouth.

The patient alleged that the dentist's departure from standard dental methods was negligence, which proximately caused the abscesses and rampant decay found around her bridgework. The plaintiff also alleged that the condition would not be present in whole or in part except for the defendant's improper fitting of crowns and jackets in an attempt to correct her bite.

The following questions identify concerns which, if answered in the negative, will dispel the charge of contributory negligence.

> Did the plaintiff exercise reasonable care commensurate with the circumstances?
> Did the plaintiff keep his or her mouth hygienically clean?

Was the plaintiff cooperative with the defendant?
Did the plaintiff report his or her complaints to the dentist as soon as they occurred?
Did the plaintiff have reason to rely exclusively on the defendant's professional skill and knowledge?

Finally, suppose the plaintiff does not permit the defendant to complete a procedure. Does that amount to contributory negligence? The question has not been answered squarely on that point in a modern dental malpractice case, but in an early case involving an extraction, a dentist had removed the crown and most of the root, and was about to remove two remaining root tips, when the patient decided to take a walk.[4] The patient had asked what the dentist was getting ready to do. When the dentist mentioned the root tips, the patient said, "No, thanks," and ran for the exit.

In a subsequent lawsuit, the dentist defended by stating the facts as described above, and added that he had warned the patient that it was risky to leave before the procedure was finished. The defense argued that to perform the standard and acceptable levels of dental treatment, the dentist required only a minimum amount of cooperation from the patient— which he never received. Without that cooperation, the dentist felt that the "fault" was the patient's.

The court's final decision is not available because the question raised in the appeal of the case concerned a procedural point. Since the dentist brought the appeal, however, it is reasonable to assume that he lost at the lower trial level. The case on appeal was whether or not the jury had been properly instructed to stick to a strong contributory-negligence standard. The court of appeal felt that the jury had been adequately instructed.

On the basis of the allegation that the patient left before treatment was completed, the court instructed the jury to consider the following: whether the cause of the injury was the result of the plaintiff's negligence or indiscretions, or of his refusal to follow the defendant's advice or to permit the defendant to complete the operation that he had commenced. If so, there could be no recovery for the plaintiff.

Given the instruction, the jury apparently found the plaintiff's story more believable than the defendant's and returned a verdict against the defendant dentist. What is the moral of the story? *Do not rely on contributory or comparative negligence in an action in dental malpractice!* Even though the theoretical protection of the law exists, courts and juries give only lip service to this historical defense mechanism—at least when it is called into use for cases where the patient's negligence corresponds in time to the acts of the defendant dentist.

On the other hand, what are the chances of prevailing on the question of contributory negligence if the acts constituting the defense occurred *after* the dental treatment? Sad to say, they're not much better.

As every dentist knows, failing to follow post-treatment advice, prescriptions, or instructions can seriously jeopardize a case. Such matters as self-care, home treatment, and returning for further examination and treatment can often determine success or failure.

This is a sample postoperative contributory-negligence instruction to the jury in a dental malpractice case: "It is the duty of a patient to conform reasonably to the necessary prescriptions and treatment and to follow reasonable and proper instructions given, and that failure to do so which directly and materially contributes to his injury will prevent a recovery in malpractice."

This instruction to the jury, used in a 1930 Connecticut case, followed testimony that the dentist was negligent in his care of the patient, but, on the other hand, that the patient did not conform to a "reasonable man" profile and thus contributed to his own injury.[5] In a 1933 Kentucky case on the allegation that the plaintiff was in pain immediately after an extraction but did not return to the dentist until four days after the extraction, the court found that the patient was not entitled to relief.[6] An instruction similar to the Connecticut case was used and the jury found for the defendant dentist.

In a 1984 case involving an Indian Health Service dentist, the lower court viewed a patient's missed appointments as evidence of contributory negligence.[7] In that case, a dentist had performed initial root canal procedures for the patient. A temporary filling was placed, and the patient was reappointed for placement of a permanent root canal filling at the next visit.

The patient failed to make the appointment and did not reappear for some three months. At that time, the dentist proceeded with treatment and placed the root canal sealer. The next day, the patient began to experience pain and swelling, and eventually required hospitalization.

At trial of the dental malpractice suit, the lower court viewed the missed appointments as evidence of contributory negligence, and decided the case in favor of the dentist. On appeal, however, the higher court focused its attention on the dentist's performance after the patient returned. It noted that reasonable care by the dentist would require him, among other things, "to wash canals with sodium hypochlorite" before placing the final root canal filling. The case was returned to the lower court for a new trial.

Case Study 1.

Undiagnosed Periodontal Disease: The Effect of Contributory Negligence

Was Mrs. V guilty of contributory negligence? This case study is a perfect example of the potential use of the theory of contributory negligence. Practicing dentists know the treatment of periodontal disease, and the outcome of treatment is totally dependent on patient cooperation. It doesn't take long to reduce a surgical masterpiece to rubbish in the mouth of a poor brusher.

The case study involving Mrs. V presented the allegation that Dr. Trustee failed to diagnose and treat periodontal disease over a number of years. Dr. Trustee will answer by describing his efforts over the years to improve Mrs. V's dental IQ. He will state his defense in one of two predictable ways.

First, Dr. Trustee will say that Mrs. V *did* have periodontal disease. He detected its presence and brought it to Mrs. V's attention. He also provided repeated home-care instruction and monitored her progress. Noting no progress, he reminded her again of the disease state and its implications for the future, but he saw no measurable improvement in her home health-care routine. Finally, Dr. Trustee's treatment lapsed into a "better than nothing" series of recall visits, where conservative cleanings were provided with the expectation that eventually the periodontally nonrestorable teeth would require extraction.

Second, Dr. Trustee might take the alternative approach by alleging that Mrs. V *did not* have periodontal disease during most of the time that he was responsible for her care. If nothing more, his skimpy records of six-month recall treatment prove that she did not have the disease for the greater part of that time. If there was evidence of periodontal disease, he would have referred her for treatment or seen her more frequently. He's not even sure that there's any disease at this time, either. After all, he hasn't seen Mrs. V for some time, and anything could have happened that he is not aware of— nor should he be!

As you can see, the first alternative, admitting the presence of periodontal disease over the years, relies heavily on the theory of contributory negligence. Dr. Trustee admits to no negligence, but alleges in defense that Mrs. V's own lack of home care was responsible for the continued development of the disease. His diagnosis and treatment were conditioned on the cooperation of the patient. Without that cooperation, he was prohibited from performing surgical treatment that would, in his judgment, be prone to failure.

Failure of surgical procedures is common if the home-care habits are not under control before initiation of treatment. With this in mind, Dr. Trustee's responsibility ends with identifying and transmitting choices to the patient. If the patient knowingly chooses the alternative that will permit the disease gradually to destroy the bony support for the teeth, the defense of contributory negligence is perfectly suitable.

Contributory negligence then becomes a matter of proof. If Dr. Trustee wishes to use contributory negligence as a defense, he must have some evidence of all the features he claims were provided to Mrs. V. His word that discussions took place may not be enough to convince the court. He needs to produce notations of the results of clinical diagnostic findings, appropriate X-rays, and perhaps notes of specific warnings to the patient. Better yet would be a carbon copy of a letter to the patient, containing the results of diagnostic tests, the alternative treatment plans, and/or the recommendation to have a second opinion—from a specialist. Such a letter would make excellent evidence supporting the defense.

The second alternative, denying the presence of disease over the years, resembles the "stonewall" defense of Watergate. It didn't work there and it probably won't work here. Such a defense can work only if Dr. Trustee's records contain evidence to support his story. Dental X-rays taken at frequent intervals, for instance, which show no change in periodontal bone characteristics, would be greatly helpful. Similarly helpful would be records of periodontal probe examinations that found no pocket depths greater than two or three millimeters anywhere in the mouth, or frequent screenings of key teeth that revealed no evidence of pocket formation, mobility, hemorrhage, or changes in color or texture. Such records would be excellent evidence for the defense. Without such record evidence, it is almost impossible to recreate information from past incidents and conversations with any kind of credibility.

Case Study 2.

Premature Crown and Bridge Failure: The Effect of Contributory Negligence

Dr. Swifty has been accused of low-quality dental work in the preparation and placement of multiple units of fixed crown and bridgework. Specifically, the patient, Mr. Newvo, has heard from Dr. Secondhand that the recently placed bridgework needs to be removed and done over. Ultimately the work will be criticized for faulty marginal adaptation, improper contours on crown surfaces, improper occlusion, and faulty porcelain application. Further, the teeth were overprepared, resulting in several instances of pulpal pathology.

How much of this was Mr. Newvo's fault? If we go back to the simple definition of contributory negligence, the questions to be answered are quite simple. Did Newvo cooperate, keep his mouth clean, report symptoms in a timely manner, and make himself available for treatment? For the sake of argument, let's say that Newvo was fully cooperative and an absolute gem in the brushing department. Let's also say that he mentioned early signs of problems to Swifty whenever they appeared. Finally, let's say that Newvo quit his job for six months so that he could drop into Swifty's office whenever it was necessary. You couldn't ask for a more cooperative patient.

What can Swifty say in relation to contributory negligence? This may be grasping at straws, but he has evidence that Newvo got into a fight at a local saloon. Could it be that a sharp blow to the mouth was responsible for the chipped and peeled porcelain? It's highly possible, but no amount of barroom battling could have created the defective crown margins, poor contours, and improper occlusion.

Contributory negligence offers little in the way of defensive comfort to Dr. Swifty. The defendant dentist's lawyer may allege the defense of contributory negligence not as a complete bar to Newvo's recovery, but as additional evidence that could cloud the issue of damages.

If the case had been in Newvo's mouth for several years, and if it was alleged that dental caries existed at the margins of the bridgework, *then* the possibility exists that the patient's oral hygiene permitted conditions to deteriorate and break down. With the facts as presented, however—the case is less than two years old—Swifty will have to defend on other grounds.

Case Study 3.

Oral Surgery Mishaps:
The Effect of Contributory Negligence

In this case Dr. Newon Block is confronted with a facial swelling and trismus, and elects to postpone treatment and/or referral to an oral surgeon. Two days later, the patient is in the hospital with a cellulitis.

What contributory negligence is present here? Dr. Block will have to spend some time in discovering whether the hapless patient took the medication, and took it according to instructions, but the greatest possibility revolves around whether or not the patient tried to communicate with Dr. Block when it appeared that things were getting worse. If Dr. Block was unaware that conditions were deteriorating, he couldn't be expected to intervene.

The patient's side of the story concerns her reliance on Dr. Block's assurances that "everything would be just fine" when she returned in three days. Did she rely justifiably on Dr. Block's words? Did she have reason to believe that the medication would eventually "take" and give her relief? These questions would be asked and answered in front of a jury, and the jury would be free to believe either side. The judge would instruct the jury at the conclusion of the evidentiary portion of the trial that the patient had the responsibility to act as a reasonable person, to cooperate with the dentist, and to report symptoms to him promptly.

It is within the realm of reason to believe that the patient acted reasonably, even though she did not contact Dr. Block. A party may seek alternative treatment (in this case, the hospital) when he or she feels that the treatment he or she is receiving is not effective. It is reasonable to go to an emergency room when treatment appears to be failing and serious illness is imminent.

Dr. Block will raise the issue of contributory negligence in order to find out whether the medication was taken properly and to test the "failure to cooperate" theory, since the patient did not contact Dr. Block when conditions worsened. Under the circumstances, this approach appears to present Dr. Block with a substantial defense, but nothing is guaranteed.

Statute of Limitations

The statute of limitations determines the length of time in which a person may bring a suit for damages. The appropriate limitations period varies from state to state, and can vary within a jurisdiction, depending on what theory of negligence is used. If the allegation of failure to provide informed consent is used, for instance, and if the jurisdiction bases this action on the old *battery* theory, then typically a shorter time period is used to limit recovery. If the action is based on the breach of an express warranty, such as when a dentist guarantees patient satisfaction with anterior crown work, then the statute of limitations is based on the typically longer *contract* statute of limitations. Such warranty cases usually require an express statement or a promise to apply the longer statute.

In cases where the incident results in immediate and obvious damage and injury, the statute begins to run from the date of the incident. Two examples are extracting the wrong tooth and instrument slippage with resulting soft-tissue injury.

Other cases, however, involve negligence which remains unknown to the patient. In such cases, the patient plaintiff may not be aware of the potential claim until the statute of limitations has passed. In recent years, the courts' interpretation of such statutes in malpractice cases has treated plaintiffs very favorably. Courts want to avoid the hardship of losing the right to sue because of the inability to bring the claim before the running of the statute. They will extend the period in such cases to a specified period following the discovery, or to the time when the patient should have discovered the injury and its negligent cause. In many cases, this can delay indefinitely the period of time required to file a claim.

In a 1980 Mississippi case, the courts extended "discovery" to some point after the patient knew of a lower-lip numbness following an extraction.[8] The court did not put an exact time on the extension, but placed it at least two weeks after the dentist had reassured the patient that the numbness was temporary.

Not all states begin the running of the time period with the "discovery" date. In a few cases, the state has adopted a slightly longer period to file the action. If the average discovery period is three years in most states with discovery extension, the nondiscovery states will adopt a strict four-year limit starting from the date of the incident.

An exception to the rule occurs when a patient is under the continuous treatment of the defendant for a period of time after the incident. If the actual injury occurred in year X, but the patient stayed in the practice of Dr. Y for four years and wasn't aware of the malpractice, the statute would not begin until the patient left the practice. The rule also requires that to invoke the "continuous treatment" extension, the patient must be under treatment for the same disease, injury, or occurrence. In a 1985 periodontal case, the patient was allowed to consider each routine recall visit as "a separate opportunity to discover periodontal problems."[9]

One state, Michigan, has gone so far as to consider a telephone call that took place after the last treatment visit as the starting point for the statute.[10] In a 1984 third-molar extraction/paresthesia case which depended totally on the strict interpretation of the statute, an Idaho court decided that the time period started on *the day of the incident,* not the day when the patient returned to have stitches removed.[11]

In addition, if one Michigan practitioner refers the patient to another, and makes arrangement to pay for the second dentist's treatment at his or her own expense, the statute does not begin to run against the first dentist until the treatment is finished in the office of the referral dentist.[12]

Finally, the statute will be *tolled* (temporarily but deliberately stopped) if any evidence can be proved that the dentist concealed information or otherwise led the patient to believe that no negligence or malpractice had occurred. (See Chapter Ten, "Guarantees, Warranties, Contracts, and Fraud.")

If the patient is a minor child, the statute is usually tolled until the minor reaches the age of majority plus two or three years, depending on the jurisdiction.

A final exception is found in the rare case when the plaintiff knew of the injury, but did not know that the injury was caused by negligence. It has been argued successfully that mere knowledge of the injury does not automatically start the statutory time period. The starting gun is fired when the patient knows of the injury and is aware that the cause was professional negligence.

An unusual 1982 dental case in Tennessee illustrates this point.[13] This case involved contraction of hepatitis by a dental patient. The dentist had hepatitis, and he simultaneously lacerated his finger and the patient's lip, causing their blood to intermingle. The court said that the patient's right to take action against the responsible party accrued not simply when he discovered that he had contracted the disease, but when he discovered the occasion, manner, and means by which the breach of duty occurred that produced the injury. In addition, time starts when all the above elements and the identity of the defendant who breached the duty become known.

All the above exceptions are in the patient's favor when it comes to deciding the exact starting time. Thus it may not help you to count a simple two or three years from the date of an incident before breathing a sigh of relief. In order to take advantage of the rule, you should tell the patient what has happened if it is not clear from the circumstances. No effort should be made to minimize or conceal information. All dental records and X-rays on problem cases or known injury cases should be maintained indefinitely in order to assist in your defense at a potential trial, which might not come until years after the "statute" has expired by your way of counting.

Case Study 1.

Undiagnosed Periodontal Disease: The Effect of The Statute of Limitations

This case presents an exception to the rule of limitation of dental malpractice cases. As you will recall, this case involves the scenario of a patient in a practice for a number of years, for whom no diagnosis of periodontal disease was made. The discovery comes in another dentist's office, and the patient asks, "When did I first have the disease?" The records maintained by Dr. Trustee may reveal the signs of the disease in X-rays taken in the early years of treatment. Can Dr. Trustee then depend on an early sign of the disease to start the running of the statute of limitations? Not usually. Two exceptions to the standard rule, namely *discovery* and *continuous treatment,* will act to lengthen the period for the plaintiff.

Discovery takes place in the office of Dr. Gardner. Typically, the plaintiff will have the statutory period to bring a claim from the date of discovery. If the state doesn't permit the discovery extension, the date for the start of the statutory period will most likely be the last date of treatment in a continuous series of visits in Dr. Trustee's office.

Case Study 2.

Premature Crown and Bridge Failure: The Effect of Statute of Limitations

Discovery in this case takes place simultaneously with the end of treatment and with the adjustment series of visits following placement of the bridgework. As in the Tennessee case described earlier, however, the patient needs to know that the failure of treatment was due to negligence.

That information cannot be assumed by the plaintiff, Mr. Newvo. He may think that the problem is negligence, but confirmation is required and it must come from a qualified person. The statute would most likely run from the time when Dr. Secondhand tells Newvo that the bridgework is defective in the aspects described in the case study. From that point on, Newvo will have all the information required to institute a legal action, and that's when his clock starts to run. He'll have the full statutory period from the discovery of the information that the bridgework was defective.

In states that deny "discovery" extensions, the statutory period begins to run at the end of treatment in Swifty's office as long as the treatment for the bridgework was continuous— not intermittent—and for the same problem (bridgework).

Case Study 3.

Oral Surgery Mishaps:
The Effect of the Statute of Limitations

As in the other cases, the series of events may lead to small differences of opinion as to the exact running of the statute of limitations, but the differences will be immaterial. The statute will run from the time Ms. Innocent discovers from some authority that the care provided by Dr. Newon Block was below the standard. If some hospital personnel are critical of the treatment, or if a subsequent treating dentist is critical, the statute runs from the day Totally puts it all together. She knows she has suffered an injury (hospitalization) for the infection, but she may not have known that the injury could have been avoided with timely intervention by Dr. Block. Ms. Innocent may get some information from unqualified sources that the care provided by Block was negligent, but she cannot count on that in court. She doesn't really have actual knowledge of the breach of any duty until a qualified source is found. That's when the statute begins to run.

For states without the "discovery" extension, the statute begins to run with the last communication between the plaintiff and the defendant, assuming that Ms. Innocent does not go back to Dr. Block after the hospitalization.

References: Legal Defenses

Contributory Negligence
1. Ellering v. Gross 248 NW 330 (Minn., 1933).
2. Alonzo v. Rogers 283 P 709 (Wash., 1930).
3. Mendlson v. Ginder 180 NYS2d 879 (N.Y., 1958).
4. Welch v. Page 154 NE 24 (Ind., 1926).
5. Chubb v. Holmes 150 A 516 (Conn., 1930).
6. Tanner v. Sanders 56 SW2d 718 (Ky., 1933).
7. LaRouche v. U.S. 730 F2d 538 (8th Cir., 1984).

Statute of Limitations
8. Pittman v. Hodges 462 So2d 330 (Miss., 1980).
9. Schneider v. Brunk 324 SE2d 922 (N.C. App., 1985).
10. Shane v. Mouw 323 N.W. 2d 537 (Mich., 1982).
11. Masi v. Seale 682 P2d 102 (Idaho., 1984).
12. Strong v. Pontiac Hospital 323 NW 629 (Mich., 1982).
13. Foster v. Haris 633 SW 2d 304 (Tenn., 1982).

3
Dental Defenses: Record Keeping

Dental records—how much do you say, how long do you keep them, and who owns or has access to them? The accumulation of information in a dental office is potentially limitless. Reams of material could be generated on one complex case involving treatment from each of several dental specialty areas. As the saying goes, there are a million stories in the naked city, and there's at least one "story" in every new dental patient.

The whole study of record keeping in dentistry can be summed up in three short rules:

1. If it's important—record it!
2. If in doubt—don't throw it out!
3. If authorized—pass it on!

These simple guidelines will stand the test of time; they'll answer ninety percent of the most commonly asked questions. Theoretically, all significant findings and most communications would be best recorded for posterity. If you can't remember how long to keep a particular record before disposing of it, don't dispose of it. Finally, if the patient authorizes the release of his or her record, you should pass the material on to the next practitioner or to the patient.

There are exceptions, of course, and there are always questions as to what is important and what should be included.

The careful counsel would advise his or her client to record all data related to diagnosis and treatment of the patient. In a perfect system with unlimited time to spend before, during, and after patient encounters, it would be great to record every scrap of information gained in even the most routine of appointment visits. Yet efficiency says, "Just record the significant information, and be quick about it." Go ahead and abbreviate; go ahead and use checklists—but don't forget to leave room for "remarks" in case something comes up that doesn't fit the standard mold.

At what point does a fact become "significant" and eligible for recording? This chapter will examine the realities of record keeping, including basic charting requirements, history taking, ownership, and length of record maintenance following the end of the dentist-patient relationship. A special section will deal with the effect of alterations to the original record after notification of a pending suit involving dental care provided in the office.

Primarily, records are used to document the course of dental diagnosis and treatment. Records provide a means of communication for the dentist and other professionals who are contributing to the patient's care. They offer a basis for analysis and evaluation of the quality of care provided. Records enable those providing treatment to maintain continuity of care on subsequent visits, and furnish documentary evidence of the course of treatment.

Another purpose of dental record keeping, of course, is to protect the legal interests of the dentist and the patient. They are personal records, personal to the patient, and must be regarded in that light. Even so, their formulation and their "flesh" belong to the dentist.

The historical interpretation of dental records revolves around a property right that carries the power to exercise dominion and control over the use and possession of the record. In the 1970s, various state courts started to write opinions stating that "the fiducial qualities of the doctor-patient relationship require the disclosure of data to the patient or his agent on request without resorting to legal proceedings." A "fiducial" relationship means that one person holds some tangible item in trust for another. In this case, the court meant that the dentist had possession of important information about the patient, but only held it in trust, and that trust meant that the dentist could use the information only for the patient's benefit, not for his or her benefit.

The decisions of the 1970s, which have continued into the 80s, invariably permitted the practitioner to retain actual physical dental records, a position consistent with the traditional view of dental records as property. In addition, the courts determined that in limited cases practitioners could still withhold information deemed harmful to the patient. Patients who could not see their records because of this "harmful information" exception were required to institute legal action to gain access to their charts.

To summarize, patients do not have a blanket right to obtain and possess their original dental records. They do, however, have a right to inspect and copy records; in most states such access is open and easy unless a "harmful information" exception is encountered.

Regarding ownership of dental X-rays, the traditional view was expressed in a 1935 Michigan case.[1] The court reasoned that as radiographs cannot be interpreted by laymen, and as they are a part of the records made by the practitioner, and as they constitute evidence in the event of a professional liability claim, all ownership rights rest with the dentist.

What about the patient's rights? In the Michigan case, the doctor was willing to allow others to come to his office and view the X-rays. This willingness was probably considered sufficient to protect the rights of the patient.

What about the fact that the patient paid for the radiographs? Again, the court felt that the doctor's ownership rights were paramount. Quoting from a section of the opinion:

> In the absence of an agreement to the contrary, there is every good reason for holding that X-rays are the property of the [dentist] rather than of the patient or party who employed such [dentist], *notwithstanding the cost of taking the X-rays was charged to the patient or the one who engaged the [dentist] as a part of the professional service rendered.* (emphasis added)[2]

Court opinions in the late 1960s and early 70s favored the patients' access to their records. One such case, from New

York, expanded on the rule in a case where a deceased physician directed the executor of his last will and testament to burn the office records.[3] The patients' welfare was a prime concern to the court in that case. The counterbalancing consideration, of course, was the physician's desire to maintain the confidences that he had protected so well during his long career.

The court looked to the AMA's *Code of Professional Responsibility*, which states that a patient's welfare is best protected if a physician makes his or her records available to succeeding physicians. Naturally there are *Code* provisions to protect the patient's confidences, but the court's final ruling directed the executor of the doctor's estate to maintain the records and make them available upon authorized request.

In 1977, another New York court considered this question again.[4] An attorney asked a dentist to release copies of his treatment records and X-rays for the purpose of investigating allegations that the dentist had misdiagnosed periodontal disease.

The dentist refused, and the dentist's attorney said in defense of the refusal that there was no current statutory requirement forcing the dentist to allow examination. Furthermore, the dentist argued that the patient could file a dental malpractice suit and then use normal legal channels available to any litigant in a pending court matter. The plaintiff's attorney was looking for evidence to determine whether a lawsuit was meritorious. Obviously, consultants to the plaintiff's attorney had told the lawyer that the case would rise or fall depending on what kind of evidence was available in the dentist's periodic file of radiographs.

The court looked to other trial rules and found some procedures that permitted the taking of testimony and evidence before the commencing of a suit, but those procedures required a court order. At that point, the court sidestepped tradition and created some new law. The court went further than any previous court and found that *the patient has a property right in the dental record*—enough of a right, according to the court, to allow direct access without filing suit.

For the first time in a dental case, the court described the dentist's rights not in terms of property, but as a mere custodial right. This time *the patient* had the so-called "property right," sufficient to afford reasonable access to the dental record. This right did not depend on the rules of discovery or upon whether litigation was even contemplated. The trend started to appear in other state court rulings, and now most states allow release of copies of dental records and X-rays upon request.

Alteration of Records

Both dentists and physicians have been known to make alterations in records and charts after an untoward incident brings a request for documentation. Alteration takes place when the "author" has the benefit of hindsight. In a 1982 Alabama case, the defendant produced two copies of a medical record on a child he had treated.[5] The original had mysteriously "disappeared." Without his knowledge, however, the hospital administrator had made a separate copy of the record before the original was lost. The "copies" presented by the defendant were not even close to the hospital executive's copy, and the court imposed sanctions against the doctor in the amount of $45,000 for tampering with the evidence.

In a 1978 Massachusetts case, a suit was initiated based on a doctor's failure to recommend certain diagnostic procedures when the patient first complained of problems.[6] The patient won a settlement, partially on the basis of altered records. In this case, the defendant had submitted original records for all days except the day in question. That page of the records was a copy, made sometime *after* the date when the patient brought the problem to the physician's attention.

The literature contains numerous other cases where medical and dental records were altered after litigation was begun.

In one case, the defendant physician wrote in the patient's chart that an X-ray of the chest had been recommended. If this were true, the defendant would have avoided a misdiagnosis of pulmonary disease, but the patient denied that any such recommendation was ever made. A professional document examiner found, among other things, that the physician had used a different ink in making the alterations.

In dentistry, the misdiagnosis of periodontal disease lends itself to the urge to make minor office-chart alterations. When litigation is announced, the dentist is tempted to "update" or fill in the record with facts that never made it to the record when the events took place. Avoid temptation. Make no alterations to the original records.

In the typical case, however, you may recall events that were not recorded. When first charged with dental malpractice, go to the record and check it for completeness. If there are omissions, make a *separate chart or list*—from memory—of significant happenings or discussions that you held with the patient. Even if you don't remember the exact date of an unrecorded happening, but only that a conversation took place during several visits, such as in "spring or summer of 1983," you should write down that fact if the incident has any bearing on the inquiry.

The legal system is notoriously slow in reaching any conclusion. By the time a trial or hearing rolls around, another two to three years may have passed. If a second chart or separate list is available for reconstructing unrecorded facts, events, incidents, and discussions with patients, the defendant dentist will have something on which to rely to jog his or her memory. President Lincoln once observed, "No man has a good enough memory to be a successful liar." The separate sheet should be turned over to the attorney representing the defendant before it is used or relied on in any manner.

There's nothing like a fully developed record to use in court. The next best thing is to state from memory any additional unrecorded details. The last—*and the very worst*—choice is to add to the record, *even if the added events or notes are fully accurate, true, and undisputed.* You can't climb out of a hole you've dug with altered records. The persons listening to the case—jurors, hearing examiners, or arbitrators—perceive record alteration as a sign of guilt. If the defendant dentist admits to changing the record in a single instance or entry, the court or the jury will wonder what other changes may have been made that weren't admitted.

Dr. John Barchilohn, a medical consultant reporting in the October 1978 *Trial* magazine, tells the story of a fourteen-year-old boy suffering from Crohn's disease. He was admitted to the hospital for investigation of a possible bowel infection. Tests including a pyelogram and barium enema were ordered by the boy's doctor.

The usual procedure for such tests is to prepare the patient by cleaning out the bowel with castor oil or another cathartic. In cases of Crohn's disease, however, the potential for perforation militates *against* the use of such cathartics for fear of forcing a breach and causing peritonitis. In spite of this potential, a hospital nurse administered 60 cc of the castor oil to the boy the evening before the scheduled tests. The cathartic soon produced severe abdominal cramps and rupture. Emergency surgery was needed to save the boy's life.

The boy's doctor told the family that he had specifically instructed the hospital staff *not* to give castor oil or any other cathartic, and blamed the error on the hospital. The family decided to change doctors anyway.

Doctor #2 requested copies of the hospital chart and the original doctor's records; these were provided immediately. Six months later, a second surgical procedure was performed to complete the surgical phase of treatment. In the six-month period between surgical procedures, however, the boy had to undergo an ileostomy and the psychological problems associated with it. After surgery he developed persistent diarrhea, which required management with fairly high doses of opiates.

Some two years passed from the unfortunate administration of the castor oil until litigation was begun. On the basis of the hospital records, the orginal doctor was absolved and the hospital found guilty of negligence. The doctor successfully defended by citing his admission note in the hospital record which contained the phrase "No Prep," meaning that the patient was not to receive cathartics.

The hospital appealed, however, and tried to demonstrate that the perforation was likely to happen shortly with or without the castor oil. In other words, the hosptail tried to demonstrate other possible causes for the perforation. In the course of the second trial, Doctor #2's records were introduced into evidence as a perfunctory matter. Among his records, Doctor #2 had a copy of the hospital chart that he had requested when he took over the case a year and a half earlier. Examination of the hospital chart revealed that the admission note did *not* contain the phrase "No Prep." The original hospital chart, however, contained the phrase.

Since Doctor #2 had requested the records after the supposed entry was made, but before litigation was begun, it became clear that the entry "No Prep" was added later when the original doctor was named as a defendant in the malpractice case. He had not, however, been able to alter Doctor #2's photocopy.

A handwriting expert was called, and he verified that the phrase "No Prep" was added later than the rest of the admission note. The expert magnified the entries in photographs, which clearly demonstrated a difference in the characteristics of the pen stroke for the admission note and for the phrase "No Prep."

All attention then focused on the original doctor; his credibility was now questioned seriously. Would it have been better to leave the document alone? Yes. The original doctor could have testified that he had given verbal instructions or that the usual procedure was to withhold cathartics unless specifically requested. Either defense would have been better than the mess created by the alteration.

Medical History

"Are you allergic to novocaine? No? Well, then, we can get started..." So, with a verbal health history completed, Dr. X swiftly begins treatment. Having honed his inquiry into the patient's medical past down to a very abbreviated form, the dentist feels comfortable because he has completed exactly this treatment on innumerable patients with no previous problem. Therefore, everything else is an unnecessary waste of time. Right?

Is Dr. X proceeding on safe grounds? Is his anecdotal experience of "no previous problems" enough evidence to proceed safely? For Dr. X, it's enough. As a rule, though, it's an invitation to disaster.

There's no telling how many times that same limited verbal health history, or something criminally close to it, is used in dental offices each day. It's safe to say that it happens all too frequently. As a defense, Dr. X may say, "Well, I took a health history when I first saw the patient," but that may have been ten or twenty years before.

In the meantime, the patient has suffered chronic back trouble, which was treated with various narcotics, muscle relaxants, and finally surgery (laminectomy). The same patient has gained twenty pounds, suffered from gall bladder disease resulting in the surgical removal of the organ, and has developed an intolerance to aspirin. In light of the new facts, one can forget the outdated health history!

If that's not enough, consider the many cases of valvular heart disease that have been attributed to dentally induced bacteremia. In a 1979 New York case, the patient's medical history indicated a history of cardiac disease, which had necessitated a mitral valve replacement procedure seven years before the dental treatment in question.[7] The dentist failed to administer antibiotics before performing a routine prophylaxis and before the insertion of a crown. The patient developed bacterial endocarditis and died four months later.

In a 1982 Michigan case, a dentist treated a patient who had stated a history of being told about a "heart murmer."[8] The dentist failed to ask further questions or follow up this "trigger statement" on the medical history. Unfortunately no precautions were taken, no antibiotics were provided, and treatment continued for an abscessed tooth. The patient developed bacterial endocarditis and ended up suing the dentist.

There are few dental procedures that don't elicit some amount of hemorrhage. Even placement of a rubber dam clamp may cause a small laceration, in the marginal gingival tissues—enough of a lesion to introduce minute quantities of bacterial microorganisms into the body. Because of the possibility of bacteremia, every practitioner should know about the patient's cardiac history. Because of the possibility of anaphylactic shock, every practitioner should know about drug intolerances. The list goes on...

The fact that a dentist has practiced for years without any problems is not sufficient reason to justify a short verbal health history. In today's legal climate, and because of the increased amount of information about how drugs interact and how treatment procedures affect the body systemically, every dentist must gather much more information from the patient than in the past. The dentist has a similar responsibility to update the information regularly and periodically. It is his or her responsibility to be aware of the patient's *current health status* at every visit.

When we look outside the dental community for guidance, we find that hospital rules require a complete health history for each admission. If the patient returned to the hospital every six months or so, the hospital would still be required to retake the health information. Hospital rules and good sense dictate that no major surgical or medical treatment proceed without it. The hospital wouldn't rely on the health history received six months earlier, and the same logic should hold in dentistry. Dentists have no right to assume that the patient's health history remains static from one routine recall prophylaxis visit to the next.

In truth, the majority of dentists take a better health history than Dr. X took in the example cited above, but there is no standard format. More and more self-administered questionnaires are used today than previously. As more information is needed to place the patient in a "treatment" or "no treatment" category, more information needs to be collected. Because dentists see an average of 16 patients per day, it may be unrealistic to take as much time for a dental medical history as for a hospital admission. Therefore, the patient-completed questionnaire may be the most ideal vehicle for dentistry.

In the best of all worlds, the patient would take the time to complete the form each time intraoral dental treatment is to be performed. Exceptions would be made for a series of treatments in a limited period of time, as when a patient returns for a series of restorations that were recommended at a routine recall examination visit a week or two earlier.

When a significant period of time elapses between visits, however, the health history should be repeated or updated. The dentist may analogize the health history to the standard of care in taking a full-mouth series of dental X-rays. It is universally accepted that the full-mouth series is required to aid in diagnosis of a new patient to the practice, but it is not required at each periodic recall treatment visit. The standard for repeat X-rays is left to the judgment of the clinician, but that does not mean that the clinician can disregard the X-ray. The competent dentist would repeat dental X-rays as clinical signs and reported symptoms require.

Standard medical-history forms of all shapes and varieties are available from specialty printers, dental supply houses, dental schools, and even the American Dental Association. The ADA form won its approval from the Council on Dental Therapeutics a number of years ago. It includes two forms, a short version and a longer one. They appear in the publication *Accepted Dental Therapeutics*. One state dental society, the Wisconsin Dental Association, has produced a multipage record-keeping system. The Wisconsin package includes two medical-history forms, one for persons under eighteen years of age and another for adults.

Recently, the University of Southern California School of Dentistry used the 1956 ADA form as the basis for an effort to update the history in "response to contemporary advances in physical evaluation *and* to increasing malpractice claims." The USC medical history was published in the October 1985 issue of the *ADA Journal*.

The USC update, produced in consultation with dental and medical school faculty, was guided by the special assistance of a trial lawyer experienced in dental malpractice cases. Upon completion of the form in practice, the patient is asked to read and sign a reminder that gives the following warning:

> To the best of my knowledge, all of the preceding answers are true and correct. If I ever have any change in my health history, or if my medicines change, I will inform the doctor of dentistry at the next appointment without fail.[9]

This is an obvious effort to shift the burden of responsibility to the patient in bringing new medical information to the attention of the dental staff. As a matter of fact, this is an area where the responsibility should be shared, but the patient's failure to volunteer new medical history information at each visit will not completely absolve the dentist for failure to update the history.

Much of the lay community does not appreciate how medical information relates to dental care. (Some practitioners, sad to say, are also unfamiliar with this relationship.) Therefore, when the question of responsibility is presented to the jury, it is more than likely that the court will find that it was *the dentist's* responsibility to ask the questions and elicit the answers that would bring the medical history up to date.

At best, the signing of the reminder agreement would assist the dentist in those states where comparative negligence assigns fault on a percentage basis.

Once a record is established, it must be used in an efficient manner. If the record is created solely to satisfy the standard of care in the area, its usefulness will be negated by failure to pay attention to the answers.

In a 1984 case involving a government hospital, the patient underwent a surgical procedure that later proved ill-advised.[10] In an earlier admission, the patient had undergone exploratory surgery and was advised that she had Crohn's disease. Five years later, additional surgery was done, and two years after that a rectal biopsy was performed on the woman in an effort to discover the source of recurring abdominal pain. The biopsy was ambiguous, and the pathologist's report listed Crohn's disease as a possible factor.

Shortly thereafter, the woman underwent a third session of surgery, and a lengthy period of postoperative infections developed. Subsequently, the woman sued the surgeon. At trial, the physician who performed the surgery testified that he would not have done so if he had been aware of the diagnosis of Crohn's disease. No evidence was presented to show that any of the physicians involved in the patient's current series of treatments had consulted records of the woman's previous operations. The court then found the defendant negligent and liable for the consequences of the surgery, even though the performance of the surgery could not be faulted.

Case Study 1.

Undiagnosed Periodontal Disease: The Effect of Inadequate Records

Mrs. V (for victim) was a patient of Dr. Trustee's, for many years. While the dentist was vacationing at a practice management seminar in Wiki Wiki, Mrs. V had a dental emergency. The new dentist informed her that she had signs of periodontal disease. Mrs. V was shocked; at the new dentist's suggestion, she went to a periodontist for confirmation. Now she faces the prospects of losing a number of teeth, multiple sessions of periodontal surgery, and expensive restoration.

Could this situation have been avoided? Mrs. V says, "Yes!" After all, she followed Dr. Trustee's advice for years. She went to his office for a cleaning and checkup whenever he told her to so do. She felt she was taking good care of her mouth so she *wouldn't* lose her teeth. "Dr. Trustee never said diddly about periodontal disease. If he did, I would have done something about it. I'm going to sue the bastard!"

Is Dr. Trustee in hot water? Perhaps. Let's look at the first line of defense—Mrs. V's chart.

This is where diligent record keeping pays off! It simply is not enough to *say* you were aware of the periodontal disease in the patient's mouth. If you've got it in black and white, you may well scotch a lawsuit at the outset. Since no one can safely predict where the next potential plaintiff will come from or whom it may be, the only safe practice is to make a *record notation regarding periodontal conditions at each and every patient encounter.*

> Note when home care changes.
> Note all patient-reported symptoms.
> Note pocket depths (survey selected teeth).
> Note mobility, color, texture.
> Note patient admissions: "I know I should floss, but..."
> Note all clinical findings, even if all findings are within normal limits (WNL).

Then record a diagnosis and be specific as to the location of problems. If you have a diagnosis, you must have a treatment plan. Put that in writing, too.

For the average adult patient, you may develop more written material in clinical findings and diagnosis/treatment planning for perio than for all restorations, root canals, and extractions combined over the same period. But that's okay. Use a separate sheet. Never mind the growing size of the filing system. Gone are the days of keeping records on 3 × 5 file cards.

Next, review your dental X-rays. If the patient has signs of periodontal disease, diagnostic X-rays are required. If the patient refuses, you have some choices, but the refusal must be placed prominently in the record. This is not to suggest that you should simply ask and then, if you encounter refusal, give in to the patient.

Dr. Wimpy: "Mr. N? Uh, I'd like to take some, uh, X-rays..."

Mr. Knowitall: (in his best bully baritone) "Forget it, Doc, you're not gonna take any X-rays on me 'til I get a toothache. I don't need the radiation, and besides, you took an X-ray seven years ago."

Dr. Wimpy: "Well, okay."

Under these circumstances, even if Dr. Wimpy did write the refusal into the body of his records, he may still lose the point in a lawsuit based on failure to take adequate diagnostic dental X-rays. Why? Because the patient's refusal was uneducated and made out of unfounded fear of either excessive radiation or fear of being overtreated.

The record entry should mention something about the effort to change the patient's mind. You need to do several things. First, you must address the patient's fear; second, you must explain the risk the patient takes by refusing the diagnostic service. After the explanation, the records should reflect what the patient's continuing objections were, what efforts were made to obtain compliance, and that the patient is aware of the risks.

Still, refusal doesn't mean that the patient is automatically *persona non grata,* although removing the patient from the patient list *is* an alternative. The patient can be managed on a more strict recall basis if you are working without the usual X-ray diagnostic test results. In that case, more meticulous use of the periodontal probe is indicated.

One final point: if the patient refuses to have dental X-rays at sometime in the dentist-patient relationship, that does not mean that the patient will never change his or her mind. To find out how the patient currently feels about radiation, you should ask at each visit whether dental X-rays can be taken. Do not assume that the patient will oppose the procedure for the rest of his or her life.

In a related medical case, a female patient was diagnosed as having cervical cancer. Some years previously, she had admitted that she had refused to have a Pap smear, but she returned to the doctor on several occasions after the refusal and before the cancer was detected. Now the patient wants to sue the doctor, but she must first address his defense that she had contributed to her problem by refusing diagnostic procedures. One court has ruled that such a refusal in the remote past will not protect the clinician from a charge of negligence. In this case, the court decided that the practitioner should have tested the patient's resolve not to have the Pap smear *at every subsequent appointment.*

The lesson for dentistry is clear. One refusal, even if plainly marked on the dental record, will not suffice to prevent a lawsuit based on failure to diagnose dental disease.

If a patient has apparent signs and symptoms of periodontal disease, that fact must be communicated to the patient. Tired old phrases like "You've got a little problem around your back teeth, Mrs. Jones" will not cut it. Patients are now rightfully insisting that the dentist not act as a father figure, trying to sugar-coat a problem. Once the bad news is out in the open, the diagnosis and treatment plan must also go on the record.

Of course, the record must also show evidence of actual treatment. Prophy visits every six months hardly qualify as treatment in the average case of moderate to advanced periodontal disease. Perfectly healthy individuals hit the dental offices at that pace. If you expect to get ahead of the problem, and if you feel you are qualified to treat the problem, then treat it! Have the patient come back for scaling, deep scaling, and root planing; do it in small segments under local anesthetic, or, if necessary, do it on an accelerated basis—three, four, or more times per year. *But do it!*

There's nothing more lame than to hear a dentist try to defend a case of undiagnosed periodontal disease with index-card records that show two "pro" visits a year over a ten-to-twenty-year period. If there is evidence that serious periodontal disease existed during the same period, it is extremely difficult to demonstrate the therapeutic value of twice-yearly recall treatment. Such a situation leaves the clinician with two embarrassing choices.

One alternative is to claim that *no periodontal disease was present.* If there had been clinical evidence of disease, the visits would have been more frequent, but since there were only two visits per year for prophy appointments, that can be interpreted to mean that the clinician didn't feel any more were required. Then the claim must be made that the periodontal disease mysteriously appeared between the time the dentist last saw the patient and the first time the patient saw another practitioner.

The second choice is to claim that the defendant dentist knew of the presence of periodontal disease, but *the patient refused treatment* or refused to take any recommendations for improved home care. The dentist might go a step further and claim that the patient not only failed to comply with reasonable home-care instruction, but refused to come to the office on a more regular basis. Some dentists who choose this defense also like to use the excuse that because the dentist knew the patient so well, he or she also knew that the patient couldn't afford any more sophisticated treatment: either a referral to a specialist or more frequent conservative treatment in the general dentist's office. That may have been true at some earlier point, but patients' financial fortunes often improve as time goes by.

None of these excuses or last-minute defenses are worth much if there is nothing in the written record to substantiate them. This brings us back to our point: record every treatment suggestion. Then record every reaction—positive and negative—and keep doing it as long as you are the dentist of record. As long as you keep the patient in your practice, you are responsible for the diagnosis of oral disease. You can't expect the average patient to find out for himself. Patients rightfully rely on their dentists' words or silence. They have no reason to get a "second opinion" when the dentist says, "Everything looks great. See you in six months."

Case Study 2.

Premature Crown and Bridge Failure: The Effect of Inadequate Records

This is the case where Mr. Newvo, an up-and-coming corporate executive, went to Dr. Swifty to have multiple units of crown and bridgework placed. Shortly after the work was finished, problems developed that were never fully resolved.

Newvo ended up seeing a second dentist, who informed the young executive that the work had to be redone. The allegations of dental malpractice in this case were (1) that the crown and bridgework placed by Dr. Swifty were below the standard of care, and (2) that the materials used (the porcelain/metal system) were substandard.

Adequate record keeping would provide several avenues of assistance to Dr. Swifty in a case like this. Initially, the records would be most helpful if they include notations at the outset of treatment advising Mr. Newvo that even the best restorative crown and bridgework may not last a lifetime without exquisitely meticulous home care by the patient. Second, if there are notations in the chronological treatment sections of the records showing that Mr. Newvo *missed appointments* by either canceling on short notice or missing the appointments altogether, they might explain some of the problems, or at least sensitize an independent reviewer to some extraordinary problems with patient cooperation.

Other instances of noncompliance, placed prominently in the records, may also have some effect on the lawyer's decision for the plaintiff to go ahead with the case. If there are indications, for instance, of a sudden deterioration in Newvo's ability to take care of his own mouth during treatment, a situation that could easily change the prognosis, then the records would have been well worth keeping for that bit of information alone. If the records show a combination of these two problems—that is, *missed appointments* and *deterioration of home oral hygiene*—then it is safe to say that the attorney for the plaintiff and any expert witness will think twice about coming to the assistance of the plaintiff. This will be true especially when the experts are apprised of Newvo's erratic and contributorily negligent behavior while undergoing the treatment in Dr. Swifty's office.

In addition to the above, you may make a notation at the outset of treatment about the financial considerations that go into selection of treatment alternatives. If Mr. Newvo's financial capabilities at the time of the treatment affected the selection of material or the techniques used in completing his case, that information would be helpful in determining how Dr. Swifty's best efforts ended up as the subject of controversy.

In relation to the patient's financial capability to obtain the restorative services, you may make a notation in the record as to the prognosis offered by Swifty before starting his work. In other words, if Dr. Swifty knew that something about the treatment plan would not provide a so-called "permanent" solution to Mr. Newvo's problem, a word about it in the records would be most valuable. If Dr. Swifty had elected to provide some kind of *provisional* restorative crown and bridge in an effort to stabilize the patient's teeth while awaiting a change in the patient's underlying oral hygiene or financial capabilities, that would be some consideration in compromising the final product.

In other words, the final product really wouldn't be *final,* but only a step in a greater treatment plan which would lead to "permanent" restorative work in the patient's mouth. Without some kind of qualifying statement at the outset of treatment, however, it would be safe to assume that the patient received what Dr. Swifty would describe as the final product—there was nothing more to follow.

In a 1984 Maryland Health Claims Arbitration case, a practitioner relied on his understanding of his patient's financial capabilities to determine an intermediate treatment plan for the patient.[11] In this treatment the dentist provided the patient with several units of acrylic and stainless steel crowns for posterior teeth. Placement of acrylic and stainless steel crowns is an appropriate form of treatment under certain conditions, as long as the patient understands that such treatment is not necessarily a permanent type of restoration.

Acrylic and stainless steel are acceptable in the short run or for an intermediate period of time while under the close scrutiny of the treating dentist. In the case at hand, however, the dentist apparently failed to communicate the nature of the work to the patient.

The allegation that the dentist put in substandard "permanent" dental work was not the only problem. The case presented further complexities, which came out in the trial of this matter in 1984. It appeared that in addition to placing the acrylic and stainless steel crown work in the patient's mouth, the dentist also constructed a cast partial denture framework that used some of the temporary crowns as abutments for the clasps and rest seats of the removable device.

There was conflicting testimony as to what exactly the dentist said about materials and longevity during the first several visits. The dentist, of course, professed that he had not promised the patient that the treatment would last a lifetime. The patient, on the other hand, claimed that the dentist said, "This will take care of your problems," or words to that effect, and she understood this to mean that the work was intended to last many, many years. The teeth that were crowned with stainless steel and acrylic eventually became carious at the margins, resulting in the loss of one key molar, endodontic treatment on another molar, and jeopardy to the restorability of several other teeth.

When the hearing panel looked at the dentist's records of this patient's care, they were led to believe that if the dentist's statements were true, there was nothing in the records to substantiate them. Without any notation in the records to support the dentist's statement, the patient's word was as good as the dentist's. It then became a matter of the witnesses' credibility when they were called to testify about their understanding of the projected "permanency" of the dental work.

Dentists who later treated this plaintiff were called to testify. Each of them testified that they felt the patient was an honest and truthful person, at least in their own relationships with the patient. These dentists also criticized the use of stainless steel and acrylic restorations as abutment teeth in the overall restored case, especially for the cast partial denture that used these particular restorations.

The case of Mr. Newvo and Dr. Swifty presents another problem beside the careless and apparently substandard creation of the crown and bridgework: the choice of material, or the material itself, may have been faulty. The allegation of faulty material, in addition to the allegation of negligence, is also the practitioner's responsibility. Because the dentist is the last person to review laboratory work before it is placed in the patient's mouth, he or she is prevented from using the defense that the laboratory work was below par.

On the other hand, if a reasonable dentist cannot see or detect a hidden flaw in the porcelain or metal in careful review of his or her restorations before insertion, he or she can hardly be responsible for the ultimate failure of that restoration. In such a case, where the porcelain peeled or cracked away from the restoration, if it is apparent that the cracking, peeling, or chipping was not caused by improper occlusal relations (which the dentist controls), the responsibility for the failure moves back to the laboratory. Since the patient has no direct relationship with the laboratory, however, he or she must take his or her complaint to the dentist. If evidence at trial indicates that the dentist could not have discovered the flaw in the underlying work, then he or she is permitted to bring in the laboratory as another defendant in the case or later to sue the lab separately on the basis of breach of contract, breach of warranty, or misrepresentation.

The records can help in this kind of case if the practitioner inspects major crown units and marks all potential problems in the record before attempting insertion and adjustment. If the record lists some flaws that are not in critical areas, but fails to note defects in the porcelain, the court could reasonably conclude that the dentist *did* make a good-faith inspection of the work, *did not* find any obvious defects, and was unable to find any sign of potential porcelain weakness. That's all that is expected of the reasonable dentist—reasonable inspection of the work for obvious errors. If no record entry exists, however, before the attempt to seat the case, the court may conclude that *no effort* was made to inspect for flaws that would have caused problems such as those in Mr. Newvo's case.

Case Study 3.

Oral Surgery Mishaps:
The Effect of Inadequate Records

What elements of record keeping would have been helpful to Dr. Newon Block in this case? As you will remember, the case concerned a general dentist who elected to provide oral surgery services in the form of extraction of an impacted third molar in the mouth of a young female patient. The patient, Ms. Totally Innocent, was symptomatic at the outset of treatment, and that fact gives us the key to the important elements of record keeping to protect Dr. Block.

The symptoms and the signs that Dr. Block identified in the assessment of the case should all be listed in cryptic, yet complete, detail. For instance, all the signs gathered at the clinical examination should be listed, so there will be no doubt at any future date that the treatment was necessary and that the recommendation was appropriate. Many practitioners add mention of any obvious external facial swelling, the presence or absence of palpable lymph nodes, and the patient's body temperature, along with any history of elevated temperature in the previous 48 hours.

Second, a chart entry indicating that appropriate X-rays were taken *and viewed* would be helpful. The radiographs, especially if they show the inferior alveolar canal in close proximity to the apex of the third molar, deserve a special indication in the patient's record.

Third, the records should contain information about the series of factual events during the procedure that dealt with the placement of the incision and the manner of retraction. If indicated, the identification of the lingual nerve and a phrase attesting to its protection during retraction would obviate a number of borderline dental malpractice claims in the eyes of attorneys and their consultants in the dental field.

Finally, the fact that the patient was symptomatic and showed evidence of inflammation and possibly elevated body temperature led to the common therapeutic recommendation to prescribe antibiotics. The medical history comes in handy here; the practitioner should not only provide the appropriate antibiotic, but give the patient details about the drug so the patient can tell if the medication is accomplishing its purpose. A simple verbal discussion is standard, but a note in the record about the instructions could be valuable. If the practitioner is using preprinted sheets with basic warnings and information about drug taking, the name or number of that instruction sheet should be entered in the record to prove that such materials were, in fact, dispensed to the patient.

Checklist for Record Keeping

Registration. You must include a general information page and additional pages for medical and dental history as needed. The general information page should contain enough information about the patient to describe him or her easily or make contact readily, should the need arise. The registration card should list current name, address, and telephone numbers. Other relevant items include the name and phone number of the patient's general physician and the name and phone number of any specialty practitioner the patient is seeing.

Medical history. The medical history form should include *identifier information* so that if it is misplaced from the record, it can be located and replaced without trouble. The history must be *dated clearly* when first taken or filled out by the patient. The patient should *sign* the form to authenticate the answers, should any question arise at a later date. The typical preprinted form includes too few places where handwritten answers are needed, making it difficult to prove that the patient did in fact fill out the form, unless the patient's signature appears on the piece of paper. Even if a staff member takes the information verbally and fills in the form for the patient, an effort should be made to have the patient sign the form.

Dental History. A dental record is not complete without some consideration of previous dental history. Several relevant items of dental history should be gained and recorded, including whether or not the patient has had previous orthodontic dental treatment and whether or not a patient has suffered any form of trauma in a previous dentist's office. Most patients are not shy about relating such incidents to the new dentist.

If the new dentist makes a point of defending the previous dentist's behavior, the patient may become defensive and withdrawn. On the other hand, if the new dentist reacts with sympathy for the patient's experience, the patient is apt to relax.

If the new dentist is asked to comment on an incredible story or set of facts, it is better to ignore temporarily the possible defenses for the previous dentist's behavior, at least at the initial visit. If the statements are significant for the dental work done, however, and are likely to be relevant to future treatment or necessary retreatment, caution is advised. Many patients will want the new dentist to pass a quick judgment that something is terribly wrong with the way the previous dentist behaved or with the work that was done.

It is all too easy to nod and agree with everything that a new patient says—but be cautious. Be sympathetic toward a long and anguished tale of woe, but do not automatically follow the patient's lead. The patient's true and complete agenda may not be apparent from initial conversations.

Dental histories can be taken verbally by asking the patient a number of leading questions in order to draw out all experiences and all fond or unpleasant recollections of previous dental care. Ask enough questions to determine whether there were any major problems with previous dental treatment; if so, inquire further.

Clinical Exam. At some point, the results of the clinical examination must be placed in the record, the closer to the time the findings were made, the better. The usual hospital practice of dictating information and reading the transcript later can sacrifice a lot of precision. Both initial and recall examinations should include a screening procedure for periodontal disease. Such a screening exam includes the use of the calibrated periodontal probe or explorer. The results of probing completely around previously determined key teeth (at least one in each quadrant or segment) should be entered in the physical record as a baseline for periodontal pocket depths at the outset of treatment. Other clinical signs and impressions should be recorded, including color, texture, tooth mobility, and the myriad of abnormal findings that exist in the average mouth. Some preprinted forms have a checklist of commonly seen conditions, but simply to check off that "calculus" is present may not be sufficient, unless the check means the problem exists everywhere. If there is a small space on the chart after the name of the condition, list the teeth where the particular problem occurs.

In a number of legal matters, defendant dentists have admitted that their records were not adequate in itemizing all findings from their examinations. It doesn't do the defendant any good to have to say, "Yes, I remember, the patient reported spontaneous bleeding from the gingiva on several recall appointments. I agree that bleeding is a significant finding or symptom. But no, I didn't record it on my chart." Whether or not the bleeding, or lack of it, had an important bearing on the case is immaterial. The point is that *the jury or the court will begin to draw inferences from the failure to keep adequate records*. Those inferences will not favor the dentist.

Chronological Treatment Record. The bulk of the treatment will be recorded in chronological sequence. The record should identify the date and details of the service or services provided. If anesthetic is administered, make a note of the type, amount, and concentration of vasoconstrictor used, along with the location or type of injection (block, infiltration, or intraligamentary).

As specific teeth are treated, list them clearly, using the universal numbering system. If some condition causes the restoration to be less than ideal, a note is required. If the level of anesthesia, for instance, is inadequate to prepare the tooth to an appropriate depth, or if decay remains near the perceived pulpal tissues, note that fact in the record, along with any medications, bases, and restorative materials used. If a direct or indirect pulp cap is used, the patient should be advised and the communication noted and dated.

No blank lines should be left between individual entries, unless blanks are left uniformly between all entries. This format will tend to show that the existing notes were all made at the time of treatment, as the next dated entry precludes any opportunity to add material at a later date.

Finally, if your records are requested or subpoenaed to court, make sure your name appears on each and every page that is transmitted. All too often, the dentist's name and office address appear only on the registration or the medical history form. If these forms with names are separated from the multiple treatment pages, some bizarre results could occur, which will take time to straighten out. Also, some offices have a habit of leaving out the year on the date of the treatment visit. If your office is in this habit, make sure that the year designation appears at appropriate places in the record.

In connection with transmission of dental records, it is permissible to send a separate typewritten page translating the handwritten copy into comprehensible English, but *do not* add to the record in the translation. You've certainly heard the old saying, "It loses something in the translation." Well, the opposite, adding to the translation, is equally prejudicial against the practitioner's honesty and integrity. It *will not help* your cause to send typewritten versions of your original dental records, which purport to enhance them. Such efforts will only come back to haunt you. *Do not panic.* Leave the record alone.

References: Record Keeping

1. McGarry v. Mercier, 262 NW 296 (Mich., 1935).
2. Ibid.
3. In re Culbertson's Will, 292 NYS2d 806 (N.Y., 1968).
4. Application of Polly P., 399 NYS2d 584 (N.Y., 1977).
5. May v. Moore, 424 So2d 596 (Ala., 1982).
6. Rehill v. Goodman, Norfolk Cty Super.Ct. No 115125 (Mass., 1978).
7. Petrizzo v. Olsen, No 78Civ 3625 US Dist Ct., S.D.N.Y., June, 1979.
8. Vincent v. Vanker, No 80-199-458 Oakland City Michigan June, 1982.
9. McCarthy, Frank M., "A New Patient-Administered Medical History Developed for Dentistry." *JADA* 111:595, October, 1985.
10. Haley v. U.S., 739 F2d 1502 (1984).
11. Bryan v. Griffith, Mont. Cty. Cir Ct. Law #65633 (Md., 1984).

4
Informed Consent

Dentists and dental office staff are roughly familiar with the concept of "informed consent." The general presumption is that the patient should not be treated until two things have happened: (1) the patient understands the proposed treatment, and (2) the patient then agrees to proceed with the treatment.

For the majority of dentists, this information is conveyed verbally, and the typical response from the patient is a nod or a shrug of resignation. As long as the patient remains in the chair, the assumption is that he or she has agreed to the treatment. This is a "captive audience" patient. For years, dentistry has played the father/teacher role, promoting and performing that which is "best for the patient"—usually with justification, but not without some legal jeopardy.

From a legal viewpoint there are two types of consent: *plain* and *informed*. Plain consent is required to claim valid exemption from liability for battery (unlawful touching). Informed consent, on the other hand, is a principle of tort (negligence) law with respect to the requirement that a patient be apprised of the nature and risks of a medical procedure.

The difference between plain consent and informed consent is critical to dentists in practice. In dentistry, the performance of any procedure without the patient's consent is technically a battery (the civil equivalent to the criminal charge of assault and battery). In legal terms, assault is an unwarranted trespass against a person, and as such is reason enough for a patient to bring suit in most states.

The patient/complainant who alleges failure to obtain plain consent may recover a money judgment, whether or not he or she has benefited from the procedure. An expert witness is not necessary, and the patient does not have to prove any specific monetary damages.

Having patients sign preprinted consent forms provides only thin protection. At best such forms are useful only against charges involving plain consent. These simple forms, of themselves, will not absolve a dentist from charges of professional negligence.

Informed consent, as opposed to plain consent, has nothing to do with assault. Failure to obtain the patient's *informed* consent constitutes *negligence* on the part of the dentist. As discussed in Chapter One, negligence or professional negligence by a dentist is synonymous with "malpractice." Negligence is grounds for a patient to sue for damages in a state or federal civil court.

In dental malpractice cases, plaintiff's lawyers will often split the charges into two main categories: (1) the charges stemming from the treatment or diagnostic failures, and (2) a second count concerning the failure to obtain informed consent.

Count 1 (Negligence)

On or about February 21, 1985, defendant Dr. Schmidlap did attempt to remove a lower third molar tooth on Plaintiff Ms. Totally Innocent. Midway through this excruciatingly painful and lengthy procedure, defendant did ask of his staff why they had not taken a preoperative X-ray. Shortly thereafter, following a loud snapping sound, defendant told plaintiff that her jaw had been broken.

As a separate charge against the dentist, the plaintiff's lawyer would then allege that the dentist was negligent in an entirely different manner, not associated with his lack of skill in oral surgery or with the failure to take a preoperative X-ray.

Count 2 (Informed Consent)

Plaintiff incorporates all the facts and allegations in Count 1 and states further that defendant did negligently fail to inform plaintiff of the possible adverse outcomes (and specifically breaking of the jaw) of the extraction procedure he initiated on February 21, 1985, and in so doing, failed to obtain the informed consent of the plaintiff to the procedure, all to the detriment of the plaintiff.

This is called *pleading in the alternative*. It allows the plaintiff a "backup position": if the jury doesn't find negligent conduct in the performance of the procedure itself, it can still find the defendant negligent in failing to inform the patient about the possibility of jaw fracture from the procedure.

Informed consent used to be the weakest argument a lawyer could make in a medical or dental negligence case. If there was little or no evidence of obvious procedural negligence, the lawyer would not readily take a case solely on the basis of failure to obtain informed consent. Frequently the evidence was weak on the plaintiff's side and not usually verifiable. On the defendant's side, the "community practice" rule permitted evidence from other doctors that the usual practice was similar to the defendant's. In other words, the brief, unrecorded statements that the defendant said he routinely made to patients facing similar treatment were accepted as standard procedures among area dentists.

Yet, as in a number of other areas of the law, the rules of informed consent are rapidly changing. Cases decided in the last five to ten years have provided plaintiffs with a greater opportunity to prevail on the question of informed consent. Courts frequently refuse to allow the defendant to rest on the argument that all the other practitioners in the community are saying the same thing. They are inclined to require that the information be tailored to fit each individual plaintiff's special needs, the professional community notwithstanding.

Requirements of Informed Consent

Before we look at common areas of miscommunication with dental patients, it would be helpful to explore the exact requirements of informed consent. Health-care providers of all disciplines must inform patients of the nature of the proposed treatment, the benefits and risks of such treatment, and the benefits and risks of the alternatives to such treatment, including nontreatment.

After that information has been provided, the patient must choose the method of treatment. The patient's decision is final. The patient who claims a lack of informed consent must prove: (1) that the dentist had a duty to provide the information to the patient, (2) that the dentist failed to provide some or all of the information, (3) that the patient would *not* have consented to treatment if the dentist had made a full disclosure, and (4) that the dentist's failure to disclose information was the cause of the injury to the plaintiff.

What is the required scope of the information to be given? How much must a patient be told? Should the dentist attempt to provide all the information he or she possesses about a subject? Obviously not, but the requirements can be quite inclusive and encompassing.

The Professional Standards Test

Two theories of informed consent are used today in American courts. The first and older theory, commonly called the *professional standards test* or *community standards test*, requires that each practitioner disclose or supply patients with the same information that would be provided by a reasonable dentist in similar circumstances. Dentists must pass this test if they are to prevail at a hearing or trial where they have been accused of failure to gain the patient's informed consent.

The professional standards test means that dentists must expose their patients to the same amount of information that the average dentist of similar training and licensure is providing to his or her patients. This theory permits the court to accept testimony from like practitioners regarding what everyone else is telling patients who have the same diagnosis or who need similar services.

Those who testify are termed *expert witnesses*. They are called to testify what the professional community is doing in regard to disclosure. Both the plaintiff and the defendant will identify expert witnesses, who will describe as well as they can what the community standards are.

In this explosive new area of malpractice in general and dental malpractice in particular, the experts often disagree sharply on the requirements of disclosure. The judge and jury are left with the task of deciding which of the competing experts was the most convincing and the least prejudiced.

The community standard theory is observed in the majority of American jurisdictions, but only a bare majority. Historically, the community standard was the first fully described disclosure law in the United States.

The Prudent Patient Test

The other theory, which is replacing the community standard theory in an ever-increasing number of states, is the *prudent patient* or *material risk* test. Those states that do not apply the community standards test maintain that a dentist must reveal *all information that is material to the patient's decision* to undergo treatment.

The *prudent patient* or *material risk* standard did not exist before 1972. Before then, all jurisdictions that recognized lack of informed consent as a basis for malpractice used the professional standards test.

In the years since 1972, an increasing number of states have adopted the "prudent patient" standard. As of this writing those states include California, Indiana, Louisiana, Maryland, Massachusetts, Michigan, Minnesota, New Mexico, Ohio, Oregon, Rhode Island, Texas, Utah, Washington, West Virginia, Wisconsin, and the District of Columbia. (Pennsylvania limits "prudent person" informed consent to surgical procedures only. Oklahoma requires that it is a physician's duty to disclose information pertinent to a *particular* patient.)

Also in 1972, the American Hospital Association published a *Statement of Patient's Bill of Rights*. In this statement the Association declared that the patient should receive enough pertinent information to arrive at a decision based on the specifics of the treatment, not on the basis of information usually provided by the community of professionals.

The influential case that triggered these developments was a 1972 District of Columbia case, *Canterbury v. Spence*.[1] For the first time, application of the informed consent rule did not depend on what local dentists or physicians usually tell their patients. Informed consent in *Canterbury* was based on a general or lay standard of reasonableness, set by law and totally independent of dental community custom. The court concluded, "The duty to disclose...arises from phenomena apart from medical custom and practice."[2]

The prudent patient rule requires the practitioner to disclose what he or she knows or should know to be the information required by a patient. This information is *what the patient requires* to choose whether to not to undergo proposed medical or dental treatment.

In other words, the practitioner should reveal any and all risks that would be material to the patient's decision. A material risk was defined in *Canterbury* as follows:

> A risk is...material when a reasonable person, in what the physician knows or should know to be the patient's position, would be likely to attach significance to the risk or cluster of risks in deciding whether or not to forego the proposed [treatment].[3]

Thus the *material risk test* is the other name ascribed to the prudent patient test for informed consent. By either name, the amount of information necessary to obviate a charge of failure to provide informed consent is *patient-based*—that is, whatever the patient *believes* is material to the decision. Material risk or prudent patient disclosure is not based on what the professional community has decided to reveal in like circumstances, but rather on what the patient needs to know to make a decision that is prudent *for himself or herself*.

States that still adhere to the professional community standard require both sides to provide testimony from expert witnesses to establish the standard. An expert can be anyone with a similar professional license, who by training and/or experience is competent in the eyes of the court to testify on professional standards.

Expert testimony is required only when the subject matter is technical or medical. In *Canterbury*, the plaintiff presented no expert evidence of the community practice on informed consent. The case involved a laminectomy (vertebral disk excision) and the patient's subsequent paralysis. When the plaintiff in that case testified that the defendant did not reveal the possibility of a resulting paralysis, and that the patient did, in fact, develop paralysis, the court held that the defendant was negligent, without the aid of expert testimony. The negligence lay in not informing the patient of the material risk of paralysis, not in any actual negligent action in the procedure itself.

The Trend Toward the Prudent Patient Test

Why have jurisdictions changed from the professional community standard to the prudent patient-material risk test? The answer lies in four considerations.

(1) The courts now believe that there really is no consensus among practitioners. The existence of a discernible custom is subject to serious question. Two dentists graduating at the same time and practicing in the same community will have two entirely different protocols in dealing with patients. One will spend quite a bit of time with a patient before starting treatment. The other will follow the "let's get started" philosophy, answering only direct questions.

(2) Practitioners have to deal with real-world differences among patients. The patient's educational level, emotional state, and financial status make each situation different. Whether a dentist has conformed to a professional standard should be limited to areas of pure medical and dental judgment—where the issue concerns the quality of the treatment.

(3) The courts are assuming that professional standards are too often set by and subject to the whim of the dentists and physicians in a particular community. This virtually unlimited discretion is often inconsistent with the patient's right of self-determination. Again, to quote from the leading case on the subject, *Canterbury* at p. 784:

> Respect for the patient's right of self-determination
> ...demands a standard set by law for physicians rather
> than one which physicians may or may not impose
> upon themselves.[4]

(4) Finally, the courts have begun to see that there is a built-in difficulty in finding witnesses who are willing to testify for patients against their colleagues. The so-called "conspiracy of silence" has served to limit the free flow of information to the courts.

Proximate Cause: Linking Consent to Damages

The patient has one more important hurdle to jump before winning the case for failure to provide informed consent. The patient must prove that he or she would not have undergone the procedure if informed of the risk ahead of time. This is the *causal connection* between the negligent act (failure to inform) and the actual injury. Proximate cause exists when, and only when, disclosure would have resulted in a decision *against* the proposed treatment.

Without a proximate cause connecting the negligence and injury, the case most likely will be dismissed in favor of the dentist. If the patient states at the outset that he or she will undergo the treatment despite any risks involved, the complaint likewise will be dismissed.

For proximate cause, most states adhere to an objective or "reasonable man" test. That is, the jury is allowed to hear testimony and use a test of reasonableness in deciding whether or not the plaintiff would have changed his or her mind if fully informed. This test focuses not on what the particular plaintiff would have done, but on what any reasonable person would have done under the circumstances. Thus, the jury is not required to be governed by what the plaintiff says he would or would not have done if fully informed. Rather, the jury can consider what they or any other reasonable person would have done if faced with the same choices.

In the case of third-molar impactions, a common complaint is the failure to inform the patient of the possibility of lingual nerve damage. At trial, the plaintiff swears, "I would never have had the tooth out if he had said there was any possibility of tongue numbness following the surgery." In only one state does that kind of testimony bear weight: Oklahoma has criticized the "reasonable man" rule of proximate causation in informed consent. In that state, the courts have said that the rule seems to backtrack on the principle of patient self-determination developed in *Canterbury v. Spence*. In all other states, the jury is able to consider whether or not the fictional "reasonable man" would have refused the treatment if fully aware of all the possible adverse outcomes. In other words, the jury in "reasonable man" states is free to disbelieve the plaintiff and rule that a reasonable man would have consented to the extraction in spite of the warnings. This rule prevents disillusioned patients from using 20-20 hindsight to take out their frustration on the treating doctor.

In this area of dentistry, the problem is whether the tooth extraction was required by clinical conditions or performed simply for preventive purposes. In a 1983 Illinois case, the dentist's failure to warn that extraction might result in paresthesia did not negate consent.[5] In that case, the defendant produced expert testimony as to the life-threatening condition of the tooth to be extracted. The jury was permitted to disbelieve the patient's testimony that she would not have consented if she had known of the risk of paresthesia.

Diagnostic Dilemma

How far does the diagnostician have to go in transmitting results of his or her clinical and radiographic examination? A 1979 Washington State medical case may help frame the requirements in this subject area.[6]

The plaintiff consulted a physician, an ophthalmologist, concerning difficulty in focusing and blurred vision. The doctor took eye-pressure readings, which registered in the borderline area for glaucoma. In response to the patient's inquiry about the results of the pressure readings, he said he had checked for glaucoma but found everything "all right." He informed the plaintiff neither that he had found high pressure in both eyes nor that her risk of glaucoma was considerably increased. Nor did he advise her of the availability of two additional diagnostic tests for glaucoma, which are simple, inexpensive, and risk-free.

The patient visited the doctor's office on a number of occasions over the next two years with the same vision problem. By the time the plaintiff was diagnosed as having open-angle glaucoma, she was functionally blind. There was evidence that if the glaucoma had been detected earlier, a great part of her vision could have been saved.

The court eventually ruled that the doctor has the duty to advise his patient of all relevant material information concerning the condition of the patient's eyes: all the information the patient will need to make an informed decision respecting the alternative methods of examination for eye disease, the reasonably foreseeable risks of each alternative, and the risks of choosing no such alternative at all.

The court further declared that the physician's duty of disclosure arises whenever the doctor becomes aware of an abnormality which may indicate risk or danger. "The facts which must be disclosed are all those facts the physician knows or should know which the patient needs in order to make the decision. To require less would be to deprive the patient of the capacity to choose the course his or her life will take."[7]

Dental Diagnosis

It's possible that cases involving failure to diagnose periodontal disease will follow the same logic. Let's consider, for instance, a case where a dentist takes periodic bitewing X-rays and notes some advancing bone loss, but doesn't feel it is serious enough to bring to the patient's attention.

Suppose further that the clinician performed no other tests, kept the patient in the practice, and continued to observe conditions regularly. Now we have created a dental situation similar to the above medical case. In dentistry there are other "simple, inexpensive, and risk-free" diagnostic tests for periodontal disease. Frequent use and recording of periodontal pocket depths, frequent mobility checks, and checks for color and texture changes can all be taken and recorded periodically for comparison. According to the reasoning of the Washington State court, the patient should be advised when early signs of periodontal disease are observed in any diagnostic test. If the patient wishes further testing or referral, then it's his or her choice and, from that point on, *his or her responsibility.*

Can Staff Obtain Informed Consent?

Which member of the dental staff can provide the information necessary for gaining informed consent from patients? A 1983 case from Pennsylvania gives us some insight as to how the courts will rule if this question is raised in the future.[8] In that case, a patient was admitted to a hospital in 1976 for the removal of four third molars. After surgery, the patient complained of loss of sensation in her tongue and slurring of her speech.

There followed an allegation of negligence in obtaining informed consent. The courts heard arguments from the injured plaintiff to the effect that the informed consent was not valid unless the risks of surgery were disclosed *by the dentist.* The patient claimed that the dentist's assistant furnished her with the information on possible complications.

The court refused to consider the argument that the dentist must personally provide the information. The reasoning was that the scope of the information, not the person making the disclosure, was the key to informed consent.

Children: Consent and Informed Consent

Consent to specific behavior-management routines in pediatric dentistry—such as the hand-over-mouth exercise (HOME), restraining devices, and physical restraint by dental personnel—may require separate approval by parents. The usual expectation of parents who entrust the care of their children to the dentist is that the child will be treated with the least amount of physical contact possible.

From a legal standpoint, the specific nonpharmacologic control procedures mentioned above should be used only after the parents have been alerted that such restraint may be necessary. In a legal case arising out of a similar incident, the parents are presumed to have no special knowledge of dentistry. Therefore they have only the average citizen's view of what can or should take place in a dental office regarding the care and treatment of their child. Since adult restraint procedures are not commonly used, there is no reason to expect a parent to know about the specific behavior-management techniques that dentists occasionally use.

For this reason it is prudent to make specific your anticipated treatment regimen concerning possible problem behavior in child patients. You might educate parents about the different types of control with a descriptive pamphlet describing each procedure and its limits on the physical trauma involved. You should also emphasize the advantages of treatment versus no treatment. Finally, you should note your views on the long-term benefits versus the short-term drawbacks, as well as your opinion on the effects of the restraint on the child's future relationships with the dentist.

Can a Child Consent?

Children, before they reach the state statutory age of majority, are incapable of giving consent to dental treatment. In the case of an emergency, the child may be treated to the point of bringing his or her condition to a point of stability.

Then treatment should be suspended pending the receipt of verbal or written consent from a parent or adult guardian. In cases where a neighbor or another juvenile brings a child for treatment, the case should be treated as an emergency and only necessary treatment provided.

Most states recognize one exception to the minor consent rule: the case of minor children living apart from their parents. These so-called "emancipated minors" may contract with dentists for necessary treatment. The law then protects the practitioner from accusations of failure to obtain plain consent and protects the fee charged for the services under contract law.

Consent in Emergencies

Exceptions to the general rule of full disclosure include emergencies where the patient is unconscious or incapable of consent. In this situation, the practitioner must feel that some harm from failure to treat is imminent and outweighs any harm threatened by the proposed treatment. These situations might be expected to arise in the offices of oral surgeons or in hospital dental practices where dental personnel are included in trauma teams. Such emergencies can occur or arise out of the specific dental procedure, such as surgery, or from a patient's injury or illness.

The following is a familiar set of circumstances. An oral surgeon contemplates removal of an impacted third molar. The two-dimensional X-ray film shows part of the impacted tooth crown overlapping the root of the second molar. When the surgeon exposes the field to direct view, he or she finds a large nonrestorable defect in the distal aspect of the *second* molar root.

Now the surgeon faces a dilemma. Before the operation, the patient had signed a document giving the surgeon "general" consent for the surgical excision of the impacted third molar, along with other language consenting to "any additional treatment the surgeon feels necessary." No discussion had taken place regarding possible injury to the second molar.

Can the surgeon safely—that is, legally and defensively— remove the second molar while the patient is under the effect of the intravenous sedation? The answer is no. Nonrestorable or not, and despite the fact that in the surgeon's opinion the second molar would have to be extracted eventually, the patient should be aroused, told of the new findings, and advised of the poor prognosis of the second molar. No particular emergency exists and no imminent harm is evident. If we assume that the area was sympton-free preoperatively, there is no justification for imposing the surgeon's will on the patient's decision-making prerogative in this case.

A second alternative would be to obtain the consent of the patient's accompanying family member, if such a person is available. Technically, that person has no right to make a decision for the patient, but the fact that the surgeon brought the family member into the process, gained his or her approval, and completed the extractions on the still sedated patient will go a long way toward forestalling a subsequent lawsuit.

Obviously there are benefits to removing the molar during the first procedure. By doing so, the risk of a second procedure is eliminated. Sticking to the rules—bringing the patient up to full consciousness and then resedating—mandates a second session of life-threatening general anesthesia, a less desirable sequence of events.

Consent Forms

Some clinicians have experimented with special forms listing consequences of treatment. In 1977, two New Jersey dentists, specializing in providing full-service dental procedures under general anesthesia, asked patients to read a list of "possible aftereffects and consequences of general anesthesia."[9] The list contained 36 adverse possible consequences of the use of general anesthetic, ranging from hiccups to circulatory collapse. The doctors then offered to discuss any of the potential problems with patients in detail.

To those who believe that the public will balk and refuse necessary treatment when confronted with serious information about the possible aftereffects of treatment, this fact should be instructive: in the year that the dentists kept records on the subject, *not one* of the prospective patients turned down the suggested treatment.

Patient Reaction to Full Disclosure

If you believe that too much information will only confuse the major issue of whether or not to undergo treatment, note the following. The presumption should always be that all patients are fully capable of deciding what dental procedures to undergo. The informed consent doctrine need not unduly frighten patients who are about to encounter surgical treatment.

In a major study of patients about to undergo angiography (a radiographic study of blood vessel patency), the patients were asked to sign an informed consent form that listed a number of serious reactions.[10] The consequences included the loss of an organ, a death rate of 4 in 6,500, and a complication rate of 1 in 500. Some 900 patients took part in this 1971 study; only 1% decided against the procedure.

Interestingly, 75% of the study participants found the information useful, and over 70% either felt more comfortable or were not emotionally affected. Some 25% admitted to being troubled by the information, but decided to go ahead anyway. The study concluded that it is wise to inform the patient well in advance of a procedure. This step allows the patient time to think over what is being proposed, weigh the risks, and make an informed decision.

Case Study 1.

Undiagnosed Periodontal Disease: The Effect of Informed Consent

This is the case where Mrs. V (for victim) alleges that Dr. Trustee failed to diagnose and treat her over a number of years for a chronically progressive periodontal disease. How does an allegation that Dr. Trustee also failed to inform Mrs. V of the presence of periodontal disease fit into the litigation? Again, plaintiff's attorneys will plead both concerns. First, that there was a failure to detect or diagnose the condition. (Also, because Dr. Trustee didn't know of the presence of the disease, he failed, of course, to treat the condition.) Second, the pleadings will allege in the alternative, that Dr. Trustee *did* know of the presence of the disease, but failed to inform Mrs. V of its presence, its consequences, the alternative types of treatment available, and the progress, or lack of progress, of his own treatment.

During the pretrial period, each side will question their opponents on this issue. Since the allegations usually cover a large number of years, testimony about what was said or done years earlier may be lost to memory. If the dentist's records contain notes about conversations concerning periodontal health, that helps the provider. If no notes were made, the dentist is left with his or her recollections and possibly with his or her usual customs and habits.

No records of conversations with the patient about periodontal disease will help the plaintiff when he or she says, "I never heard the term 'periodontal disease' in all the years I went to Dr. Trustee." Further, the dentist may remember telling Mrs. V about the disease and even offering to give her a referral, but if the notes don't contain any mention of a referral, and if Mrs. V testifies that none was made, the jury is free to believe Mrs. V's version. In the same vein, if Dr. Trustee remembers, but none too clearly, that Mrs. V refused to take a referral and refused to come in regularly, his notes should reflect those thoughts in writing, as they are important pieces of information.

All these considerations make the written record of the patient's treatment all the more important to the defense of claims concerning failure to diagnose periodontal disease.

Case Study 2.

Pathetic Prosthesis:
The Effect of Informed Consent

This case study involves the hasty and less-than-careful placement of multiple units of crown and bridge. Dr. Swifty was more than adequate in extolling the virtues of new crowns, but the risks of failure—unaesthetic porcelain, adverse soft-tissue reaction, and the possibility of endodontic treatment—went by the wayside.

Here the patient-plaintiff, Mr. Newvo, will say that the possibility of root canal treatment was never made a part of the pretreatment discussions. Dr. Swifty will counter either that he did in fact mention the possibility, or that the possibility was too remote to mention. In either case, the plaintiff will plead lack of informed consent as an alternative count in the complaint.

In this case, the jury will take a close look at whether or not Newvo would have refused the treatment if he had received full disclosure. Under the objective test in most communities, the jury will be able to consider how an average person would react when advised of the possible root-canal complication.

In this particular case, only two of the twenty teeth prepared by Swifty required endodontic procedures. Would Newvo have refused the crowns if Swifty had told him in advance that two teeth would probably need root canal treatment? The "reasonable man" on the jury might very well say, "No!" Therefore, Newvo can expect to lose on that count. There is no guarantee, however, that juries will see things in a logical manner. The plaintiff will probably not give up the slim chance to obtain a jury verdict on informed consent under these circumstances.

Case Study 3.

Oral Surgery Mishaps:
The Effect of Informed Consent

As you will remember, this case study involves Dr. Newon Block and Ms. Totally Innocent. Ms. Innocent needs treatment of an infection around a partially impacted lower third molar. As a preventive measure, the opposite lower third molar is extracted at the same session as the symptomatic tooth. As a postoperative complication, Ms. Innocent complains of numbness of the edge of the tongue on the side of the asymptomatic tooth extraction.

Here the plaintiff will allege that the dentist failed to inform her that tongue numbness might be a possible outcome of the treatment. She will argue further that Dr. Block knew or should have known that she was a wine taster by occupation. At the very least, she will allege that she wrote her occupation on the dentist's registration form and/or that they discussed her unusual occupation and/or that she may have brought him some wine at an earlier visit. Anything will be done to help the jury recognize that this particular patient had a greater stake than usual in the possible adverse outcome of tongue numbness.

Then Ms. Innocent will allege that the treatment was of a nonemergency nature. She will state that the tooth on the opposite side was the symptomatic tooth, and that removing the tooth that led to the lingual nerve damage was purely and totally elective.

Putting the two factors together, that Ms. Innocent was a special patient and that the procedure was elective, will give Ms. Innocent an advantage before a jury. Both those facts give credence to the need for the information and the high probability that she would not have agreed to the elective extraction if informed at the outset about the possibility of numbness.

As a defense, Dr. Block may be able to show that there was a discussion of nerve damage. If his records lack that particular information, however, he will have to rely on a very tenuous defense of habit and custom. If he can't remember the particular circumstances, he may use his custom and habit of telling each and every third-molar extraction case about the possibility of nerve damage. This is not the strongest defense, but if verifiable, it may even the score a little and help the jury decide in the dentist's favor.

Summary

In general, a dentist should disclose information that he or she knows, or reasonably should know, concerning hazards of the proposed treatment. Even so, the practitioner cannot be held liable for the unknown. The dentist cannot be held responsible for failing to warn about injurious results of unexpected occurrences, such as when the unexpected hazard is improper execution of the procedure. In that case, the negligence would be in the procedure itself, not in failure to tell the patient that he or she could be hurt "if I botch the job."

In dentistry, the "unexpected" may happen when the patient experiences pain and makes an involuntary movement. If the practitioner is also the anesthesiologist, however, the responsibility for the failure of anesthesia would be related back to him. Many sources believe that control of the patient's movement is the responsibility of the dentist. Various methods are available to assure that anesthesia has "taken," allowing the practitioner to move ahead safely with treatment.

Furthermore, the dentist need not communicate those risks of which the average patient of reasonable sophistication would be aware, such as postoperative infection or the necessity of taking pain medication. It's not prudent to omit these important facts from a case presentation involving surgery, but some courts have felt that such failures have not led to any legal liability. In the same light, if the patient has already discovered certain information, as through a previous experience, then those risks need not be disclosed.

In determining which hazards should or should not be presented to the patient, the courts have looked to the seriousness and danger of the possible injuries. Thus, where extremely serious injuries may occur, even if the potential incidence is extremely small, the court will generally require disclosure. Also, if the danger is statistically high, then the danger must be disclosed even if the injury is minor or temporary.

Finally, if the danger is both remote statistically and minor or temporary, the dentist need not reveal its possibility. In a dispute about what should or should not have been revealed, however, the court will allow the jury to decide.

The same rules govern the prescription of drugs. Any known serious side effects must be revealed before the patient agrees to take such medication.

Finally, where an unorthodox or radical treatment method is proposed, the fact that the treatment departs from the professional community standard must be disclosed, along with any potentially serious dangers inherent in the procedure. This category includes techniques and procedures not presently recognized by a national testing agency or association such as the American Dental Association, the National Bureau of Standards, or the U.S. Food and Drug Administration.

References: Informed Consent

1. Canterbury v. Spence 464 F2d 354 (D.C. Cir., 1972).
2. Ibid.
3. Ibid.
4. Ibid.
5. Gemme v. Tomlin 455 NE2d 294 (Ill., 1983).
6. Gates v. Jensen 594 P2d 919 (Wash., 1979).
7. Ibid.
8. Bulman v. Myers 467 A2d 1353 (Pa., 1983).
9. Drs. Kroll and Stone, East Orange, New Jersey 07018.
10. Alfidi, Informed Consent: A Study of Patient Reaction 216 JAMA 1325 (1971).

5
Abandonment

Termination of treatment occurs daily in almost every dental office in the land. This cessation takes many forms and occurs for a variety of reasons. In our mobile, dynamic society, patients are continually leaving, or not returning to, their dentists.

If discontinuation of treatment is due to patient whim, it does not give rise to liability on the part of the dentist. In some instances, in fact, such cessation may be viewed as a factor in contributory negligence on the part of the patient. (Contributory negligence by patients is treated in the chapter on legal defenses.)

If the termination is caused or initiated by the dentist, however, then the allegation of *abandonment* is heard, and as such can be considered a cause of action in negligence—malpractice.

Most of the litigated cases of abandonment arise against hospitals in the context of overcrowded emergency rooms. The usual fact pattern is as follows: (1) the patient is refused treatment; (2) the patient's condition is allowed to worsen because of the failure to treat the patient promptly; or (3) the patient is treated superficially and released, only to become worse or die outside the hospital.

Unless a dentist is part of a comprehensive treatment facility which customarily accepts emergency dental cases, such "emergency-room" situations do not apply. In this chapter, we will limit the topic to instances of abandonment in private offices or in group clinic settings.

The law on termination is fairly simple. Once a dentist has established a relationship with a patient, the practitioner must continue treatment until there comes a time, or until circumstances require, that the relationship justifiably be ended. There is no obligation to take any new patient into your practice, but once you have done so, you are obligated to continue treatment until a logical stopping point is reached. That stopping point may be different from the one that was established initially as the treatment objective.

Termination can occur if the patient decides to "fire" the practitioner. It can also occur at a point where the dentist cannot continue treatment under the circumstances. Before the dentist may terminate treatment short of completion, however, three obligations must be met if abandonment is to be avoided.

First, the dentist may not discontinue in the middle of a distinct treatment phase. For example, a dentist may not prepare a tooth and then refuse to complete the procedure. Although there are times in the life of every dentist when he or she would love dearly to do that, the law would frown on such behavior. The dentist must continue to treat the patient until it can be said legitimately that the patient is in a "stable" treatment phase. In other words, nothing more is pending in the current series of treatments.

This does not mean that the ultimate objectives of treatment must be achieved before a patient can be terminated. Rather, it means that the dentist *must complete what he or she has started*—it's as simple as that. If the dentist begins a series of planned visits to provide a full denture, the denture must be delivered. On the other hand, if the patient has a number of problems, and if the treatment plan calls for preventive or prophylactic services, followed by restorative work, followed by crown and bridge, the answer to when a dentist may terminate safely is not so simple.

If trouble occurs between the dentist and the patient before any restorations are done or even started, then, with proper attention to the other considerations in terminating a patient, the work can stop before the restorations are started. The same does not hold true, however, for trouble that occurs *during* restoration. At that point, efforts must be made to continue the restorative phase to completion. The idea is that the patient should not be forced into making a quick decision to find follow-up treatment. The courts, for example, find it unfair to stop treatment in the middle of placing a number of fillings. The patient knows that such work must be completed and that conditions are likely to deteriorate if left unattended. A case can be made, however, for terminating after the completion of simple restorative procedures and before beginning complex procedures, such as crown and bridgework or removable appliances.

In cases where treatment responsibilities are shared with one or more specialists, the question of termination can be complex. Suppose you have referred a patient of yours to a periodontist. Upon the periodontist's recommendation, the patient enters into a treatment plan that includes a number of surgical sessions over a protracted period of time. Before the surgical phase of treatment begins, the plan calls for the placement of "provisional" restorative care, usually temporary crowns replacing defective existing restorations.

What happens when a breakdown occurs between the general dentist and the patient after the provisional treatment is placed and the surgery is begun, but before the final restorative care is rendered? The question has probably not been litigated, but peer review committees around the country have heard this complication. What happens, for example, if at some point during treatment the patient fails to return for treatment, or fails to make good on promised payments? What, then, if the dentist doesn't reschedule the patient promptly or if the patient feels that he or she has been spoken to in an insulting manner? Communication ceases, that's what. Is that abandonment? Quite possibly. The dentist may be more at fault than the patient because he or she is the professional—the player in the drama who is expected to control his or her behavior.

In dentistry, abandonment isn't always as easy to understand as leaving a baby on a doorstep. Breakdowns in communication are more subtle. Nuances of communication can destroy feelings of trust and respect between parties. If the dentist is found to be more responsible for the breakdown than the patient, then the dentist is responsible for the abandonment.

In order to make a case for abandonment in dental malpractice, however, two additional elements must be proved by the patient. First, the patient must show that the abandonment led to the damages claimed. Second, of course, the damages must be measurable. Straight abandonment, by itself, will not suffice to carry a case of malpractice. Damages must be proved, and it must be established that they occurred because of the abandonment. Practitioners should not rely on lack of damages when confronting an abandonment action. Abandoned patients have claimed successfully that psychological damages resulted from arbitrary terminations by dentists.

Damages caused by delay in treatment are easy to prove in questions of oral disease. The two most common oral conditions, caries and periodontal disease, are known to be progressively destructive. Time and inattention to treatment, both home care and professional care, inevitably lead to worsening of these conditions. The professional knows this.

The patient, however, is not necessarily aware of this information. If a case is deteriorating for one of these reasons, the facts of the situation must be explained to the patient before things go too far. Here again, record keeping plays a significant role in protecting the dentist against subsequent lawsuits that are based on abandonment and lack of informed consent.

Vacation Coverage

There's also the possibility of abandonment when the dentist is on vacation. If no coverage has been provided, the patient in need of treatment is left with some poor choices. One choice is to wait for the dentist to return. A second choice is to try to get help from an alternative medical source. A third option is to involve another dentist in the dental care, either temporarily or permanently.

The first choice is appropriate if the problem is not too serious, such as when a piece of filling chips off. If the problem is swelling in the jaw and throat, however, waiting can be very dangerous. Pain, swelling, and temperature elevation are symptoms that can lead to serious illness, sometimes requiring hospitalization.

Some dentists, on learning that a patient with serious symptoms elected to await their return, have been heard to say, "If it was that serious, why didn't the stupid patient go to the hospital?" Doctor, there are two possible explanations. First, you never told your patients what to do in case of emergency. Second, many people—physicians, accountants, judges, and other highly educated individuals—are reluctant to seek medical assistance even when they suspect they should. As a corollary, patients know that many conditions are of short duration and self-limiting, so they choose to "wait it out till Doc gets back."

Nature *can* heal many problems without medical intervention. It's understandable for patients to delay emergency visits until they're convinced they won't get better on their own. Besides, the dentist may have said some reassuring things that convinced the patient to wait or treat the problem at home. After an extraction, for instance, the usual instructions about bleeding and infection are frequently accompanied by reassurances that "in a few days you'll be able to eat and function normally." What does that tell the average patient? It says, "Nature will take its course. Don't worry if you're uncomfortable for a few days. You'll get over it because Dr. X said so. Don't bother him at home; he's already told you you're going to feel better even though you may feel like death warmed over until enough time has passed."

Even worse, doctor, there are other things you may have done to discourage a return visit by a troubled patient. Suppose you have anticipated a problem of postoperative complications, and have provided the patient with some low-strength, prophylactic antibiotic. Over the weekend you're at the beach, the patient religiously takes the empirical medication with only a statistical probability that it is appropriate for the complications that arise. The patient has not only your reassurances, but also *your medicine* to keep him from calling you, or anyone, while his condition steadily worsens.

The lesson for dentistry is clear. In order to avoid the charge of abandonment in the event of postoperative complications, some means of contact with dental professionals must be available to the patient. This responsibility may be met through the organized efforts of the local dental society or by an informal understanding among a group of dentists, but some arrangement for such coverage *must be in place*.

Follow-up Care and Abandonment

In dentistry, the greatest number of abandonment cases occurs when dentists fail to provide follow-up attention after

treatment. The classic example comes from a 1960 Massachusetts case in which a dentist failed to follow up after the
extraction of teeth, even though he knew that root tips had
been left in the patient's jaw.[1]

In that case, the dentist examined the plaintiff's mouth
and then stated that two wisdom teeth needed to be extracted.
He said the patient should be admitted to the hospital the very
next day to have the procedure performed. The patient com-
plied, and the surgery took place on the second hospital day.
The surgery was performed under a general anesthetic and the
patient was discharged one day later.

At home, the left side of the patient's jaw started "throb-
bing like a toothache." The jaw tightened, and the patient
could not eat on the next postoperative day. The plaintiff's face
was greatly swollen, and she was in severe pain. She tried to
get in touch with the dentist, but without success. The
swelling and pain persisted, and she was unable to open her
mouth.

Eventually the dentist was contacted, and diagnosed an
abscess. During the first ten post-op days, the plaintiff saw the
dentist numerous times at his office. The dentist lanced the
abscess and prescribed warm salt-water rinses.

The patient's condition continued to deteriorate, and the
left extraction site began to hemorrhage spontaneously. On
two occasions, the patient was taken to the hospital emergency
room for treatment. Because of the severity of her complications, the patient was admitted to the hospital and remained
there for 12 days. After discharge from her second hospitalization, the patient was able slowly to resume her normal
activities.

About a year after the procedure, the patient was still
experiencing occasional discomfort in the left jaw, so she saw a
new dentist. The new dentist took an X-ray and immediately
referred the patient to an oral surgeon. The oral surgeon
discovered a root tip at the site of the earlier extraction, and
removed it.

Until this time, the patient did not know that a root tip
had been left in her jaw. When she learned that this was the
case, she changed titles—whereas she had been a "patient,"
she now became a "plaintiff."

At the trial, the first dentist admitted that no preoperative X-ray had been taken, but admitted that pre-op X-rays are used to give the dentist valuable information. He then told the court that although he had intended to take out the full tooth at the outset, he was forced to discontinue the procedure because of the patient's poor respiration and severe hemorrhage. The dentist further admitted that it was common practice to remove the full tooth, but that in this instance he had not removed the root tip either initially or subsequently.

The plaintiff's expert was the oral surgeon who had found and removed the root tip. He testified that the pre-op X-ray was vital and that if the root tip had been removed soon after the original surgery, the plaintiff probably would not have had any problem. The judge ordered a verdict for the dentist, but on appeal, the court reversed itself and found in favor of the plaintiff.

At the first trial, the court had chosen to disregard the relevance of the pre-op X-ray by reasoning that the failure to take the radiograph was not the cause of the patient's postoperative complication. The court overlooked the defendant's decision to discontinue the operation by reasoning that all practitioners would behave similarly under similar circumstances (poor respiration and severe hemorrhage).

The appeal court, however, would not allow the defendant, the one person with the knowledge of the remaining root tip, to get away with keeping that information to himself. The court found that the defendant had the facts and had the patient under his care for the first ten post-op days, plus the 12 days she was in the hospital for the swollen jaw. Yet during that time, and for several visits after the second hospital admission, the defendant dentist *never told the patient about the root tips* and took no steps to remove them.

The defendant also testified that after the patient had ceased to see him, he tried without success to contact her with the thought of removing the remaining root tips. This was a classic case of too little effort, too late.

The court held that the dentist had, in effect, abandoned both his responsibility and his patient. By withholding information and treatment, his behavior was tantamount to termination of care. He had failed to provide the required explanation and he had failed to try to find alternative sources of care for the patient.

Who's in Charge?

Even a temporary distraction that takes the practitioner away from the focus of his or her responsibility can lead to a charge of abandonment. Any such lapse in treatment can give rise to this allegation, but, again, only if some damage or injury occurs in the period of lapse and is a result of the lapse.

In a famous 1967 Washington State case, a case indirectly involving dentistry, the court ruled that the physician who admitted a patient to the hospital and then entrusted the case to an oral surgeon was negligent and responsible for the anesthetic accident that occurred during the surgical procedure.[2] The physician left the hospital before the oral surgeon had performed the surgery to set the plaintiff's jaw. Anesthesia was administered by a nurse-anesthetist, but an error caused severe brain damage due to anoxia.

This case has had strong repercussions in the health field. Fewer hospitals now require one health-care professional to supervise the activities of another, because such bureaucratic layering exposes more professionals to liability. The rule is fairly clear and unambiguous: if one practitioner has the major responsibility for patient care and turns that care over to another, then any subsequent act or omission by the second person will reflect on the person with the major responsibility.

A similar principle in employment law states that the employer is responsible for the acts of his or her employees while they are conducting company business. The same principle holds true in health care. In the case at hand, it may have been a hospital rule that brought the physician into the picture in the first place. Perhaps he only signed off on the work of the oral surgeon. To the patient and the court, however, the M.D. was "in charge," albeit in name only. Theoretically, the physician "selected or employed" the oral surgeon to carry out the treatment of the patient.

In ascribing ultimate negligence, no one is ever totally free of fault. The plaintiff is permitted to sue anyone in the chain of responsibility. In a case like this, the patient would have a case against the nurse, the oral surgeon, the physician, and the hospital. The hospital was the actual employer of the nurse, which makes the nurse the hospital's agent. The hospital may be sued on the theory of negligent hiring, or negligent supervision of the system or of the particular persons involved. Under the rules of agency law, the employer must answer to the charges of negligence by its employee. If the agent was acting *outside* the bounds of employment, the hospital may be able to recover from the nurse. If the nurse is deemed to be acting within the bounds of employment, however, then the hospital cannot recover against the nurse.

Late-Night New Patients

What about those late-evening phone calls from persons who are having pain because of long-neglected oral care? Dispensing advice over the telephone is dangerous, especially if the advice is to postpone treatment until the office is open or until some other practitioner can see the patient.

In a 1960 New York medical case, a patient went to a hospital emergency room seeking relief from pain.[3] Apparently the house physician was not present, and the patient used the hospital phone to talk to him. The physician told the patient to go home and to come back to the hospital in three hours, when the plaintiff's own physician would be there. The plaintiff died before he could return. The court said that the jury could decide whether the defendant undertook to diagnose the patient's condition during the brief telephone conversation and then abandoned his responsibility to treat or to refer the patient for treatment.

The lesson for dentistry is clear. If the telephone call comes from a stranger, there is no rule of law that requires the dentist to accept the patient.[4] Once the call is accepted, however, the law requires that certain steps be taken in order to terminate.

Even if the patient declares that this is an emergency and that he is in great pain, health-care professionals are under no obligation to accept the patient. It may be unethical to turn one's back on a fellow human being in distress, but the law is clear. There is no duty to accept patients. A dentist may reject any patient except for reasons that would violate the person's civil rights.[5]

If a stranger calls in the night, you need not take him or her into your practice, so long as that person is truly a stranger to your practice. Even so, the way in which you handle the discussion can be critical. If you listen to the patient's complaints and then say you can't see him or her, you may have inadvertently accepted the patient by the act of receiving a medical or dental history. Involvement to the extent of forming an opinion or diagnosis could be construed as acceptance. If you then refuse to see the patient, the charge of abandonment becomes a possibility.

The best way to handle such situations is to have at your telephone a list of emergency centers with 24-hour dental capability. Even if the facility is not nearby, suggesting an available emergency treatment center will salve your conscience and provide the patient with an alternative to waiting for normal business hours.

The conversation should go something like this:

Prospective patient: "Hello, Dr. Dogtired? I'm sorry to bother you at 2:30 in the morning, but I'm in terrible pain. My name is Wade Toolong, and I know you don't know me from Adam but..."

Dr. Dogtired: "Hold on there, Wade, I can't see you, but I can give you telephone numbers of (hospital emergency room, clinic, or practitioner with advertised 24-hour phone number). Got a pencil?"

Wade Toolong: "But this is an emergency, and my cousin's girlfriend goes to you and said you're a real push... I mean a real great guy and..."

Dr. Dogtired (interrupting again): "I'm sorry, I can't see you. These telephone numbers will get you in touch with someone who will be able to help." (Gives numbers.) "Good night."

In this example, the dentist had already decided not to take any information from the caller. His polite but firm refusal and his provision of alternative sources of care will act in his favor if the patient does not find relief, or if his condition worsens because of the delay and he decides to sue for abandonment. The dentist's defense would be that he did not undertake any patient acceptance activities and did not receive any medical or dental information from which to make a diagnosis. Without a diagnosis, the dentist could not have abandoned the patient's care.

In such instances, when the dentist is at the office the next morning, he or she should make a memo detailing the early-morning call, the decision not to accept the patient, and the provision of the alternative numbers. Such a memo will help the dentist remember how the call was managed. There is wisdom in maintaining a separate file of such emergency calls and their disposition. Such memos could prove to be valuable.

Late-Night Regular Patients

Now let's change the circumstances a bit. The middle-of-the-night caller is Granny Goodwitch, one of your oldest and most loyal patients, who has been up for hours with pain and discomfort. She has tried to hold off until your office hours, but now her jaw won't open and she tells you there is swelling in her face and under her jaw.

You saw Mrs. Goodwitch three days ago for the extraction of a lower molar, and you suspect that the symptoms are the result of a postoperative infection. You also know her health history. You ask additional questions, and find that her temperature is elevated and has been for 12 hours. You had prescribed a low-dose penicillin V, and she has taken the pills faithfully.

If you move to intervene promptly, you might avert a lengthy hospitalization and unnecessary airway surgery. On the other hand, you could tell her you will see her first thing in the morning. The only legally defensible position is to over-react and move aggressively in the face of potentially serious complications. The expense of a hospital emergency room is insignificant compared to the possible need for a surgical procedure to establish an airway, and an attendant hospitalization costing thousands of dollars.

You recommend that Mrs. Goodwitch go immediately to the local hospital, and tell her, "I'll meet you there."

Some years ago, a dentist performed a combined service of extractions and the placement of a temporary partial denture, a "flipper," for a patient with periodontally hopeless teeth. The extracted teeth included several upper anterior teeth and a maxillary third molar. The flipper was designed to replace the upper anteriors, and covered only a portion of the anterior palate.

After the morning surgery and placement of the prosthetic device, the patient was discharged from the office with the flipper in place for hemorrhage control in the anterior region and a gauze pad at the third molar site. Early in the afternoon, her daughter called the dentist to report that some bleeding was still occurring. The dentist asked the daughter to bring her mother back to the office, and suggested that in the meantime, gauze or tea bags be placed between the lower teeth and the surgical sites and that moderate pressure be applied.

The daughter said she would try to get the patient back to the office, but that the patient's husband, and only driver, had gone to work and could not be reached. When the dentist did not hear again from the daughter, the patient, or her husband, he closed the office at 5:30 p.m. and went home. Upon arriving home, he received another call, this time from the patient's teenage son. He said that "Mom" felt ill, *but that there was no more bleeding*. The dentist gave instructions to have the mother eat some liquid preparations and get some sleep.

An hour later, the teenager called again, this time nearly hysterical. Mom had collapsed, and an ambulance had been called. The son handed the telephone to the ambulance attendant to speak directly with the dentist. The ambulance attendant said the woman was on the floor. She had a pulse, her mouth had been inspected, and *no bleeding was evident*. The dentist said to take her to the hospital, where he would join them.

At the hospital, the dentist talked with the emergency-room personnel. They reported that the patient had arrived with no pulse. They'd done some quick resuscitation, completed blood tests, and were presently infusing blood into the patient. The patient had vomited blood in such quantity that the hospital staff felt she was bleeding from the stomach. Her blood tests indicated leukemic levels of white blood cells. There was no bleeding from the mouth. This was one sick lady—or so the hospital thought.

To his credit, the dentist was there, consoling the family and trying to interpret the meaning of all this. The dentist rolled up his sleeve and offered to donate blood on his patient's behalf.

At first, the husband blamed himself because he had not been available to bring the patient back to the dental office in the afternoon. Later, when everyone was convinced that the mouth was not the problem, the husband blamed himself for not paying attention to his wife's frequent complaints that she was having heavier and heavier vaginal bleeding during her periods.

The patient was taken to the intensive care unit, where she remained through the night. The next day, an upper GI series ruled out any gastric bleeding, and the preliminary diagnosis of leukemia was also ruled out. The technicians who did the GI series, however, noted that there was bleeding from the upper wisdom-tooth socket. The upper front surgical site was dry.

When advised of this, the dentist returned to the hospital the evening of the second post-op day and received a special waiver of privileges from the staff. An ICU nurse, working with a flashlight, assisted the dentist in placing gelfoam and sutures over the posterior site, and the bleeding was stopped. After that the patient began to improve, and a week later she was dismissed.

No one had noticed that there were two distinct surgical areas. Every report to the dentist said that "the mouth" was not bleeding, but the reporting sources had only viewed the front part of the mouth; they never thought to look in the back. The dentist had trusted those reports. He hadn't examined the patient's mouth at the hospital and he hadn't asked the staff to check the posterior molar extraction site.

No litigation arose from the incident, probably because of the dentist's decision to drop everything and get involved in the case with the patient and her family at the hospital. Although the postoperative complications were apparently of dental origin, the dentist's responsiveness met everyone's expectations.

Now let's take a look at some other circumstances and see how the courts have viewed the question of abandonment.

Leaving a Broken Piece of Tooth in the Jaw

A dentist, after seeing the patient on several post-op visits, changing the packing in the socket, and administering penicillin, apparently became fed up with the case and told the patient's parent that he, the dentist, "didn't want to fool" with the case anymore.[6] When the patient's parent inquired whether or not an X-ray of the extraction site might be helpful, the dentist refused and said again that he, the dentist, had done everything he could for the patient and that the family had "fooled with" him. "I'm not going to fool with that case anymore. I can't help it; I am through!"

A second dentist, of course, took an X-ray and found a root tip. After the offending root tip was removed, the post-op complications resolved quickly—but not, however, the legal complications. The court decided that it is a dentist's duty to use an X-ray or other means of determining the advisability of a supplementary operation or other special treatment to effect a cure or correct conditions which developed after an initial operation or treatment. If the dentist fails to do so, the allegation of negligence based on abandonment is appropriate.

Failing to Fill a Prepared Tooth

In a 1947 West Virginia case, a dentist was preparing a tooth for a filling when the patient began to scream and cry uncontrollably.[7] The dentist removed the patient's bib and pulled her from the chair. He then ordered the patient to leave the office and not to come back until she had regained her composure. Naturally she did not come back, but instead consulted her lawyer. A case in malpractice was made, claiming that the dentist abandoned his responsibilities by undertaking to care for the patient and then arbitrarily terminating treatment.

Other Abandonment Cases

In related medical incidents, here are some cases of general interest.

In a 1976 Connecticut case, an obstetrician left the side of his critically ill patient to write orders, confer with specialists, and see other patients.[8] Although he wasn't gone long, even minutes can make the difference in critical care cases, and the patient died. The defense that the patient was left in the hands of other competent health-care personnel did not protect the primary practitioner from liability.

In a 1963 Iowa case, an ophthalmologist, after removing pieces of steel from the plaintiff's eye, failed to tell the patient to return the next day.[9] As a result, the eye was lost. Follow-up is a critical step in medicine and dentistry; as long as resolution of the disease or injury is not full and complete, follow-up procedures must be maintained. Even if only the telephone is used in the procedure, the case remains open until the patient is free from disease or the injury has healed. Leaving the responsibility of follow-up with the patient is permissible only if the patient or the patient's guardian is competent to recognize the warning signs of reinjury or deterioration.

Case Study 1.
Undiagnosed Periodontal Disease: Effect of Abandonment

In this case Dr. Trustee had provided routine dental care to a long-time patient, Mrs. V (for victim). When Mrs. V discovered that she was suffering from an apparently long-standing case of chronic periodontal disease, she sued her dentist, alleging either misdiagnosis of the condition or mistreatment.

If the allegation is one of misdiagnosis, the practitioner's defense would be that the condition simply was not there during the time he had responsibility. If Dr. Trustee takes the position that he *was* aware of the presence of the disease, his defense is that the patient's home care was either the sole cause or a major contributing cause of her condition.

The latter set of facts and the contributory negligence defense read like an allegation of abandonment. The requisite elements for abandonment are there: the practitioner accepts the patient and makes a diagnosis, but fails to treat the disease state. The mere fact that the practitioner makes himself or herself available periodically to reexamine the patient doesn't change anything. The "diagnosis and no treatment" fact pattern makes an arguable case for dental malpractice based on abandonment.

As stated earlier, the best defense to the allegation of abandonment in untreated periodontal disease is a record full of notes containing key findings, coupled with indications that the information was conveyed to the patient and descriptions of the efforts that were made to gain compliance with good oral hygiene practices.

Abandonment in the context of periodontal disease can be blocked effectively by a record of attempts to induce the patient to accept a referral to a periodontal specialist. Better yet, if the patient has been evaluated by a periodontist, has received a treatment plan from that specialist, and has refused to go through with the plan, then he or she has received the best and clearest information on his or her own disease as well as the best plan of treatment. Refusal in light of these kinds of efforts surely will provide the dentist all the protection he or she may need to raise a defense of contributory negligence and avoid the charge of dental abandonment.

Naturally, the same principle of periodic reminders is required here as in the case of the patient who has refused dental X-rays in the past. The fact that a patient refused periodontal referral or a periodontal treatment plan in the past does not provide endless protection. Periodically, the dentist must retest the patient's resolve not to undergo the procedures, always reminding the patient of the adverse risks of the course he or she has selected.

Case Study 2.

Premature Crown and Bridge Failure: Effect of Abandonment

Mr. Newvo's crown and bridge did not last very long, and some of the prepared teeth now need endodontic treatment. The units are losing their porcelain veneers, and the occlusion has been ground flat. In addition, there are marginal errors, leading to periodontal problems and carious breakdown.

Dr. Swifty blames Mr. Newvo's erratic behavior and poor appointment record for causing him to rush to completion a case that should have taken more time. He laments that he offered to make any necessary correction, but he did. Even so, the patient won't come back. Dr. Swifty claims that the broken porcelain is the patient's fault because he heard that Newvo was in a fight shortly before the porcelain was fractured.

In the situation described in the example, there would be no specific allegation of abandonment. It would seem more appropriate for the angry dentist to charge the patient with abandonment. Patients, however, have no duty or obligation to return to a dentist where treatment has not been effective.

If the work was actually done as badly as the plaintiff says, and if the dentist, Dr. Swifty, refused to see Newvo any further, there would be a case for abandonment.

It is common practice for dentists to place major cases and then make some adjustments and alterations in the mouth. When such adjustments seem endless, however, there comes a time when the dentist looks at the balance owed by the patient and decides to stop providing adjustments until the bill is paid. The dentist may even go so far as to file a lawsuit in small claims court.

The lawsuit ploy works in only a small portion of cases. In a significant number of instances, the patient not only doesn't pay, but countersues. Then, in addition to the allegation of poor work, the patient alleges abandonment. The abandonment comes from the fact that the patient is ready, willing, and able to return to the office for adjustments, but the dentist refuses to grant an appointment until the bill is paid.

Courts in a number of jurisdictions have found this practice reprehensible. From the classic case where a dentist repossessed a set of dentures from a slow-paying patient, "accidentally" dropped them on the floor, and stepped on them, to the orthodontist who refused to remove arch wires and bands from a young adult who had fallen behind in payment, the courts will not tolerate self-help collection tactics. Payment or lack of payment is not an adequate criterion for terminating service to a patient. Once a procedure has been started, it must be completed.

The courts reason that the dentist can use alternate remedies to obtain payment. The dentist can use his or her right to sue the patient under a contract theory in small claims court. Good public policy would militate against the refusal of health-care practitioners to provide services contingent on the full and immediate payment of the fee for those services.

Be aware; do not use slow or delinquent payments as an excuse to terminate dental services.

Case Study 3.

Oral Surgery Mishaps:
Effect of Abandonment

Dr. Newon Block had a problem with the nerve damage caused by surgical removal of an impacted third molar. This negligence occurred when a possible adverse outcome was not mentioned to the patient at the outset of treatment. No allegation of abandonment could be upheld on the facts or circumstances described.

If the facts were changed just a little, however, they would fit the pattern of post-op infection, a common problem with third-molar surgery. If Dr. Block disappears from view after an extraction, he may be liable for abandonment *if* the patient is injured by the delay.

You may ask, "How could a patient in a large metropolitan community possibly argue abandonment when the telephone book lists hundreds or thousands of dentists in the immediate area?" The answer is that the patient may rely on his or her own personal dentist for quick and immediate access if a problem arises. The patient has no such expectation from any other dental office. Furthermore, the patient may believe that the condition is self-limiting and will resolve itself before Dr. Block returns. Finally, Dr. Block may have provided reassurance through the provision of pain medication and antibiotics, which the patient presumes will overcome the pain and swelling.

The patient who lacks dental or medical training has no way of knowing when antibiotics are not working effectively against a developing infection. The court reasons that the dentist who leaves town without coverage has jeopardized his patient's treatment and, at least in theory, has effectively abandoned the patient.

References: Abandonment

1. Berardi v. Menicks 164 NE2d 544 (Mass., 1960).
2. Pederson v. Dumouchel 431 P2d 973 (Wash., 1967).
3. O'Neill v. Montefiore Hospital 202 NYS2d 436 (N.Y., 1960).
4. Coleman v. Middlestaff 305 P2d 1020 (Calif., 1957).
5. 42 USC Section 1983.
6. Butts v. Watts 290 SW2d 777 (Ky. 1956).
7. Wellman v. Drake 43 SE2d 57 (W.Va., 1947).
8. Ketsetos v. Nolan 368 A2d 172 (Conn., 1976).
9. Barnes v. Bovenmeyer 122 NW2d 312 (Iowa, 1963).

6
Liability for the Acts of Others (Vicarious Liability)

In the course of a career, a dentist works with and for a number of other parties in a variety of settings. The law has principles for regulating these relationships and for establishing responsibility, should an innocent person be injured by such parties acting in concert or independently of one another.

When a client claims that a dentist or dental hygienist treated him or her negligently, the average trial lawyer will try first to identify the negligent party—in legal parlance, the *tort-feasor*. Next, the lawyer will try to determine whether the person who performed the substandard service was, in fact, the employee or partner of another. If there is some indication that the person was an employee, the lawyer's responsibility is clear. The *employer must* be sued as an additional named defendant. If there is reason to believe that a partnership exists, the partnership and partners also must be named.

Let's start with an example to illustrate some of these principles. Suppose that the following signs are placed prominently at a dental office, both outside and inside:

Dr. Trustee and Associates. PC
General Dentistry
Wayne Trustee, DDS PC
Stuart Swifty, DDS
Newon Block, DMD

Here we have three dentists working in the same office. From the appearance of the signs, that's all we can say with

97

any certainty. If Dr. Swifty produced some bad crowns, is Dr. Trustee liable in any way? How about Dr. Block? If Dr. Trustee misdiagnosed periodontal disease, would the other two dentists have any reason to worry? Suppose Dr. Block abandoned a patient after performing an oral surgery procedure. Are the other two dentists implicated in any way?

As you can see, there are various possibilities to consider in the chain of responsibility. The names on the door, however, give the victim little help in deciding who is responsible for what. Plaintiffs' lawyers have a dilemma, too. If they name the wrong parties, they are liable for counteractions by the parties improperly named. If they omit a party who turns out to be a principal, and if the error cannot be rectified in time, they are liable to their client for jeopardizing the case.

Because of the potential for *legal* malpractice, it is dangerous for the lawyer to omit any party who might be culpable. Medical and dental malpractice defendants will often adopt the tactic of blaming omitted parties for the injuries about which the plaintiff is complaining. In addition, if the statute of limitations has passed and if the lawyer is prevented from naming the omitted parties, the lawyer is in malpractice jeopardy.

The legal principle that permits lawyers to name persons not actually involved in the commission of the act is called *vicarious liability*—liability for the acts of others.

There are strict rules that keep this legal principle within reason. For instance, not everyone in the room where a negligent act occurs is guilty simply by reason of proximity. If a stranger walks into a dental office while a dentist is ineffectively applying CPR to an overmedicated patient and walks out again immediately, the stranger is not necessarily liable. The stranger's presence at the time when the negligence was occurring does not automatically make him or her a potential defendant. The nonparticipating stranger is not liable for the act of the dentist.

Now let's change the facts somewhat and make the stranger a CPR instructor at a local college. The "stranger" has enough expertise to know that the dentist is not performing the CPR correctly. If such a person walks away from a situation of this type, many courts would find the behavior negligent. The so-called "good Samaritan" statutes were enacted to protect physicians, dentists, and other health professionals from suits arising out of failed attempts to aid accident victims. With that protection, however, comes the expectation that persons with medical knowledge will use their skills to assist accident victims.

In this example, the dentist is potentially liable for *commission* of negligent acts, while the CPR instructor is potentially liable for *omission* or failure to act. Vicarious liability does not apply here; both the dentist and the CPR instructor are independently negligent.

Let's change the scenario again and make the stranger another dentist who works in the office. Is the second dentist vicariously negligent? Possibly.

To connect the two dentists legally, the courts would look to the public perception or outward appearance of the practice before delving into the specifics of the working arrangement. Is the associate dentist an employee or an independent contractor? Is he or she a partner, corporate officer, or joint venturer?

Let's go back to the office of Dr. Trustee and Associates, and let's assume that the dentist performing the poor CPR on the compromised patient is the "associate," Dr. Newon Block, a name prominently displayed on the office signs. The person walking onto the scene is Dr. Trustee.

Is Trustee apt to be a named defendant in a potential legal action? Yes! The courts are likely to assume an employer-employee relationship based on the obvious practice arrangement, coupled with the fact that there was no specific warning that the "associate" was anything other than an employee.

In this context, many hospitals with emergency rooms now have prominent announcements in their waiting rooms, something like this:

This emergency room is operated by
XYZ Independent Emergency Room Company
which is not related to this hospital.
None of XYZ's employees are employees of
the hospital.

The associate in Dr. Trustee's office may well be an independent contractor for other purposes. That relationship, however, will probably not insulate Dr. Trustee from any negligent acts of Dr. Block because the principal, Dr. Trustee, will be held responsible for the want of due care by his agent, Dr. Block.

The law of agency was created not to absolve a careless employee, but *to add* the party who stands to profit the most from the employee's work. Without such protection, neither victims nor salaried employees would benefit. With only the poor working stiff to sue, victims would not be compensated adequately and workers would not be able to bear the brunt of litigation and/or judgments.

There is a difference, however, between an employee and an "independent contractor." In order for the agency principle to come into play, the dominant party must *have control* over the way in which a task is performed. In the dental office, a true independent contractor is the dental equipment repairman. If a service person comes to repair the dentist's chair, lights a blowtorch, and accidently burns a patient's shoes and feet, the patient can *try* to connect the service person's negligence to the dentist. The dentist's defense is founded on the lack of agency between himself and the serviceman.

The service person is truly independent in that his work is undirected and unsupervised. If the dentist requests special control, as in asking the service company to lend the technician for a specific custom-made addition, the technician becomes a "borrowed servant" and the *dentist's* agent. In that situation, any act that causes injury to another is the dentist's responsibility. Keep this point in mind before making special requests of your service people.

Dental associates most often come under the definition of agents or employees, even though the associate is often autonomous for tax purposes and pays his or her own income taxes and Social Security contributions. There is a certain amount of unsettled law in this historic dental arrangement, but in the context of responsibility for negligent acts, it is safest to assume that the associate is an employee. The argument can be made that the associate is independent in the sense of performing unsupervised in the dental office. By virtue of his or her license, an associate could and should act independently in the best interests of his or her patient.

If the negligent dentist is a true independent contractor, however, the employing dentist will not be held responsible. The jury may end up deciding that question as they sift through the various ways dentists have structured their practice arrangements. For instance, if the associate "rents" space and supplies his or her own patients, uses his or her own hand instruments, and conducts his or her own business (appointments and billing procedures) separate from the "landlord" dentist, *then* there is good reason to defend on independent contractor status. To gain acceptance of this defense, however, this kind of separation and some notice to the public are required.

Employees' Negligence

When the employee or agent is a dental assistant, hygienist, or technician, it is seldom difficult to establish a master-servant relationship. Those individuals are usually on the dentist's payroll and clearly act on the dentist's behalf. Therefore any act of negligence by the employee will be imputed to the dentist. Keep in mind the basic agency principle: the employer is liable under *respondeat superior* ("let the superior reply") only if the employee is directly liable. In other words, a jury cannot find the employee innocent of the negligence and hold the dentist vicariously liable. If the employee is found innocent, the dentist is innocent as well.

Liability of Partners

In the example of the improperly administered CPR we have determined that Dr. Trustee, whose name appears prominently on the office door and who, in fact, has contracted with the associate, would be vicariously liable under the circumstances as outlined. Let's change the situation somewhat and make the negligent dentist (improperly performing CPR), Dr. Stuart Swifty, a *partner* in the office of Dr. Trustee and Associates.

A professional partnership operates under the same legal principles that apply to business partnerships. Ordinarily, dental partners are liable for the malpractice of the partner dentist. Individual partners are *jointly and severally* liable for each other's acts of malpractice. The term "jointly and severally" means that the nonperforming partner would be liable for the full amount of damages if the performing negligent partner was unavailable to pay the damages. Each partner is the agent of the partnership. The partnership is liable for torts committed within the scope of the agency on the principle of *respondeat superior* in the same way that an employer is responsible for an employee's negligence.

In the example cited earlier, Dr. Swifty was performing negligently. Dr. Trustee, as the other partner, would be liable, as each member of a partnership is responsible for the care provided by all other members of the partnership. If Dr. Swifty should take off for South America shortly after a dental malpractice judgment was announced against him, the plaintiff could collect the entire judgment from Dr. Trustee.

Liability insurance offered by most underwriters, however, has a separate rider for partnership concerns. In this context it is often asked whether or not the assets of the partnership would be attached before a judgment was satisfied out of personal assets. The answer is that partnership assets would be taken first if there wasn't enough insurance to cover a judgment. Collecting malpractice judgments from practitioners is typically a matter of contract arrangements with the insurance company. In a business context, if a judgment is achieved against a partnership, the partnership assets will be taken first. If such assets are inadequate to satisfy the judgment, then the creditor may attach the personal assets of any partner. This is what makes partnership arrangements somewhat risky.

Even so, appropriate liability insurance coverage can protect against all but the most flagrant acts of negligence. There have been some incredibly high judgments, which have overwhelmed normal liability coverages.

Liability for Office Sharing

Suppose Dr. Trustee and Dr. Schmidlap made an arrangement to share office space. Would Dr. Trustee, who simply rents space to Schmidlap, be responsible for an act of negligence by Dr. Schmidlap?

The answer is "probably not." To avoid any misunderstandings, however, signs or information should be provided to all patients of Dr. Schmidlap to indicate that there is no connection between his practice and the practices of Dr. Trustee and Associates. If no indication is made to the public that Dr. Schmidlap is not an associate or partner or employee of Trustee, the public may reasonably assume that such a connection exists.

Indemnity and Contribution

Let's look again at the example in which Dr. Swifty, as a partner, performed negligently and the subsequent lawsuit named Trustee as copartner. If Dr. Trustee was required to pay the judgment based on Swifty's negligent act, then the nonnegligent defendant, Trustee, has the *right of indemnity* against his copartner for the latter's actual negligence. In the same regard, if more than one partner is actually negligent but only one is sued by the plaintiff, the defendant partner has a right of contribution from his or her fellow negligent partners. This situation creates concern among insurance companies when individual partners are insured with different companies. If the partnership and each individual are covered by the same company, then the problem is only one of bookkeeping.

Liability of Corporations

To change the example one more time, suppose that P.C., the practice of Dr. Trustee and Associates, is a *corporation* with Dr. Trustee as president, Dr. Swifty as vice-president, and Dr. Block as secretary. These three are the only shareholders of the corporation. Would Dr. Swifty's act in performing the negligent CPR be attributable to Dr. Block or Dr. Trustee? In the corporate arrangement, the answer would be "no." Dr. Trustee and Dr. Block would not be named independently as joint tort-feasors. The plaintiff, however, would have another entity to sue, namely the corporation itself, in addition to Dr. Swifty, the one defendant who performed the negligent act. The corporate structure has this advantage over other forms of practice.

Liability of "On-Call" Dentists

To turn to a different topic, what is the responsibility of dentists when they leave the area temporarily and provide substitutes to take emergency calls and treat their patients?

Generally, dentists are not liable for the negligence of other independent dentists who substitute for them during a period of temporary absence or unavailability. Naturally, if an act of negligence occurs in a substitute dentist's office, the plaintiff's lawyer will make an attempt to connect the two dentists.

Liability for Referrals

In the matter of referrals between general practitioners and specialists, the law is quite simple. When a general dentist refers a patient to a specialist, the general dentist will not be held accountable for the negligence of the specialist as long as he or she has no control or gives no direction to the acts and decisions of the specialist.

A distinction may be made between "referring out" and "bringing in a consultant," a term used in medicine. As long as the referral is made to a practitioner or specialist whom the general dentist knows or reasonably believes to be competent, no negligence attaches to the standard dental referral.

On the other hand, if an arrangement is made such that the specialist is brought *into* the dental office, and if the specialist uses the general dentist's equipment and materials, and, further, if the general dentist advises the patient that a certain procedure needs to be done and that it should be done in his office by the specialist, *then* the general dentist may have some liability for any negligence of the specialist performing the tasks discussed.

Such a case occurred in a 1978 medical case in Rhode Island, when a general practitioner consulted with a surgeon concerning specialized surgery for gastric ulcers.[1] In the course of the surgeon's procedure, an injury resulted. The plaintiff patient felt that the adverse risks and alternatives had not been explained appropriately. The general rule is that practitioners employed together by the patient, who diagnose and treat the case together, owe the same duty and are jointly liable to the patient for any negligence. Thus a general practitioner may be held jointly liable with a specialist when the facts reveal some concert of action between the two, as in the Rhode Island case.

In a 1976 Montana case, however, an orthodontist was held not liable for the negligence of an oral surgeon he recommended to the patient.[2] In that case, the plaintiff, a twenty-year-old unemployed stockbroker, went to an orthodontist to "reduce the gaps between his teeth."

There is conflicting testimony as to how and why the plaintiff came under the care of the oral surgeon. The plaintiff says that the orthodontist diagnosed a "tongue-thrust" problem and recommended a surgical procedure to correct it. The orthodontist states that he never recommended the surgery, but only made a consultation appointment for the plaintiff with the oral surgeon. The orthodontist sent X-rays and study models to the oral surgeon, all without comment or communication.

The oral surgeon made a diagnosis of congenital macroglossia, scheduled the surgery, and performed it in June. The plaintiff spent five days in the hospital, and although he was scheduled to see the oral surgeon regularly post-op, only went to see him once, on July 20. The oral surgeon said that the plaintiff was sympton-free on that visit.

In addition, the oral surgeon testified that he *did* tell the plaintiff about the possible loss of tongue mobility, speech impairment, and loss of taste, and that the surgery might not correct the tongue-thrust. Furthermore, the oral surgeon testified that at one post-op visit the plaintiff had normal taste and mobility, such that he "could lick his lips."

After the surgery, the plaintiff returned to the orthodontist for six more months of treatment, and then moved to a new city. Some months later, the plaintiff had his tonsils and adenoids removed. The physician said that although the glands were enlarged and infected, in his opinion the infection was chronic and was not causing the restricted mobility of the tongue.

Apparently the plaintiff became disillusioned with the oral surgeon and the orthodontist, and a lawsuit was filed. Among other things, the plaintiff accused both the oral surgeon and the orthodontist of negligence—the oral surgeon for negligence in the performance of the procedure, and the orthodontist for failing to inform him of the adverse risks of the surgery.

In defense, the orthodontist relied on the facts as stated in testimony. He did not recommend the surgery, but merely referred the plaintiff to the oral surgeon for an *independent* consultation, where the surgeon and the plaintiff could come to their own understanding on diagnosis and treatment selection. Since he had no idea what diagnosis the oral surgeon would reach or what treatment would be selected, he, the orthodontist, could not possibly provide the plaintiff with information on the ultimate surgical treatment. Without this definitive information, there could not have been, and there was no effort made to gain, informed consent.

The court found the orthodontist free of any vicarious liability, and set down three major points for the referral issues in this case:

1. Absent a partnership, employment, or agency, a referring practitioner cannot be subjected to liability in regard to his referral; the recommended practitioner is an independent contractor liable for his own torts.
2. Plaintiff, on whom an operation was performed by the oral surgeon, could not recover from the referring orthodontist on the theory that he was negligent in failing to warn plaintiff of the seriousness of such operation.
3. Practitioner, who prepares to perform a medical or surgical procedure, rather than a referral doctor, has the obligation to explain the procedure to the patient.

Thus the Montana decision reaffirms and clarifies the responsibilities in a routine referral transaction in dentistry. The legal responsibility rests with the party who expects to perform the treatment and the services.

References: Vicarious Liability

1. Francis v. Hopper Newport County Superior Court, No. C.A. 75-154, Oct. 13, 1978.
2. Llera v. Wisner, et al., 557 P2d 805 (Mont., 1976).

7
Expert and Fact Witnesses

Other than as a defendant, there are two ways that a dentist can appear on the witness stand in a dental malpractice case. One is to be called as an *expert witness,* a person who expresses an *opinion* on an allegation of negligent diagnosis or treatment. The other is as a *fact witness,* one who simply provides *information* on the diagnosis and treatment of the patient.

Expert witnesses are professionals who have similar training and licensure to that of the defendants. Their role is to examine records, exhibits, X-rays, and, in some cases, the plaintiffs' mouths in order to arrive at opinions as to whether or not the defendants' care and treatment was of standard quality. Experts assist judges and juries in understanding the dentistry and by making their opinions known on the issue of negligence. These witnesses are paid a fee for the time spent in the performance of their review and for any time required for depositions or in-court testimony.

The *fact witness* is a dentist who has treated the plaintiff, usually after the treatment by the defendant in the case. The fact witness is asked to testify as to the clinical and radiographic findings, the diagnosis and treatment plan, and the status of the work in progress or completed for the plaintiff. Anything contained in the fact witness records is fair game for questions at trial. This witness does not receive any special compensation other than a courtesy fee for the time and expense of making an appearance in court.

In some states, the roles can overlap. In others, the roles must be separate and distinct. In an illogical constitutional twist, plaintiffs sometimes call *defendants* as the plaintiffs' experts. The reasoning is complicated and the rules pertaining to questions differ, but the dentists on trial are occasionally asked to give information and opinion about the standard of the care that they, themselves, provided to plaintiffs.

It is legal dogma that any person who has knowledge of any fact important to a lawsuit may be required to appear as a witness in court, whether or not he or she wants to appear. The court can subpoena the appearance of the reluctant witness. Failure to comply subjects the person to a possible bench warrant, which permits the sheriff to take the witness into custody and remove him or her to the court. A dentist has no special exemption when called to testify in any legal matter. Avoiding the service of process (subpoena) will only delay the inevitable.

If you are to testify as a fact witness only, you need to understand a few things at the outset.

You may expect the ordinary witness fee (usually for transportation only), but no other special fee for your time or inconvenience is required. You may, however, arrange with the party who calls you for a reasonable fee for your time. The calling party is not required to compensate a fact witness, and if the information about payment comes out in court, the jury may consider the dentist's testimony in a different light.

If you are going to testify from dental records, become familiar with them before you enter the courthouse. There is nothing more unsettling than to sit and watch a witness silently read his or her own records to find the applicable notes.

Make sure the records you bring to court are the ones requested in the subpoena. Any other papers you refer to in court are open to inspection by the lawyers and possibly the jury.

Refresh your recollection of times, dates, and data. You may want to discuss your testimony with your staff if they have relevant information. *Do not* try to develop a common story if members of your staff may be called as witnesses. Testimony must be what is recalled personally, not what has been decided upon.

At the Courthouse

Dress in neat business attire and bring a copy of the subpoena. Be prompt, but do not enter the courtroom. Fact witnesses are usually *not* allowed to sit in the room and listen to other testimony. Send a message to the attorney who called you to let him or her know you're in the hall.

On the Stand

Speak slowly and clearly. Answer the lawyer's questions and look at him or her or the jury in explaining your answers. Use conversational language and, as much as possible, avoid using technical jargon. Keep your answers short and civil, but expand on your answers if necessary. Do not argue or attempt sarcasm. Listen to each question; pause before you answer. This pause will permit the other lawyer to interpose an objection if there is a reason to object.

You may correct an earlier answer in your testimony. The effect of letting a mistake go uncorrected can be significant to the case, especially if it appears that you are withholding information.

Cross-Examination

If you are asked whether you have discussed the case with anyone, be straightforward and say you talked to the lawyer, the patient, your staff, and/or anyone else with whom you've discussed the matter.

If you are asked whether you are being paid, you can say that you received the witness fee or a small fee for your time out of the office. Try to avoid the simple, unembellished "yes," as it may be misinterpreted by the jury.

If the session is long, ask for a short break if you feel tired or short-tempered. A cross or sarcastic answer may undo all the good work you have done up to that point.

Finally, act professionally. You will make the best impression if you appear to be a forthright, interested bystander, not simply an advocate.

If you are called as a *fact witness* in a dental malpractice case, can the lawyer ask questions about the standard of care or the negligence in the matter? In some states, the answer is "yes" and the lawyer need not pay for your "expert advice." In other states, rules prevent asking "loaded" opinion questions of friendly fact witnesses.

As an example, suppose you are Dr. Secondhand in Case Study #2, "The Pathetic Prosthesis." That case requires your testimony. From the fact pattern, you have determined that Mr. Newvo's bridgework was defective and needed replacement.

You have agreed to be a fact witness on behalf of Mr. Newvo in his malpractice case. You have already sent *copies* of your dental record and X-rays to the lawyers.

You have spoken with Mr. Newvo's lawyer, and he has agreed not to serve a subpoena in return for your assurance that you will be available on an hour's notice on a predetermined morning or afternoon. The lawyer has also volunteered to pay your reasonable hourly fee for your time out of the office.

On the afternoon reserved for your testimony, you are sworn to tell the truth. The questions start flying: Who are you? When did you examine Mr. Newvo, and what were your clinical findings? You find your nervousness wearing off. You're really rolling, explaining and demonstrating, and then comes the surprise...

Lawyer: "Based on your exam of Mr. Newvo, was the bridgework below the standard of dentistry for this area?"

Secondhand: "I wasn't aware I was here to make a judgment."

Lawyer: "Doctor, you're here voluntarily. As long as you're here and as long as you have the information, and as long as you're a qualified dentist, tell us if the work Dr. Swifty did was substandard."

Secondhand: "Your Honor, I was told I was to come and tell what I saw in Newvo's mouth, my findings and all. No one said anything about my opinion of the work."

Judge: "Well, you wanted to replace it all, didn't you? Go ahead and answer the question. You're here to assist the court in the ultimate question."

In a situation where the adversary lawyer didn't object to your becoming a "surprise" expert, and the judge was inclined to hear your opinion, you must answer or risk contempt of court. Next time get your understanding *in writing* or you won't cooperate at all.

Serving as an Expert Witness

You've been asked to be an expert witness to examine the allegations of Mrs. V in Case Study #1. Before you accepted the role, you inquired about the autonomy you would have if, after reviewing all the evidence, you found that no case had been made out against Dr. Trustee. You asked for that assurance in writing.

The lawyer for Mrs. V sent you a letter incorporating that understanding, along with additional records, X-rays, and correspondence. After careful review, you believe Mrs. V has a legitimate claim.

To make a statement concerning negligence, the potential expert must consider all the available records and evidence. The expert witness in a dental malpractice action will have to testify under oath that on the basis of some factual evidence (examination of plaintiff, examination of records and X-rays, or both) the expert has developed an opinion on the question of negligence. Thus the expert must become intimately familiar with the case record. Normally a proposed expert would be asked to look over the following documents:

A. Records and testimony of defendant
    1. defendant's complete dental record
    2. any dental X-rays taken or used by defendant
    3. any answers to written interrogatories from defendant
    4. any transcript of an oral deposition of defendant

B. Records and testimony of current treating dentist
    1. records and X-rays
    2. interrogatories, answers, and transcripts of depositions
    3. clinical and radiographic findings at first visit (of prime interest). Such information provides the best independent picture of the condition of plaintiff's mouth shortly after leaving the defendant's care.

C. Chronology of significant events
    1. prepared by plaintiff or plaintiff's attorney
    2. not considered evidence
    3. hints at testimony the plaintiff will provide

D. Court documents
    1. original complaint or statement of claim
    2. correspondence stipulating to undisputed facts and/or admissions.

E. Plaintiff's deposition and answers to interrogatories

F. Miscellaneous medical records or information
   1. other expert reports
   2. second-opinion records
   3. statements of family members

A review of a dental malpractice case can begin before the medical records are assembled by examining the patient plaintiff and taking a detailed dental history. Giving the plaintiff time to outline his or her whole story will often put him or her at ease. Few other people are willing to listen to the story of dental care gone wrong.

The examination and history taking gives the proposed expert an early chance to see whether the plaintiff's story has the ring of truth. Asking polite but leading questions at the end of the recitation can help you get to the crux of the matter and test the plaintiff's story.

Francis X. Pert, proposed dental expert, questions the unhappy patient as follows:

Q: "Surely Dr. X told you about your gum condition after each cleaning, didn't he?"
A: "All he ever said was, 'see you in 6 months.' "
Q: "Prepared 20 teeth in an hour and a half? Come on, you probably mean two teeth in that time. Right?"
A: "Nope, I mean 20. He told his assistant that would put him in the *Guinness Book of World Records!*"
Q: "Now, about the assistant that said to the dentist, 'Doctor X, we don't have any of those elevators you asked for sterilized, but this one looks clean.' Do you remember the assistant's name or can you give me a description of her?"
A: "Her name was Rose, the heavyset fortyish blonde with a tattoo on her arm."

The expert is searching for blatant or obviously false statements from the unhappy former patient, or instances of substandard care and treatment. Naturally, the plaintiff is trying to persuade the expert that Dr. X's acts or omissions were extreme, perhaps calculated, and certainly substandard.

Some plaintiffs have been misguided by friends and relatives who have urged the unhappy patient to sue the dentist. Some of the well-meaning counsel even comes with credentials: "My neighbor, the tax lawyer, says you have a $100,000 case."

Some stories do not merit follow-up, and in such cases the best service a professional can perform is to inform the proposed plaintiff that there is no breach of any standard of dental care, even if everything the injured person said about the incident is true. It's not easy to tell an emotional and frustrated person that he or she has an incorrect basic perception of dentistry and negligence, but it's not really helpful to be noncommittal in face-to-face discussions and then critical after the person leaves.

Some investigations, however, can and should proceed. If the unhappy patient presents the nucleus of a case in negligence, further evidence should be gathered and reviewed to substantiate the claim. An expert looks for deviations from the standard of care. Somewhere in the stack of assembled paperwork and other records will be the information to support or deny the plaintiff/patient's story.

The proposed expert should itemize all instances of faulty diagnosis and/or treatment and be able to describe the time and circumstances of *each such deviation*. Then the expert will be required to explain what the *proper* diagnosis or procedures should have been. Finally, he or she will want to be certain that the faulty treatment *proximately caused* the damages claimed. If all the elements are present, the expert then should review the pertinent area of dentistry to pick up all the latest developments and to go over the basics and terminology.

After an exam/interview with the potential plaintiff, an examination of all available records and X-rays, and a review of the dentistry, a report letter can be compiled. The letter should state the exact records and X-rays used in the review, followed by a brief history of events. Then the expert should indicate where the purported negligence occurred in the defendant's treatment. The final section of the report should state briefly but clearly that Dr. X's diagnosis or treatment was below the standard of care and that Dr. X's negligence was the proximate cause of the injuries and damages incurred by the plaintiff.

The letter should be truthful, brief, and convincing. The letter may be circulated to the defendant and the experts hired by defendant's lawyers. Therefore it must be capable of withstanding criticism from the professional community.

If, in your opinion, negligence was found, you will be identified as an expert by the plaintiff's lawyer and will have to give a deposition at some point. At that time the defense lawyer will have the opportunity to interview you in the presence of a court reporter, who will take a verbatim transcript of questions and answers. You will have to answer questions, under oath, on a wide variety of subjects. In most jurisdictions, the expert is paid for the actual time of the deposition by the defendant's lawyer, but firm arrangements should be made at the outset.

Most lawyers who call on an expert are reputable, and will pay a reasonable fee for the time involved. Others, however, those who represent financially unsound clients, may simply pass the bills for deposition time over to the client, and he or she may not pay. Since it's the client's ultimate responsibility to pay for the deposition time of the expert witness, check with the lawyer for the side that retained you to learn what you should do.

The deposition questions will center around three main areas:

1. Your credentials and the records you used in your review.
2. Your knowledge of the dentistry.
3. Your findings and opinion on the case.

The credentials and the dentistry are a cinch, but the opinion part can be hairy. At some point, the expert must say that the care provided by the defendant did not live up to professional standards. Each instance of substandard treatment must be identified and an explanation offered as to how the diagnosis or treatment should have proceeded. All the instances of negligence that proximately caused the damages must be identified.

Now your opinion is on the record. The written transcripts cost about $1.50 or $2.00 per page to produce, and an hour of your time may produce a deposition of 75 to 100 pages. The expert can see the transcript before a copy is filed in court, but he or she may change only the typos or misspellings made by the court reporter. The deposition is now part of the evidence of the case.

If the case is not settled shortly afterwards on the basis of the expert's opinion, the matter is scheduled for trial. At trial, plaintiff's lawyer will direct the first set of questions to you. Enough questions will be proposed to place all the facts and your opinions in the trial record. Then you will be cross-examined by the defendant's lawyer. That lawyer will have a transcript of your deposition, which he or she will use to see if any of your answers have changed since the deposition. You can avoid that trap by preparing in advance and rereading your own deposition. At trial, your fee as an expert is paid by the plaintiff and lawyers for the plaintiff. Again, specific arrangements are needed in advance to avoid misunderstandings.

Legal Requirements for Experts

Some recent cases have raised questions about the need for expert testimony.

1983, Alabama

During a root canal procedure, the dentist dropped a file into the patient's throat. It was admitted that the dentist had not used a rubber dam (which would have prevented such an accident). Further, the dentist failed to obtain emergency medical services immediately after the accident.

The question that was taken up on appeal of this case was whether an expert was required to state that failure to use a rubber dam and failure to obtain emergency services were below the standard of care. The Alabama court held that the expert testimony was essential to the case.[1]

1983, Michigan

The allegations in this case were that the dentist ground down the patient's occlusion unnecessarily and excessively. The plaintiff alleged further that the grinding resulted in pain, change of appearance, and the necessity for subsequent dental repair work. The court, in analyzing whether or not expert testimony as to the standard of care was necessary, came to an alarmingly novel conclusion: laymen are capable of recognizing such a manifest lack of professional care. In other words, no expert was required to set the standard, let alone testify that the dentist's actions were below the standard.[2]

1983, Vermont

In this complicated case, expert testimony was unnecessary to establish negligence: the dentist failed to examine his patient, whose cheek he had lacerated, and did not prescribe antibiotics or warn the patient of possible complications. The same court, however, found that the plaintiff failed to prove a causal connection between the negligence and the plaintiff's damages, which were the expenses of the hospital visit that followed the dental treatment. In other words, this case permits a court to dispense with expert testimony in areas that are close to common knowledge, but continues to require testimony that the negligence actually caused the damages claimed by the plaintiff.[3]

1984, Florida (Medical, Not Dental, Prosthesis)

The Florida court, in this medical case, found that no expert testimony was required in the failure of a hospital to check components of a prosthesis to be installed in a patient's knee. The failure to check the components resulted in the surgeon's implanting a prosthesis with unmatched (different-sized) components. The court felt that the failure to check, and the resulting mismatched kneecaps, were an obvious breach of duty that would be apparent to "persons of common knowledge." The court felt that expert testimony was unnecessary in this case.[4]

References: Expert and Fact Witnesses

1. Sprowl v. Ward 441 So. 2d 898 (Ala., 1983).
2. Sullivan v. Russell 417 Mich. 398 338 N.W. 2d 181 (Mich., 1983).
3. Baker v. Titus 458 A. 2d 1125 (UT., 1983).
4. Florida Patient's Compensation Fund v. Tillman 435 So. 2d 1316 (Fla., 1984).

8
Dental Cases by Specialty

Periodontics in Litigation

A number of recent decisions involving misdiagnosis of periodontal disease or failure to provide periodontal treatment have been reported from around the country. The following histories represent a few selected cases.

"Bridge Over Troubled Waters"

In a 1979 New York case, the allegations of undiagnosed periodontal disease and failure to treat or refer the patient led to a decision by the court to award the plaintiff $31,600. The defendant dentist had the patient under his care for a period of 18 years. During that time, the dentist had placed crown and bridgework on all the plaintiff's remaining upper teeth. One such fixed device was placed in 1959 and then replaced in 1976.

Immediately after the replacement, the plaintiff moved from New York and became the patient of a California dentist. The new dentist found "advanced periodontal disease, including abscesses, severe mobility and extensive bone loss with periodontal pockets up to 7 to 9 mm in depth."

That diagnosis was made *before* the periodontist had seen the case! The periodontist removed the less-than-year-old bridgework, extracted three hopeless teeth, and arranged to have the remaining teeth treated endodontically and reduced to act as foundation abutments for an over-denture.

The allegation of failure to diagnose, failure to treat, and failure to alert the patient to the presence of the disease formed the basis of the lawsuit. In addition, a further claim was raised that the bridgework was ill-advised and improperly constructed.

Testimony was received that the conformation of the crowns caused irritation to the gum and bone tissue; that the crown margins were, as described by the new dentist, "so open I could put a very large instrument in them"; and that the lack of embrasure space restricted the patient's ability to clean adequately around the abutment teeth.

The defendant dentist, however, didn't roll over and play dead. Although he admitted the existence of overcontoured crowns, both the defendant and the defendant's expert witness offered several explanations. The court, hearing the case without a jury, leaned toward the plaintiff's experts in reconciling the conflicting expert statements.

Regarding the periodontal aspects of the case, the defendant stated that he saw the plaintiff two to three times a year, took periodic dental X-rays, and noticed progressive bone resorption. He stated that he treated the plaintiff's periodontal condition by regular cleanings, including scaling of the teeth and "ultrasonic therapy," and he claimed that he curetted and medicated the tissues. Both sides gave testimony on alternative treatment choices in periodontal disease and the usefulness of referral to specialty care for treatment. The defendant admitted it would have been below the standard of care not to suggest that the plaintiff see a periodontal specialist, but he testified that he *had* suggested the plaintiff see a specialist, although he could not remember exactly when he had done so.

On that point, the plaintiff vigorously denied ever hearing about the disease, any special warnings about the disease, or any special home care instructions. She particularly denied ever hearing a suggestion that she see a specialist concerning the disease. The court found the plaintiff's good record of visits to the dentist and the fact that she conscientiously took her daughters to the New York dentist for regular checkups as strong evidence that she would have gone to a specialist if so advised.

Two errors on the part of the dentist probably spelled the difference in this litigation. First, the dentist failed to record the suggestion that the plaintiff visit a specialist for treatment of the periodontal disease. The doctor's story changed on this point, which caused further trouble. This problem could have been avoided if a short note had been placed in the record: "Ref to Perio - Pt refused," or the like.

Second, in a deposition taken sometime before the actual trial, the dentist had testified under oath that he "never referred plaintiff to any other dentist." That statement was inconsistent with his statement at trial that he "suggested that she go see a specialist." The explanation for the inconsistency made the distinction between "a recommendation" and a "referral" and the fact that he, the defendant, had not referred the plaintiff to a periodontist because "she could not afford specialists' fees."

The judge who wrote the opinion allowed that the inconsistency was never fully explained away, and he wrote that the defendant's credibility on the issue was "undermined by his testimony at trial." The judge also found fault with the defendant's lack of enthusiasm for the referral, which he stated would have been unnecessary at the time he saw her. Finally, the judge was disappointed with the defendant's testimony that he had made the suggestion of seeing a specialist only "a long time prior to 1976," but had *never repeated* the recommendation or discussed the potential consequences of noncompliance. As with the refusal of dental X-rays, a dentist is expected to repeat his or her advice on the need and usefulness of diagnostic X-rays at each recall visit.

The court awarded the plaintiff damages for the loss of three teeth ($20,000), pain and suffering ($10,000), and the cost of the bridge made by the defendant ($1,600) for a total of $31,600.[1]

Standby CPR

In this 1979 Florida case, a 37-year-old male sales manager suffered brain death as a result of insufficient oxygenation during periodontal surgery. The plaintiff was admitted to a clinic for elective periodontal surgery. In the course of the surgical procedure, the plaintiff received the following medications: Demerol, Innovar, curare, Pentothal, nitrous oxide, succinylcholine, Sublimaze. All the drugs were administered by an anesthesiologist. In addition, the dentist infiltrated locally Xylocaine with epinephrine.

The operation went smoothly during the first hour of general anesthesia. Then the plaintiff's pulse rate began to fluctuate and tachycardia ensued. After that his pulse rate fell rapidly and he went into cardiac arrest.

The anesthesiologist attempted to resuscitate the plaintiff by using cardiopulmonary resuscitation (CPR). The anesthesiologist was attempting one-person CPR, however, and apparently not very efficiently. The anesthesiologist was compressing the plaintiff's chest with one hand while squeezing an ambubag with the other.

The periodontist did not aid the resuscitation attempt, apparently because he did not know how to perform CPR procedures. As a result of the cardiac arrest and the inefficient CPR, the patient suffered brain death caused, according to the coroner's office, by cerebral anoxia.

Naturally, the plaintiffs claimed that the patient had become hypoxic because of inadequate ventilation during surgery. Hypoxia was due in part to the number and combination of drugs administered to the patient before the surgery, all of which are known to depress respiration. In addition, the hypoxia was caused by the failure to perform two-handed CPR.

This particular case was tried before a mediation/arbitration panel, and the plaintiffs were successful in convincing the panel of the merits of their case. The anesthesiologist and the clinic settled with the plaintiffs and then sought contribution from the periodontist. The court awarded $923,500 to the estate of the 37-year-old man for his wrongful death while undergoing periodontal surgery.[2]

Extraction Alternatives: Referral Scam

In a 1980 California case, a 58-year-old woman accused her dentist of unnecessarily extracting 14 teeth and failing to detect, inform, or treat periodontal disease around her nine remaining teeth.

The plaintiff went to the defendant dentist for treatment of one or two cavities. The dentist, to his credit, diagnosed bone and gum disease and recommended that all the patient's remaining 23 teeth be removed by an oral surgeon. The defendant said to the plaintiff that she was going to lose all her teeth anyway. According to the plaintiff, the dentist denied that the disease was also known as "pyorrhea," which the plaintiff knew to be treatable. After some negotiation, the defendant dentist and the oral surgeon agreed to leave nine lower teeth in the plaintiff's mouth. All the remaining upper teeth were extracted and an ill-fitting upper denture was placed.

After trying to adapt to the device, the plaintiff sought dental care in the office of a prosthodontist. At that appointment, the plaintiff learned that her upper teeth may have been extracted unnecessarily and that her remaining teeth showed evidence of periodontal disease (pyorrhea). Shortly after that, the plaintiff sued the defendant dentist and the oral surgeon, alleging negligence and failure to take a dental history, failure to take adequate X-rays, failure to take adequate clinical findings and record them, and failure to refer the patient to a periodontist. At the end of a jury trial, the plaintiff was awarded $72,000.[3]

Minor Injury, Major Damages

In a 1981 North Carolina case, the patient sued her dentist for undiagnosed periodontal disease. In this case, the plaintiff was under the care of the defendant general dentist for a period of eight years. During that time, the plaintiff was not treated for periodontal disease, even though she complained of bleeding and swollen gums.

When finally referred to a periodontist, the plaintiff was diagnosed as suffering from periodontal disease. The allegations of negligence in this case included failure to diagnose plaintiff's condition in timely fashion, failure to treat the condition, and failure to refer the plaintiff to a periodontist. At the trial, experts for the plaintiff testified that the disease was apparent on dental X-rays taken by the defendant six years before the present litigation. At the conclusion of testimony, the jury found for the plaintiff in the amount of $76,600. Although no teeth were lost, plaintiff experiences permanent sensitivity of the teeth and pain caused by sweets and hot and cold foods.[4]

Periodontal Disease Uncovered by Accident

In a 1984 Florida case, a 43-year-old housewife was under the care of one dentist from 1975 to 1982. During those years, she was never treated or diagnosed as having periodontal disease, but the defendant dentist performed a number of endodontic services.

Sometime after 1982, when the plaintiff was involved in an auto accident and sustained dental injury, another treating dentist discovered that she had extensive periodontal disease. Largely as a result of the accident and partly as the result of her weakened periodontal situation, the plaintiff lost several teeth. In addition, most of her root canal teeth had to be redone because of the poor quality of the prior work. All told, the plaintiff incurred expenses of $15,000 to place her mouth in stable condition.

A lawsuit initiated by the plaintiff alleged that the defendant failed to diagnose and treat the periodontal disease and performed root canal work negligently. The court never had an opportunity to decide the issues, as the case was settled out of court at a reported figure of $190,000.[5]

Periodontal Misdiagnosis, Punitive Damages

In a 1985 Texas case, a jury awarded punitive damages against the dentist for failure to treat periodontal disease adequately. In this particular case, the patient claimed that the dentist made her problems worse by removing teeth and crowns without her fully informed consent. In addition, the plaintiff alleged that the dentist performed inadequately and failed to refer her for treatment of an abscess that caused prolonged infection and excessive drainage.

The court said that the evidence supported the patient's claim that the dentist was negligent in failing to refer her to a specialist. In addition, experts for the plaintiff testified that the dentist's salt and soda treatment of infected soft tissue was below community treatment standards. The experts also testified that if an infection was not improving, a prudent general dentist should refer the patient to a specialist.

There were other allegations of improper or substandard work, including the construction of a temporary acrylic splint that proved unstable because of lack of support from the underlying tooth structure. Experts also testified that allowing the periodontal condition to deteriorate was below community standards.

Initially, the patient received a judgment of $174,000 in actual and punitive damages in the malpractice action against the dentist. On appeal, the court reduced a portion of the award by $43,000, but left intact the $125,000 in punitive damages against the dentist. This is one of the few cases in which significant punitive damages have been awarded in dental malpractice.[6]

Prosthodontics in Litigation

Dentists and patients often have decidedly different views of the fit, look, and feel of fixed and removable prosthetic appliances. When communications reach an impasse, litigation sometimes follows.

Backfire of Collection Attempt

In this 1984 Louisiana case, a dentist had provided a 49-year-old patient in 1974 with a number of units of crown and bridge over her existing upper teeth. At the time of treatment, the patient had multiple missing teeth and others in need of root canal treatment. Most of the teeth had some decay, and few were totally unaffected by dental disease.

In 1979, the patient and the dentist agreed to replace the upper bridge and to place crown and bridgework on the remaining lower teeth. When the work was completed, however, the patient had much pain and difficulty. She was apparently unable to get any satisfaction from the dentist. In November of the year the work was placed, the dentist sued the patient for $7,000, his unpaid services, and he added an additional 25% for the attorney's fees necessary to collect the unpaid balance.

As might have been predicted, the unsatisfied patient responded with a claim for dental malpractice. Expert testimony was presented, which demonstrated that the dentist's work was substandard. The patient lost four of the teeth treated by the dentist, and two other teeth deteriorated as a result of the work placed. Also as a result of the substandard work, the patient was no longer able to support fixed bridgework in the lower arch. At trial, the jury awarded the plaintiff $13,374.

The patient appealed the finding; the appeals court affirmed the finding of negligence by the dentist and found that the patient was entitled to $15,000 in general damages over and above the $7500 that was necessary to remove and replace

the work done by the dentist. The total award for the patient
turned out to be $23,424.

This case demonstrates what can be expected if a dentist is
not absolutely sure that the work in contention has the
absolute support of the entire dental community and that no
expert would find the quality of the work below the standard.
This case changed a simple collection lawsuit for $7000 plus
attorney's fees into a loss of nearly $25,000 for the dentist's
insurer. It hardly seems worth the time and effort to attempt
collection when the possibility exists that the plaintiff could
obtain testimony that the work being sued for *was substandard.*[7]

Plaintiff Aided by Dental Technician's Testimony

In this 1983 Alabama case, the patient went to her dentist,
and for a period of time he attempted to prepare teeth, provide
temporary coverage, and take impressions for the fitting of
some fixed bridgework. The dentist tried and failed several
times to obtain adequate impressions of the patient's prepared
teeth. He also failed to obtain a proper occlusal relationship. In
addition, a number of attempts to provide temporary coverage
failed during this period. After 14 months of this misadven-
ture, the patient left the dentist and went to another office,
where the treatment was completed successfully in about a
month.

The patient sued the first dentist for taking all that time
for nothing. The dentist, after receiving the complaint, filed a
legal action attempting to have the case dismissed. He claimed
in this motion that everything that was done for the patient
was done according to accepted standards and that the failure
to obtain a final result was not necessarily negligence. He
signed an affidavit to that effect, and the patient was forced to
find an opposing viewpoint or risk losing the lawsuit.

Apparently the second dentist was neither willing nor able
to fault the first dentist for the delay in providing the fixed
bridgework. The second dentist's dental technician, however,
was willing to state that he saw the work from *both dentists,*
and that the first dentist's work was far below normal. The
dental technician stated that he had been in the business for
22 years and was familiar with dental standards governing
the preparing and taking of impressions for the construction of
crowns and bridges. He had been asked by the first dentist to

construct four different bridges and at least ten crowns for the patient, all of which had been unsuccessful. The technician stated that the impressions weren't adequate to construct work that would fit properly.

This technician was also engaged by the second dentist, and as such was in an excellent position to state that the impressions taken by the second dentist immediately provided the foundation for excellent work.

The court, in reviewing the affidavit of the dentist and the affidavit of the dental technician, determined that the court should grant the dentist's requests for dismissal, but the patient appealed the decision.

On appeal, the dentist said that his affidavit was essentially unchallenged by an expert or by *equivalent* expert testimony. The court found, however, that the technician's affidavit raised at least a *scintilla* (small amount) of evidence supporting the patient; therefore the dentist's motion should be denied. The court admitted that the dental technician's opinion was not as impressive as that of another dentist, but they found that the technician certainly had a better grasp of the information than would a layman. Therefore his testimony had some weight, and it was up to a jury to decide whose evidence had the greater credibility.[8]

Crown Preps Requiring Root Canals

In a 1985 Maryland case, a 40-year-old male patient went to the dental clinic for the preparation and placement of two three-unit bridges, one each in the upper left and upper right sides of his jaw. The dentist employee of the clinic prepared the four teeth and took impressions for subsequent construction of the units. Before the preparation of the four abutment teeth, the patient had never suffered any sensitivity or toothache.

Shortly after the placement of the two three-unit bridges, the patient complained of constant sensitivity in and around the teeth prepared to receive the abutment crowns. Shortly after the preparation visit, the dentist recorded in his dental chart that he had observed a possible exposure of the pulpal tissues on one of the four abutment teeth.

When the patient returned, complaining first of sensitivity and finally of extreme pain in one of the four abutments, the clinic employee began a root canal procedure. The first involved tooth was not the one initially suspected, but another of the abutment teeth preparations. The root canal procedure did, in fact, eliminate the sensitivity in that particular tooth.

The patient complained, however, of continuing sensitivity and worsening of the condition. When he failed to gain satisfaction, he finally changed dentists and visited a dentist in a solo practice. The second dentist, upon observing the work provided by the earlier dentist, began to make preparations for new bridgework and also provided root canal treatment on all four abutment teeth. The second dentist was able to find and diagnose the need for endodontic treatment on three of the four teeth. (The fourth tooth was treated by endodontics when no other treatment could provide relief of symptoms.) For three of the four abutment teeth, the second dentist was able to identify substandard preparation errors that necessitated the root canal work to preserve the teeth as abutments for the fixed bridgework.

The second dentist did not perform four root canals at the outset, but finished the root canal that the first dentist had started and began treatment of the other teeth only as symptoms required. He attempted to improve the temporary coverage to eliminate other possible sources of sensitivity, but nothing worked short of the root canal treatments.

The question is this: was the need for root canal treatment on all four teeth enough evidence in and of itself that the treatments provided by the first dentist were, in fact, negligent? The second dentist wrestled with this idea, based on his knowledge of the shape of the prepared teeth and the appearance of the teeth before the first dentist had begun treatment. (The first dentist's pre-operative X-rays were available to him.) The second dentist was able to state that the work performed by the first dentist was, indeed, substandard.

Shortly after the second dentist's opinion became known, the dentist employee settled with the patient for an undisclosed amount of money. The patient, however, continued his lawsuit against the employer/clinic operator.[9]

Endodontics in Litigation

Practitioners who perform endodontic procedures are likely to be aware of controversies over the necessity of the rubber dam, the broken instrument, and the use of paraformaldehyde pastes. The following samples represent cases involving endodontics.

Failure to Use Rubber Dam

Probably the most frequently cited case involving the general practice of dentistry is one that occurred in Kansas in 1976. The dentist, a general practitioner, undertook to provide endodontic treatment for his patient. He did not place a rubber dam. An instrument was accidentally dropped on the patient's tongue; the patient swallowed the instrument, and problems ensued.

Certainly in many cases accidentally swallowed endodontic instruments have been passed without injury, but this was not the case here. The instrument caused some significant damage.

Initially the patient was taken to the hospital, and an X-ray of the abdomen located the instrument in her stomach. A few days later, the patient experienced extreme pain, tenderness, and evidence of bleeding. The decision was made to remove the instrument surgically. While the patient was recuperating in the hospital, she developed a bladder infection, which was attributed to a catheter. After discharge from the hospital, the patient continued to have bladder difficulties and reportedly was unable to eat certain foods.

In the subsequent malpractice suit against the dentist, the patient claimed that the dentist was negligent in not using a rubber dam to prevent her from swallowing the instrument. The jury, however, returned a verdict for the dentist, and the patient appealed.

In reversing the jury verdict, the Supreme Court of Kansas said that the trial court should have directed a verdict in favor of the *patient*. The dentist, said the court, was doing the work of a *specialist* in performing the endodontic procedure on the patient. Therefore, the dentist had to exercise the skill and care of a specialist. An endodontic expert testified that the dentist deviated from the standard of care by failing to use a rubber dam. The dentist himself admitted that he was taking a chance by neglecting to use a dam.

The court also commented on the possibility that the patient was contributorily negligent. The court found that because the patient was under the influence of a sedative drug

(Valium), she could not have made any voluntary contributing movements. The case was ultimately remanded to the trial court with directions to proceed to trial on the issue of damages.[10]

Sargenti into the Sinus

In this 1985 Idaho case, a 42-year-old housewife had a root canal procedure performed on an upper posterior tooth. The practitioner, using Sargenti materials, extruded the paste past the apex of the tooth and into the maxillary sinus. Evidence was brought out that the materials acted as a foreign body in the maxillary sinus and caused neurological damage, resulting in extreme facial pain.

According to the complaint, the plaintiff felt that the defendant negligently used Sargenti paste, which contains paraformaldehyde, in his treatment procedures. The plaintiff developed testimony that alternative, nontoxic filling materials existed, which were recognized and safe. As a separate count of negligence, the plaintiff alleged negligence in forcing the materials beyond the apex of the tooth and into the sinus.

Before the court could determine the merits of the issues, the plaintiff settled the lawsuit for a reported $200,000.[11]

Sargenti into the Canal

In this 1983 Colorado case, a 28-year-old woman sustained nerve damage during root canal treatment for a lower posterior tooth. As reported in the trial literature, the plaintiff underwent root canal treatment on tooth #18. Her dentist performed the procedure using the Sargenti technique and the paste containing paraformaldehyde.

During the procedure, an overfill forced some of the paste into the mandibular canal, damaging the inferior alveolar nerve. According to court papers, the plaintiff claims she suffered a permanent paresthesia, numbness, hypersensitivity, and severe discomfort. The allegations of this case involved negligent use of the material and negligent placement notwithstanding the nature of the material itself, since it did not have FDA approval.

This case was settled for $65,000 before the court could hear the merits of the issues.[12]

Loss by Dentist and Druggist on Sargenti

In this 1984 California case, a 29-year-old nursing student claimed to have suffered paresthesia of the lower right lip and chin following a root canal treatment.

The plaintiff was in the dental office for root canal treatment. The defendant used N2, a paraformaldehyde-containing root canal sealer which was not approved by the FDA. The drug was obtained from the codefendant druggist, who sold the materials through the mail to dentists.

In this suit, in addition, the plaintiff claimed a violation of FDA regulations: the quantity supplied to the dentist (150 g.) constituted a bulk sale rather than a prescription, making the druggist a manufacturer.

The suit claimed that while filling the root canal, the dentist used an excessive amount of the caustic drug, which caused an overfill into the mandibular canal. The patient apparently noted symptoms immediately. Within a month, the plaintiff underwent neurological surgery to remove the excess material. Unfortunately, the condition remains permanent. As in the other cases, the parties agreed to a settlement before trial. In this case, the plaintiff was awarded $100,000; $65,000 was contributed by the dentist and $35,000 by the pharmacist.[13]

Broken Root Canal Instruments

In this 1982 New York case, a 19-year-old woman claims to have suffered permanent mental anguish when informed that instrument fragments were left in her jaw following root canal surgery. Unfortunately, details are not available to determine what the surgical procedure was and what instruments were involved.

The report of this case, however, discloses that the fragments were located close to the mandibular nerve, which tells us that the treatment was in the lower jaw. It was also noted that the plaintiff had been advised not to undergo any surgery to remove the instrument fragment because of the proximity of the mandibular nerve. The report notes that there is some ongoing risk of movement of the fragment. This unusual case went through a trial, and the patient was awarded a $44,000 jury verdict.[14]

Missed Appointments Not Contributory Negligence

In this 1984 case, a dentist working with the Indian Health Service provided endodontic treatment for a patient on two occasions, in October and November 1978. According to the court reports, the dentist opened the teeth to allow drainage of fluids, instrumented the canal to shape it for filling material, and closed the access opening with a temporary filling material.

Permanent filling was scheduled to be inserted later in November 1978. The patient missed or canceled four appointments, however, and did not return until March 5, 1979.

When the patient returned, the dentist cemented filling material in the canals. The patient returned the next day with extreme pain and localized swelling, and the dentist prescribed penicillin and opened two teeth for drainage. When the symptoms did not abate, the patient was hospitalized for treatment.

At the trial level, the court focused a great deal of attention on the patient's missed appointments. The defendant claimed that the missed appointments accounted for the problems associated with the acute flare-up of infection and the hospitalization. The court agreed and dismissed the case in favor of the dentist.

The patient appealed, however, and the appellate court said that the lower court should have determined whether or not the dentist used proper procedures on March 5, when the permanent fillings were placed. Apparently an expert gave testimony, indicating that the dentist may have failed to disinfect or wash the root canal with an antiseptic material such as sodium hypochloride before placing the final fillings. The appeals court returned the case to the lower court to determine whether or not the evidence was tantamount to negligence balancing the patient's contributory negligence.[15]

Endo Tooth Replaced Backwards

In this unusual 1985 Virginia case, the plaintiff, a housewife in her 50s, was in the dentist's office to have root canal work done on a bicuspid tooth. According to newspaper reports, the plaintiff became upset when she observed that the tooth on which the dentist was supposed to be performing root canal procedures was on the tray in front of her as she sat in the dentist's chair.

The dentist reassured her that it was not unusual or uncommon to extract the tooth, perform the procedures, and then reimplant the tooth at the same visit. Several weeks later the woman was in the office of another dentist, who discovered that the bicuspid had been reimplanted *backwards*. The plaintiff then charged the first dentist with negligence, assault and battery, and emotional distress. The dentist defended his procedure, stating that teeth are often extracted during the course of root canal therapy, and that he was unaware that he had inserted the tooth backwards.

A Virginia jury felt otherwise and awarded the woman $75,000 for her trouble.[16]

Temporomandibular Joint Dysfunction in Litigation

Dental treatments and procedures have only recently been blamed as initiating factors in temporomandibular joint (TMJ) disorders. Claims against dentists for initiating TMJ dysfunction are becoming commonplace across the country.

Occlusal Equilibration—a Specialty in Colorado?

In a 1983 Colorado case, the plaintiff went to the office of the defendant dentists and was advised of the need and usefulness of occlusal equilibration to improve the patient's bite. The defendants advised the patient that the procedure would be beneficial and that they were newly capable of administering the treatment.

The defendant dentists were, in fact, currently enrolled in an equilibration course being offered in their state. The patient consented to the treatment, and work began on achieving a centric relationship for the patient. After six sessions and three months, the objectives of treatment had not been achieved. The defendants recognized that the procedures were not effective, and recommended that the patient seek specialty services in a prosthodontist's office. The prosthodontist's reconstruction cost $11,000. The patient sued the original dentists for having caused the problem that required the reconstruction.

The trial court found in favor of the defendant dentists. On appeal, the patient claimed that the trial court had erred in not holding the general dentists to a higher standard of care. The patient felt that the general dentists were engaged in the "subspecialty of occlusion" and therefore should be held to a higher standard. After all, the defendants were practicing a form of dentistry that requires special knowledge and training.

The defendants countered with a recitation of the specialties recognized by the American Dental Association, and urged the court to hold them to the lower standard required of general dentists.

The court ruled that the general dental standard of care is applied to dentists "unless that person represents that he or she has greater or less skill or knowledge beyond the common in the profession. If such higher skill is represented, then the dentist incurs the obligation to have and exercise the skill and knowledge that are represented."

Therefore, a dentist who represents himself or herself as a specialist in a certain type of practice is required to have the skill and knowledge common to other specialists. The same holds true if the practitioner represents himself or herself as having greater skills than the average member of the profession; the applicable standard is modified accordingly.

The court ruled that there was enough evidence to allow a jury to decide whether the dentists had represented themselves as possessing special skills in the area of occlusal equilibration, even though the subject may not be a recognized specialty.

On the premise that occlusal equilibration is a specialty skill, this would be the question: did the general dentists live up to the higher standard? If they did not, the jury could find for the plaintiff. The court returned the case to the trial court for a retrial, and one judge dissented. His point? Occlusal equilibration is not a recognized specialty, and therefore the standard of care is unknown or at least of questionable substance. You can't compare provided care to an imaginery standard.[17]

Multiple Sessions of Equilibration Leading to Failure

In a 1983 Michigan case, a patient was in the dentist's office for routine examination and cleaning. Although the patient was not experiencing any dental symptoms or difficulties, the dentist pointed out the possibility that problems might develop if an occlusal adjustment was not performed. No other clinical findings or indications for the dentist's recommended course of treatment are available.

The dentist then set about adjusting the occlusion of plaintiff's posterior teeth. Shortly after the initial effort, plaintiff began experiencing symptoms in the temporomandibular joint. The dentist attempted to correct the negative results of the grinding by repeating the procedure again and again. Eventually the plaintiff's pain became so great that she sought out a temporomandibular joint specialist, an orthodontist, and a specialist in physical medicine. These specialty practitioners diagnosed the patient as suffering a derangement and tearing of the meniscus of the temporomandibular joint. Ultimately the patient required reconstruction of all the teeth involved in the occlusal adjustment.

At the conclusion of the trial, a jury awarded the patient $600,000 for the injuries to the TMJ and consequent pain and suffering.[18]

Bad Bite Bridgework

In this 1985 Michigan case, a 45-year-old female was complaining of a loose tooth in a maxillary partial prosthetic device. The dentist decided to install a fixed permanent bridge and several additional crowns to provide abutments for a new prosthetic device. When the procedures were completed, the patient complained that the crowns were too high. The dentist then adjusted the bridge and crowned teeth to accommodate the occlusion. Apparently the plaintiff was never fully satisfied that the bite or occlusion was proper.

The plaintiff then complained that after the installation of the bridge and crowns and the unsuccessful effort to grind the new restorations to fit appropriately, she suffered temporomandibular joint dysfunction. The patient admitted, however, that with treatment, the TMJ pain disappeared with no residual damage.

A lawsuit was filed in the above case, alleging that the dentist had performed multiple unnecessary procedures instead of proposing an alternative, such as the simple repair of the existing prosthetic device. Then, once the dentist was engaged in replacing the bridgework and found that the occlusion was inadequate, he never mentioned another alternative, remaking the framework in a more acceptable occlusal relationship. He never explored this possibility with the patient and never provided it. This case was settled out of court for a reported $170,000.[19]

TMJ Not Relieved by New Bridgework

In a 1984 Indiana case, a patient began dental treatment to relieve symptoms of temporomandibular joint dysfunction. For the next two years, the plaintiff underwent the placement of several crowns and repeated adjustments of the crowns and teeth. The patient made some forty visits to the dentist's office and spent more than $5,700 for the work.

The plaintiff admitted that the treatments resulted in no permanent injuries, but she contended that she was subjected to unnecessary and excessive pain and suffering as a result of the grossly improper treatment. The plaintiff settled after a review panel issued a unanimous decision in her favor. Settlement was reported to be $23,000.[20]

Extraction Leading to TMJ Dysfunction

In a 1984 Virginia case, the plaintiff was being treated by a general dentist and a periodontist, both of whom recommended that an upper left third molar (wisdom tooth) be extracted.

As part of his examination, the general dentist took four bite-wing radiographs and sent them to an oral surgeon. The plaintiff had visited the same oral surgeon two or three years earlier for the extraction of a lower third molar.

According to the patient, the oral surgeon agreed that no additional X-rays were necessary. The upper third molar was removed, using the bite-wing X-rays only. The oral surgeon later claimed in court documents that a periapical X-ray was taken, but that it was lost and unavailable for review.

At the time of the extraction, the plaintiff was a healthy mother of two children. Shortly after the extraction, however, she was unable to open her mouth without pain. In a few more days, her ears became clogged and her head seemed filled with pressure. Sounds became annoying, and eating and speaking became difficult. She returned to the oral surgeon for assistance, but the postoperative visit did not provide any significant relief.

Some months later the plaintiff visited a neurologist, who prescribed a number of drugs that apparently gave only temporary relief of the pain and discomfort. The patient then began a prolonged search for comfort, and was in and out of the offices of a dozen practitioners. Some provided short-term relief; others provided no relief at all. All the subsequent practitioners pinpointed the extraction as the causative agent of the patient's symptoms, but none were able to provide a cure or treatments to give comfort.

The patient was advised at one time that a clinical radiographic procedure, an arthrogram of the TMJ, was available and might be able to identify the precise injury to the temporomandibular joint. After consultation with a number of other practitioners, however, the patient refused to have the procedure performed. She gave as her reason the fact that the procedure was invasive (injection of radioopaque dye into the joint capsule), and she feared that it might lead to either further aggravation or permanent injury, plus more pain and discomfort.

A medical malpractice review panel in Virginia found, on the basis of the facts presented, that the practitioner was not guilty of negligent conduct.[21]

Ground Gold Leading to TMJ Pain

In a 1984 Missouri case, the patient related that she was seen in the office of a dentist for routine dental examination. A second and separate appointment was made for minor occlusal adjustment. The reason given for the extra visit was that there was evidence of "wear" on the molars.

The patient apparently was symptom-free before the appointment for the occlusal adjustment. During that appointment the dentist proceeded to grind selectively as many as seven or eight upper and lower posterior teeth. According to the patient, she immediately began to experience trouble in the form of pain and discomfort in and about the face and jaw. She returned to the dentist two days later, and further adjustment was accomplished without any improvement in her symptoms. In fact, the symptoms grew worse.

In an effort to relieve her pain and discomfort, the patient continued to see the dentist for a period of nine months after the initial treatment. In addition, she consulted other dentists and physicians in a protracted effort to relieve her symptoms, which included face pain, headaches, and ear problems, including tinnitus, hearing loss, and dizziness. Efforts to diagnose the multiple problems ruled out a number of possible underlying medical problems and focused on one recurring diagnosis: temporomandibular joint dysfunction syndrome.

The record in this case points to an inescapable conclusion: the occlusal adjustment performed by the general dentist initiated a painful neuromuscular response in the patient. Occlusal grinding, as performed on an asymptomatic patient, apparently had the effect of upsetting the delicate tooth-TMJ balance. The record maintained by the general dentist reveals no specific indication of a valid clinical reason to change the occlusal relationships. The patient's posterior teeth had been restored previously with gold inlay-onlay restorations on the first and second molars in each quadrant. Those restorations had been made many years earlier, and the patient had accommodated to those changes.

Testimony was available to demonstrate that wear on the molars is not sufficient reason to embark on a major occlusal change. Loose, mobile teeth, existing joint pain, chronically fractured tooth cusps, or inability to put pressure on certain teeth, however, give some indication for occlusal adjustment, but only on a limited basis. Apparently none of these signs or symptoms were present. Further testimony stated that occlusal adjustment is not to be used routinely and is considered an irreversible procedure.

The explanation of the diagnosis and treatment given to the patient at the outset was clearly inadequate, and according to the patient, no discussion of potential adverse consequences took place. This lawsuit was settled out of court for an unreported amount.[22]

Local Anesthesia in Litigation

Problems with anesthetic reactions have been reported in the literature since the products first gained popular usage a number of years ago. Here is a sample of recent cases involving local anesthetic agents.

Mental Nerve Injury from Local Injection

In a 1972 Vermont case, testimony disclosed that the plaintiff had broken a lower second bicuspid tooth, which had to be removed. The dentist determined that the tooth was abscessed, and elected to attempt extraction using local anesthesia. The extraction went without incident, but postoperatively, the patient experienced continuous pain in the lower face and chin area on the side that had received the anesthetic block.

The dentist and the patient gave different testimony as to the exact site of the injection. The patient claimed that the injection was in the area of the tooth, making the site the mental foramen. The dentist insisted that the injection was given in the area of the mandibular foramen. A physician treated the patient's pain by severing the sensory nerve branch at the mental foramen.

The dentist further defended on the principle that even if the injection was given at the mental foramen, this was not necessarily substandard. Apparently he did admit, however, that the injection at the mental foramen "was to be avoided and one that was inconsistent with the standards of care generally exercised in the area."

The plaintiff testified that the dentist injected into the mental nerve area; although he did not see the injection, he did feel it.

The court acknowledged that there were inconsistencies in the testimony and alternative explanations for the injury, but felt that the jury could resolve the conflicts. The court reversed the trial court's dismissal of the action and remanded the case to that court for a new trial.[23]

Adverse Reaction to Xylocaine

In a 1983 Pennsylvania case, an eight-month-old child was injected with Xylocaine in preparation for a test for anemia that required bone marrow aspiration from the posterior iliac crest. Twenty minutes after the injection, the child suffered convulsions and cardiac and respiratory arrest. The child was resuscitated, but now suffers from permanent and severe brain damage.

At trial against the drug company, it developed that between 1964 and 1971 the corporate defendant failed to file any adverse drug reaction reports with the Food and Drug Administration, as required by law. The trial lasted nine weeks and ended in a $315,000 jury verdict for the child and family. A new trial on computation of the damages was granted, and this time a jury awarded $2,367,032.[24]

Stroke after Xylocaine Injection

In this 1979 Washington State case, a dental patient presented to the dentist for the extraction of an impacted third molar. The dentist administered Xylocaine without obtaining a current medical history. The patient suffered from hypertension, and problems became apparent after the surgery was completed.

The patient sued the dentist for failure to obtain a current medical history, failure to obtain the patient's informed consent by explaining the risk involved in administering the anesthetic, and failure to render adequate medical care when it became apparent that the patient was experiencing complications.[25]

Adverse Reaction to Marcaine

In this 1978 California case, a physician injected a pregnant 35-year-old woman caudally with Marcaine for labor pain. The patient began to convulse; apparently the doctor had inadvertently injected the anesthetic into a blood vessel, which precipitated two seizures. Thereafter, the mother went into respiratory and cardiac arrest.

There was a delay in obtaining a Code Blue team, which delayed resuscitation; the patient died. The baby was delivered by Caesarean section, but is affected with severe cerebral palsy due to the period of anoxia during delivery.

At trial, there was testimony that some eight minutes elapsed before a Code Blue team was called. It was also alleged that the physician should have had anticonvulsive medication and oxygen available before starting the Marcaine.

The lesson for dentistry is that an inadvertent injection of anesthetic could precipitate a medical emergency which, if slowly or badly managed, will spawn a lawsuit resulting in a judgment over and above the limits of liability insurance. This cased ended with a $1.1 million settlement.[26]

General Anesthesia in Litigation

Probably the highest judgments and settlements in dental malpractice come from errors and accidents involving general anesthesia or conscious sedation techniques. Here are the details of selected cases decided in favor of the plaintiffs.

Failure to Monitor Post-op

In a 1977 Arizona case, a 26-year-old father of three was in the dental office for extraction of four impacted third molars. The patient's medical history contained no contraindications to surgery.

The dentist used a combination of Valium, Nisentil, and Brevital for sedation. Xylocaine was infiltrated locally. The surgery was completed without incident, and the dentist left the room for the purpose of writing his notes, leaving the patient in the care of the dental assistant. The assistant also left the room for what she testified was "no more than five seconds."

At that point, the patient suffered a cardiac arrest. When the assistant returned to the room and noticed the lack of respirations, she took a blood pressure reading and obtained none.

Evidence was available to demonstrate that the combination of drugs could cause respiratory and cardiac depression and arrest. Because of the dangerous propensities of the materials, any patient receiving them should be monitored closely. The contention was that if there had been constant monitoring, it would have been easy to resuscitate the victim. The case was not heard by the court because a settlement for $350,000 was reached before suit was filed.[27]

Nitrous Oxide Lines Crossed

In this 1977 Maryland case, the patient, a 25-year-old law student, was in an oral surgeon's dental office for the removal of her impacted wisdom teeth. The defendant and another dentist in that office had recently begun to use a new anesthesia machine. The procedure required the use of nitrous oxide for deep sedation. The patient began to have trouble breathing on what the dentist thought was a very low concentration of nitrous oxide. The dentist tried to reverse the effects of nitrous oxide by giving the patient pure oxygen. Unfortunately, however, the plumber had mixed the nitrous oxide and the oxygen lines during construction. While attempting to give pure oxygen, the dentist, was in fact, forcing pure nitrous oxide to the patient. The patient died; the cause of her problem was not readily apparent.

After an unsuccessful resuscitative effort, it was assumed that the patient had died from a drug allergy. Some three weeks later, however, another patient had a similar reaction, but in that case resuscitation was successful.

The patient's family sued the oral surgeon and included as defendants the supplier of the anesthesia machine, the plumber who actually crossed the lines, another dentist who had also used the equipment and who had previously noted patient difficulties, but had not done anything about them, and the landlord. The plaintiff's family claimed that at least one of these parties should have performed a simple test to determine that the lines were properly connected.

Since this unfortunate incident in 1977 and a similar incident in Texas in the same year, manufacturers of anesthesia machines have changed the fittings of the hookups so the tubes are of different sizes. It now is much more difficult to cross-connect the two types of gas. In addition, a simple test can be run to assure the practitioner that only oxygen is coming through the oxygen path of the system.

Nitrous Oxide Lines Crossed (Hospital)

This 1977 Texas hospital case is a companion to the Maryland dental-office case described above. In this case a 27-year-old woman died when she was given nitrous oxide instead of oxygen after the birth of her first child in a hospital. The incident occurred on the day the hospital opened. The plumbing contractor had crossed the oxygen line with the nitrous oxide line leading to the operating room. Apparently no one performed the simple test to assure that the correct gases were flowing from the appropriate lines.

In this unfortunate case of wrongful death, the hospital reported that the death was due to amniotic fluid embolism. In this case, as in the Maryland case, the hospital was not aware of the real cause of death. Defendants in the Texas hospital-death case included the hospital, its parent corporation, the architect, and the plumbing contractor. This case originally went to the jury; they found for the plaintiffs in the amount of $2 million for compensation and $5 million in punitive damages against the hospital and the corporation that owned the hospital. Under Texas law, however, the court refused to permit the $7 million judgment, and held the award to $2 million, the amount originally demanded by the plaintiffs.[28]

Brain Damage from Dental Operation

This 1978 California case involves the administration of anesthesia by a nurse-anesthetist in the office of two dentists. No details of the type or amount of anesthesia or the services provided are available. A 43-year-old man suffered brain damage, however, and is now confined to a wheelchair as a result of what was believed to be either cardiac or respiratory arrest or both during a dental operation.

The defendants were two dentists, one the employer of the other, who were performing the extractions when the cardiac and/or respiratory arrest occurred. Paramedics employed by the city were called to the dental office to assist. The plaintiff contended that the defendants were agents and servants of each other and exhibited negligence in the administration of anesthetics, in monitoring the plaintiff's condition under anesthesia, and in rendering emergency care.

The dentist employer argued that the nurse-anesthetist was an independent contractor, and thus the dentist employer was not liable for the acts of this independent professional person. The other defendants contended that the paramedics were the ones actually at fault. Apparently the emergency service was ineffective in resuscitating the patient during the transportation to the hospital. A trial court dismissed the lawsuit against the city and the paramedics because of a theory of governmental immunity which, in some states or jurisdictions, does not permit a suit to be brought against a governmental agency.[29]

Halothane Reaction and Ineffective CPR

In this 1978 District of Columbia case, a seven-year-old child died after having an adverse reaction to halothane while in the dentist's chair for the removal of a tooth.

The dentist in this case elected to use a mixture of nitrous oxide and halothane to effect an anesthesia level on the boy. When the dentist attempted to instrument the tooth, the child "bucked" and caused an attached stethoscope to come away from where it had been strapped to the patient's arm. In spite of this, the defendant dentist continued to administer the anesthesia and finished the procedure.

Shortly thereafter, the boy developed a cyanotic appearance of the mucosa and an absence of pulse. At this point the defendant recognized the problem and attempted to perform CPR to revive him. The defendant worked on the child while he was still in the dental chair rather than placing him on the hard floor, as is usually recommended. The defendant continued to attempt resuscitation and performed a cardiac adrenalin injection, but was unsuccessful in reviving the child.

In this case it was alleged that after the failure of the anesthetic to provide an adequate level of anesthesia, as evidenced by the child's strong reflex movements during manipulation of the tooth, the defendant dentist should have known that the child was experiencing an untoward reaction to the anesthesia.

The second allegation of negligence in this particular case concerned ineffective CPR administration. Evidence was available that it is more efficient to place a victim on a hard surface in order to put appropriate compression on the chest. The defense was that the seven-year-old child didn't require that much compression, and the stability of the dental chair provided enough foundation for that kind of effort. This case did not reach jury, but was settled out of court for a reported $140,000.[30]

Inadequate Medical History

In this 1978 Missouri case, the 18-year-old patient was admitted to the hospital for the surgical removal of two impacted wisdom teeth. A nurse-anesthetist was employed to provide anesthesia for the procedure. The basic contention in this case was that the dentist and the nurse-anesthetist were not aware that the patient had a history of asthma. During the procedure, the patient suffered respiratory arrest, and efforts at resuscitation failed. The patient died and the family sued.

This particular 18-year-old had a history of childhood asthma. The dentist claimed that the information was never given to him or received by him so that it would appear on the medical history of his dental-office charts. The victim's mother claimed that on two separate occasions she told the dentist about the boy's history of childhood asthma, first at the initial visit to the dental office some seven years before, and again five years later during a tooth extraction.

In order to fulfill the hospital requirements for a physical examination before being admitted to the hospital, the 18-year-old patient was seen by his family physician, who then provided a written report to the dentist to qualify the young man for admission. The physician wrote to the defendant dentist that the boy was in good health. No mention was made of any allergy or asthma. The family physician had noted on his examination sheet an entry that read "no asthmatic breathing." The family doctor, however, testified by deposition that in 1963 the boy definitely had asthma, and that he had been treated for asthma in 1966 and again in 1967. The incident date here was 1970.

When the patient was admitted to the hospital in 1970, routine tests were performed and a history was taken by the hospital staff. One entry on a page referred to as "progress notes" states that there was a history of childhood asthma. The defendant dentist and the nurse-anesthetist, however, denied ever seeing that particular page before performing the surgical procedure on the boy later in the hospital admission.

The nurse-anesthetist made no effort to interview the patient the day before the procedure. She gave testimony that she did speak with the boy on the day of the procedure and found that the patient was nervous, with an elevated blood pressure and rapid breathing. She observed nothing, however, that suggested that the operation should be postponed. The nurse-anesthetist decided to use the drug Innovar because of the lack of information concerning a history of asthma. She also testified that if she had been aware of the possibility that the young man was currently suffering from a mild form of asthma, she would have chosen another anesthetic agent. The extraction went smoothly until the procedure was over. Then the patient became cyanotic and the staff couldn't obtain a pulse.

Two physicians administered drugs and applied external cardiac massage, but without success. An expert in pharmacology testified that the dentist and the nurse-anesthetist should have been aware of the history of asthma; if they were, the choice of anesthetic agent was improper. The patient's mother testified that she had informed the dentist of the history of asthma, and that she knew that the family physician knew of the history of asthma (because of his treatment of the victim as recently as three years before the hospital admission); on the basis of this testimony, the mother had done everything she could to bring the information to the professionals in charge of her son's care.

Further, the expert testified that the persons responsible for picking up the medical history information and passing it on to the surgical team were negligent, each in their own way. The dentist was negligent for never recording the earlier mentions of asthma from the family; the family physician was negligent for not passing on the information of the asthmatic history to the dentist in the physical he performed specifically for admission to the hospital, although he knew that a general anesthetic would be administered. The house physician employed by the hospital was also negligent; he had picked up the history of asthma from the interview with the victim, but placed the information on the "progress notes" instead of on any record to be seen and used by the dentist and nurse-anesthetist.

The major responsibility, however, lay with the dentist. As the person directly responsible for the care of the patient during the surgical procedure, he had the responsibility of gathering the information from those who had it and passing it along to the nurse-anesthetist. In addition, he had failed in his own responsibility to bring the information from his office to the surgical arena.

As for the nurse, evidence was available from the expert that her interview with the patient was superficial. During the brief interview there were signs which should have been apparent to her, indicating that the patient may have had a breathing problem requiring further questions, follow-up, and careful selection of anesthetics based on the potentially compromised respiration.

Upon the conclusion of the evidence in this case, the jury awarded the family the sum of $28,000 from the dentist for the wrongful death of the patient. Earlier in the trial a settlement was reached with the nurse-anesthetist, and the case against her was dismissed. The amount of that particular settlement was not available in the record.

This case represents a careless breakdown in communication between parties. The nurse-anesthetist should have gone through a checklist of her own before selecting the anesthetics, and should not have relied solely on the information gathered and assembled by the other actors. If there was information available to the dentist about potential or actual asthma, that should have been recorded and transmitted by him before the surgical procedure. The family physician who had treated the patient on a number of occasions before the hospital admission was culpable through giving the dentist a letter stating that the patient was in good health.[31]

CPR Ineffective as Dentist Stands By

A 1979 Florida case involved the administration of a number of anesthetic agents, which resulted in the brain death of a 37-year-old man who had been admitted to the hospital for periodontal surgery. The jury found that the anesthesia was inadequate and that the administration of CPR by the anesthetist was inadequate to resuscitate the patient, once it became apparent that the patient was suffering from respiratory arrest. A $923,500 postmediation settlement was made in favor of the estate of the deceased. (This case is discussed more fully in the section "Periodontics in Litigation."[2])

Inappropriate Intubation

This 1982 Missouri case involves an oral surgery problem in St. Louis. A 34-year-old male was in the hospital for the extraction of wisdom teeth. Apparently the intubation preced-

ing the procedure was improper, and the endotracheal tube
was inserted accidentally into the esophagus. Experts estimated that the patient suffered ten minutes of anoxia; he is now
confined to a nursing home after irreversible brain damage.

The case was settled before final judgment in this particular court action, and a $2 million "structured" settlement was
arranged with the defendants.[32]

Additional Case Citations

In a 1973 Florida case, a 17-year-old died during extractions of four wisdom teeth.[33]

In a 1979 Florida case, a 23-year-old suffered cardiac
arrest while undergoing extensive dental treatment.[34]

Oral Surgery in Litigation

The largest number of dental malpractice cases by far
arises from the performance of oral surgery services by general dentists or oral surgeons. A few cases have been highlighted
for illustration.

College Student Blinded after Extractions

In this 1976 Iowa case, a college student suffered from an
upper respiratory infection that seemed to localize as a toothache and headache on November 26. The student, the recipient
of a basketball scholarship, went to the University Hospital
oral surgery department. An oral surgeon found that two of
the student's teeth were seriously decayed, and extracted
them. A prescription for aspirin with codeine was provided.

The next day, the student returned and reported that the
symptoms had not lessened, but in fact had worsened during
the night. The oral surgery department provided the student
with IV Demerol and Phenergan. The student was permitted
to take Dilaudid pain reliever when the Demerol wore off.

Several days later, the student was brought to the infirma-
ry, where the basketball team physician examined him but
failed to request any laboratory studies. Among possible
diagnoses the physician listed mononucleosis, brain abscess,
and septicemia. Shortly thereafter, the student became vio-
lently ill and was seen by a second physician, who noticed
redness of the eyelids and palatal petechia. The second physi-

cian ordered a complete blood count, urinalysis, and mononucleosis spot test, but the tests were not scheduled until the next morning.

During the night, the patient's temperature rose to 104.4 degrees, his eyelids became swollen, and an alarmed nurse summoned the on-call physician, who prescribed Seconal. The physician referred the boy back to the oral surgery clinic the next morning.

The next morning, the student's symptoms were worse, and a marked stiffness about the head and neck was evident. His eyes appeared to be bulging from their sockets, and a neurologist was consulted. At that point, the patient was given massive doses of ampicillin and other medications. That same afternoon, physicians intervened surgically. Intensive medical care saved his life, but not his sight.

The final diagnosis was cavernous sinus thrombosis, which caused clotting in the arteries supplying the blood to his eyes and which, in turn, caused retinal damage.

A lawsuit was initiated, which claimed that the oral surgeon and physicians had negligently diagnosed and cared for the student. A trial court agreed and awarded the student damages. There was expert testimony that the physician should have performed a spinal tap, taken X-rays, and ordered a brain scan because a brain abscess or septicemia was suspected.

It was contended that prompt administration of large doses of antibiotics would have prevented the blindness. Although the real culprits in this tragic affair were the physicians who failed to pick up the developing facial-cranial infection, the lesson for dentistry is clear. The head, face, and neck contain pathways for infection that can cause serious injury in a short period of time. Follow-up and monitoring efforts are required for all surgical procedures. Taking and recording of more clinical information, coupled with earlier and more aggressive intervention, should be the rule when conditions require.[35]

Failure to Provide Post-op Antibiotics

In this 1981 Massachusetts case the patient was seen for the extraction of wisdom teeth. The allegation in the case was that the teeth were already inflamed and infected and that surgical procedure was performed inadvisably in the face of the existing infection. Furthermore, the patient claimed that no prophylactic antibiotics were administered before the surgical procedure. The major problem, however, occurred postoperatively; no antibiotics were administered, even when symptoms developed. The patient claimed that spinal meningitis occurred following the oral surgery work, and the jury awarded an amount of $2.75 million.[36]

CPR Delayed

In this 1981 California case, a 56-year-old female patient suffered respiratory arrest in the chair of the dentist extracting her teeth. The patient was unconscious for 24 hours and hospitalized for two weeks.

The patient's injuries included minimal brain damage, causing personality changes and transitory weakness of the left arm. In the lawsuit that arose out of these facts, the plaintiff claimed that the defendant had taken an inadequate medical history. After the fact it was discovered that the patient's thyroid problems and the medications she was taking had had an effect on the anesthesia that was provided to her.

In his defense, the dentist responded by saying that respiratory arrest was not uncommon with the use of Brevital as an anesthetic agent. Perhaps the most unusual defense was the defendant's statement that he did not start resuscitation efforts until he had completed pulling the teeth, saying that the pain involved in the extraction would "shock the patient into respiration."

This case was settled before trial at a reported $112,000.[37]

Improper Fixation Following Plastic Surgery

In this 1982 New York case, a 34-year-old female suffered from a bone nonunion following facial fractures during plastic surgery.

Apparently the patient had agreed to the procedure to correct a receding chin. The services were performed by a plastic surgeon in conjunction with an oral surgeon. After the procedure, the patient claims that she was left with a permanent paresthesia and TMJ pain. The allegation was that following the fracture and resetting of the mandible, fixation failed and problems resulted.

This case was settled out of court for $185,000. The plastic surgeon contributed $175,000 and the oral surgeon $10,000.[38]

Septicemia Following Extraction

In this 1982 Texas case on the wrongful death of a 43-year-old man, the defendant dentist failed to provide adequate follow-up examination and treatment of the patient. It was claimed in the lawsuit that the patient developed septicemia shortly after the extraction of two teeth. When notified that the patient was having problems, the dentist recommended cold showers to shock the lethargic patient back into wakefulness. In spite of the report from the family that the patient had a fever and was disoriented and suffering shortness of breath, the defendant dentist would not examine the man. Forty-eight hours later, the patient was dead.

Unfortunately, the report of the case does not identify the cause of death or any of the details of the 48-hour period after the time when the dentist refused to see the patient and his death. This case was settled before trial for a reported $75,000.[39]

Legal Blindness Following Blade Implant

In this 1983 California case, a 45-year-old civil engineer was in his regular dentist's office for the extraction of teeth and placement of a blade implant device. The general dentist first extracted the upper molars on the left side of the patient's mouth. After the extractions, the defendant dentist placed a blade implant near the operative site through the maxilla, perforating the floor of the maxillary sinus.

Apparently because of the complications developing around the perforation, the circulation to the left optic nerve was impaired. Optic neuritis developed, resulting in the loss of depth-of-field vision. Although the patient is not totally blind, the vision is markedly impaired in the left eye. Expert testimony was available to connect the implant to the reduced vision in the eye. This case was heard by a jury who gave the plaintiff a $500,000 verdict.[40]

Lingual Paresthesia

In this 1983 New York case, a 23-year-old college student whose right lingual nerve was severed during a third molar extraction was awarded $100,000 in a jury verdict. The plaintiff reported as permanent damages a paresthesia of the right anterior two-thirds of the tongue.[41]

Jaw Fracture During Extraction

In this 1983 California case, a 48-year-old woman was in a dental office for the extraction of a lower right third molar. During the procedure, the defendant oral surgeon fractured the mandible. After the procedure, the patient was forced to undergo ten weeks of fixation. Thereafter, according to the plaintiff's testimony, she developed a temporomandibular joint problem and a malocclusion. In order to restore her jaw and occlusion, the patient underwent the crowning of thirteen teeth and had to wear occlusal splints for almost two years.

The allegations of the lawsuit charged the defendant with negligence, fracturing her jaw, and lack of informed consent.

In this particular case, lawyers for the plaintiff had demanded $15,000 as a settlement effort before trial. The defendant was willing to pay $1,000. The jury, after hearing the evidence, returned a verdict for the woman in the amount of $91,824.[42]

Failure to Cut Arch Wires

In this 1984 Texas case, a 16-year-old girl was in the dental office for oral surgery, after which her jaws were wired together. While still in the hospital, the patient became distressed and, according to testimony provided by the patient's mother, suffered for four hours while the nurses and staff did nothing. At the end of the ordeal, the patient suffered respiratory arrest, slipped into a coma, and died several days later.

The allegations against the hospital were that the nurses failed to take notice and to institute emergency procedures to cut the wires to permit the patient to breathe normally. Other testimony was available that the mother requested that the wires be cut, but was never accommodated.

In defense, the hospital contended that the mother was contributorily negligent for failing to cut the wires herself. The jury, however, felt differently, and awarded the patient's family $1.2 million after hearing all the testimony and evidence. The award was broken down into two parts: the jury awarded $200,000 in actual damages and $1 million in punitive damages.[43]

Postoperative Bleeding

In this 1984 California case, an 18-year-old girl was in the dentist's office for the extraction of four teeth. The following day, the patient started bleeding. Eleven days later, she experienced heavy bleeding.

At 11 p.m. the plaintiff's mother called another dentist, who was also named as a defendant in the action because of the problem with bleeding. At 6:30 the next morning, the plaintiff was finally admitted to an emergency room with an estimated 40 to 50% loss of blood volume. Twenty minutes after she was admitted to the hospital, she suffered cardiac arrest.

In the subsequent lawsuit, the plaintiff alleged that the defendant extracted the teeth improperly and provided negligent postoperative care. The second dentist was also sued for refusing to see plaintiff when she was experiencing heavy bleeding. Details are not available as to why and how the plaintiffs approached the second dentist and why they didn't approach the first dentist for postoperative care.

At trial, the plaintiffs rejected a $3,000 settlement offer by the defendants. The jury awarded $300,000 to the plaintiff's daughter, and the mother recovered $125,000 for her emotional distress. The award was then reduced by 20% because the jury felt that there was contributory or comparative negligence.[44]

Delayed Diagnosis of Mucoepidermoid Tumor

In this 1984 New York case, a 19-year-old student went to the office of the defendant oral surgeon, complaining of a swelling on the roof of her mouth. After six months, the defendant hospitalized the plaintiff for the removal of the growth.

The defendant submitted a specimen to the pathologist, and confirmation of the mucoepidermoid tumor was made. Apparently the pathologist also offered the opinion that there was still tumor left in the palate.

Reportedly, the defendant did not recommend a second session of surgery at the time. Sixteen months later, however, a recurrence of the tumor required removal of the entire palate and a large portion of the maxilla.

The plaintiff must wear an obturator to replace the portion of the maxilla removed in the second surgery. In addition, the plaintiff reports that she cannot speak without the prosthesis and cannot eat certain foods.

The allegations of negligence were the delay in diagnosis initially and leaving portions of the tumor in the patient's palate. No information was available in the report of this case to indicate whether or not the defendant had informed the plaintiff that there was evidence that some tumor remained. Following the testimony and evidence, the jury awarded the plaintiff $3.5 million.[45]

Violinist and TMJ Problems

In this 1985 Washington State case, a 33-year-old registered nurse and concert violinist was in the office of an oral surgeon for treatment of jaw complaints relating to a childhood accident. The defendant performed what is alleged to have been an incomplete history, never noting that the patient was a violinist.

Subsequently the oral surgeon went through a conservative series of treatments, including the placement of an occlusal splint. When the occlusal splint did not provide complete remission, the oral surgeon performed a condylectomy.

Apparently, during the surgery, a rotary instrument that was being used to perform bone cuts caused damage to the meniscus.

After the surgery, the plaintiff not only didn't obtain relief, but experienced even more pain plus an inability to open her mouth. There were also annoying clicking and popping noises in the joint. Four corrective surgeries were required to produce an improvement in her situation. The plaintiff continues to suffer residual pain and reduced ability to perform as a concert violinist.

Expert testimony was available to indicate that the treatment of choice for a violinist would have been extensive conservative treatment. There was also criticism of the use of a rotary burr rather than an oscillating saw for the bone cuts. The suit was settled out of court for a reported $190,000.[46]

References: Dental Cases by Specialty Area

Periodontics in Litigation

1. Zaryczny v. Brimker 77 Civ 3963 (WCC) USDC SDNY, 1979.
2. McSheffrey v. Stage Fla., Duval County Court No. 78-6611-CA, Feb. 23, 1979.
3. Helms v. Curry, Cal., Los Angeles County Superior Court, No. Nc-C-11713, Aug. 20, 1980.
4. Brantley v. Hall, N.C., Wake County Superior Court, No. 80CVS 2915, May 15, 1981.
5. Costillo v. Domenech, Fla., Dade County Circuit Court, No. 83-24116, Jan. 26, 1984.
6. Costa v. Storm 682 S.W. 2d 599 (Tex. Ct. of App., Oct. 18, 1984).

Prosthodontics in Litigation

7. Baker v. Scott 447 So. 2d 529 (La. 1984).
8. Dimoff v. Maitre 432 So. 2d 1225 (Ala. 1983).
9. _____ v. Sterling Dental Centers, Md. Health Claims Arbitration, 1985.

Endodontics in Litigation

10. Simpson v. Davis, 549 P. 2d 950 (Kan. 1976).
11. Schwartz v. Robson, Idaho, Kootenai County District Court, No. 40320, Mar. 1, 1985.
12. Pierce v. Long, Colorado, Denver County District Court, No. 83CV2023, Nov. 3, 1983.
13. Kline v. Bromboz, U.S. Dist. Court N.D. Cal., No. C83 3369 TEH, June 1, 1984.
14. Battcher v. Anton, New York, Nassau County Supreme Court, Index No. 22236-80, October 29, 1982.
15. La Roche v. U.S., 730 F.2d 538 (S.D., March 23, 1984).
16. _____ v. _____, Fredricksburg Circuit Court, Va., August 22, 1985.

Temporomandibular Joint Dysfunction in Litigation

17. Short v. Kincade, Colo. App. 685 P2d 210, 1983.
18. Schlesinger v. Maza, Michigan, Oakland County Circuit Court No. 82 240231 NM, June 6, 1983.

19. Pesavento v. Golden, Michigan, Oakland County Circuit Court No. 83 270107 NM, Jan. 17, 1985.
20. Boknecht v. Ladd, Allen Superior Court (IN) No. 5-84-1175, 1984.
21. Weisshaar v. Whiston, 31st Judicial Court of Virginia Review Panel, August, 1984.
22. White v. Dan, St. Louis, Missouri, 1984.

Local Anesthesia in Litigation
23. LaRocque v. LaMarche, 292 A.2d 259, Vt. 1972.
24. Stanton v. Astra Pharmaceutical, 718 F.2d 553 (C.A. 3, Pa., 1983).
25. LeBeuf v. Atkins 594 P.2d 923 (Wash., 1979).
26. Barreto v. Justen, Cal., Santa Barbara Superior Court, No. SM 15783, Oct. 27, 1978.

General Anesthesia in Litigation
27. Colter v. _____, Phoenix, Arizona, 20 ATLA L. Rep 274, August, 1977.
28. Lord v. Harcon, 133 d District Court 987, 929 Harrison County, Texas, June 29, 1977.
29. Pittman v. Beauchamp, Cal., Los Angeles County Superior Court, No. SOC 35227, March 28, 1978.
30. Goodman v. Howard University, D.C., Superior Court, No. 11285-76, May 22, 1978.
31. McKinley v. Vize, 563 SW.2d 505 (Mo. 1978).
32. Lake v. St. Lukes Hospital, St. Louis City Circuit Court, No. 792-3656, Jan. 22, 1982.
33. O'Keefe v. Boca Raton Community Hospital, 16 ATLA News L. 170 (Fla. 1973).
34. Goodman v. Tesher, 17 ATLAS News L. 199 (Fla. 1974).

Oral Surgery in Litigation
35. Speed v. State of Iowa 240 N.W. 2d 901 (Iowa, 1976).
36. Snow v. Yavner Mass. Middlesex County Superior Court, No. 75-1863, October 6, 1981.
37. Varner v. Hall Cal., Sacramento County Superior Court, No. 278756, Mar. 30, 1981.
38. Lloyd v. Wood-Smith, U.S. District Court SDNY No. 80 CIV 3896, Nov., 1981.
39. Brian v. Kopecky Tex., Dallas County 14th Judicial District Court, N. 79-10851-A, June 11, 1982.
40. Haeri V. Foote, Cal., Orange County Supreme Court, No. 34-85-68, Dec. 1983.
41. Pascarella v. Wagner, New York Erie County Supreme Court, No. 83-812, Nov. 30, 1983.
42. Nickels v. Lewis, Cal. Napa Valley Superior Court No. 41267, Oct. 13, 1983.

43. Lorrumbide v. Doctors Hospital, Tex., Dallas County, 191st Judicial Circuit No. 81-5216-J, Nov., 1984.
44. Rajewsky v. Thomson, Cal., Los Angeles Superior Court, No. C-324, 047, Oct. 9, 1984.
45. Engstrom v. Friedman, N.Y. Nassau County Supreme Court, No. 4725/81, May, 1984.
46. McClarry v. Group Health Hospital, Washington King County Superior Court, No. 82-2-12516-4, March, 1985.

9
Communication and Termination

A patient's disappointment may be especially great when he or she discovers that a bad result is due to a calculated risk that had not been discussed at the outset. In oral surgery, this might mean that the surgeon was betting that he or she would not damage adjacent nerve tissue during a surgical excision of a lower third molar. In crown and bridge, the operator might have bet that he or she would not damage the pulpal tissues during preparation. In endodontics, the practitioner might have been betting that he or she would not need a rubber dam to protect the throat from a dropped instrument.

Although it may seem at odds with modern-day case presentation, an adequate discussion of prognosis should take *failure* into account. Dentistry has made a concerted effort over the last forty years to educate the public to a widespread understanding of modern dental techniques and materials. It is embedded in our system to reassure and explain to patients that the services being proposed are both necessary and beneficial. With such large efforts being made to reverse old myths and prejudices, there's an understandable reluctance to talk about the possibility of problems.

Even so, careful prediction of the outcome of treatment is an integral part of the comprehensive duty a dentist owes his or her patient. If the patient is expecting an outcome significantly different from that which occurs, he or she tends to attribute the difference to negligence and malpractice.

The patient may have acquired unjustified expectations from advertisements or articles on dentistry in the lay press

Unrealistic expectations may also be caused by excessively optimistic predictions on the dentist's part. Dentists are allowed some room for "education" and for giving reassurances and encouragements, but they must balance their presentations to accomplish two major objectives: first to gain acceptance of the work that needs to be done, and second to gain the patient's fully advised and informed consent to the treatment.

In this delicate balance, enthusiasm and energy can swing a case presentation toward "sales" and away from "service," so to speak. Thus the practicing dentist must take care to ensure that a seemingly innocent reassurance is not misunderstood by the patient.

Communicating with Patients

Effective communication is as essential to building a practice as are your technical training and your business skills. Through good communication a spirit and a level of understanding will eliminate the petty problems that arise continually in offices where it is lacking.

There is general communication, there is personal communication, and there are failures of both. General communication is transmitted by the outward appearance of the office, by signs and placards, and by the words and actions of your staff. This form of communication, often found currently under the heading "internal marketing," is beyond the scope of this book.

Personal communication, on the other hand, is delivered directly by the dentist to the patient, and vice versa. Personal communication is a two-way street; the dentist is alternately the speaker and the listener. Most dentists are good at one or the other of these skills; being good at both is unusual.

The best "communicators," however, are both good speakers and good listeners. They listen attentively, with good eye contact, and do not interrupt to correct the speaker or change the subject. At the end of the speaker's turn, the good listener takes a deep breath or pauses long enough to assure that the speaker is finished.

The good listener then responds to each of the speaker's questions or suggestions. Some questions may not have been stated directly, but the good listener will "sense" the inquiry or the subject that is worrying the patient. As if reading between the lines of written communication, good listeners try to understand the speaker's interests and concerns, and then integrate them with the actual words being spoken.

Communication can be written, oral, or the result of the outward appearance of the personnel and the office. We are concerned here with direct patient communication, either written or oral, and how that communication can make a difference in maintaining a lawsuit-free environment.

Of all the professions, dentistry has the most difficult challenge in trying to combine communication with office efficiency. Since dentists are generally considered to be office-oriented and technical-minded, the most efficient operators are usually thought to be those persons who can produce the most units or surfaces in the shortest periods of time. The more hours of pure "chair time" can be crammed into a busy day, the happier are our business managers and accountants.

Some have argued that dental offices are so highly motivated by efficiency that their major objectives are to say "hello" to patients and then shove them onto the assembly line. The dentist rushes in and takes a seat next to a draped, reclined, rubber-dammed, and anesthetized patient. He or she then performs the technical service and departs, leaving the auxiliaries to mop up and collect. All the while, the dentist keeps moving, doing only what he or she is best trained to do: drill and fill, cut and pull, scrape and gouge.

In such "efficient" offices there is no time for chitchat. All post-op instructions are relegated to simple preprinted messages; all consent statements are minicontracts with a lot of filled-in blanks.

Is this communication in the dental office? Not quite. Communication, in the legal sense, means a "meeting of the minds." The exchanging of preprinted forms for money may be superficial interaction, but it is certainly not effective communication. Forms and contracts are the mere trappings of communication. In a legal sense, they are only physical indications that some form of communication took place.

All important information should be expressed verbally to the patient, and reasonable attention should be paid to how the patient is receiving the information. Even if the dentist practices good listening techniques, he or she can't be certain the patient is also a good listener. Speak only as fast as your listener can follow. Measure your pace by the gleam in the patient's eye. The gleam changes to fog when the discussion becomes boring or begins to go over the patient's head. Pause every so often and ask if the patient has any questions. Such moments will occur when you're demonstrating home care procedures, outlining a treatment plan or presenting a new treatment concept, or giving post-op instructions following an extraction.

Pay attention to the verbal details, follow up with written reminders, and make adequate recordings of the specifics in the patient's dental chart. By doing so you will forestall a large number of potential lawsuits.

Not all cases or relationships go smoothly. There will be times when you and the patient are not communicating. It is predictable that dentists tend to acquire patients whose backgrounds and expectations are similar to their own. Patients with markedly different personalities and expectations are usually lost to the practice, as they search out environments where they feel more comfortable.

There are, however, a number of persons in the gray area between loyal patients and patients who are seeking another dentist. Focusing attention on this subgroup, the so-called "gray area" patients, will pay dividends in patient stability and fewer legal hassles.

The Difficult Patient

In the "loyal" group, the dentist and the patient like each other and hope for a continuing relationship. In the "seeking" group, both the dentist and the patient are looking for a way to get out of the relationship. The patient usually finds other arrangements, and the dentist couldn't care less. There's also an in-between group of patients, in which either the dentist likes the patient or the patient likes the dentist, but the feelings are not mutual.

It is a challenge to retain the patient who doesn't know if the dentist is quite what he or she is seeking. On the other hand, there's the problem of what to do with the patient who wants to stay in the practice, but whose presence produces an emotionally charged episode every time he or she appears for treatment. It can be stressful on both the dentist and the staff to have a number of such difficult patients in the practice.

In many ways the difficult patient can lead to compromised treatment. The difficult patient may not want diagnostic X-rays, may not want ideal treatment, may not take enough care of his or her mouth, or may insist on all sorts of extra attention to nonexistent ailments.

Most practitioners have seen some or all of these types a thousand times in their own practices. When confronted with such a patient on an already hectic day, the dentist can easily turn the difficult patient into a nonexistent patient. Before that happens, though, it would pay the dentist to try to express the desire to make the patient happy, so the patient has at least an opportunity to make the dentist happy.

When a difficult patient makes a combative statement, pause and ask if the patient is upset about something or apprehensive of impending treatment. If the patient fails to respond, try some assurances that you are interested in the patient's well-being, and that it's upsetting to the office to see the patient so visibly troubled. Try making some pleasant remarks about the patient to ease your way into his or her innermost thoughts. The objective is to find out what is troubling the patient: fear of pain or discomfort, a misconception about the office, or possibly something that has happened to the patient quite outside the dental environment.

Hopefully, the dentist will get a chance to listen and then, in turn, to speak to the patient's concerns. Just as important, the dentist will have an opportunity to explain gently the office's reservations about the patient's behavior. Here are some conversational examples:

On Diagnostic X-rays

"We need your trust and respect, Ms. Difficult, and we have researched the issue in some detail. We have the latest and safest X-ray equipment, and we use it sparingly. We need the information from the diagnostic X-ray to provide the best clinical service we can. Without it, we are practicing second-level care, like working in a room without light. We've known and respected your views on the use of X-rays for several years. Now it's time for you to acknowledge our views and reconsider having a series of X-rays done at this visit."

On Failure of Home Care

The wrong approach: "Your mouth and home care stink, Mr. Problem. If you don't shape up you can find yourself another dentist."

The better approach: "Mr. Problem, I've got to pause for a moment to discuss the way you're taking care of your mouth and teeth at home. It doesn't make sense to have me place and replace fillings and watch your gums get worse and worse when there is something to do about it. That 'something' involves your own efforts outside our office. If you aren't interested in preserving the work we do here, then we shouldn't continue doing it. But if you can find more time in your busy schedule for yourself—and you deserve it—you will greatly reduce your overall dental problems."

On the Demanding Patient

"Ms. Demand, we know there are problems with any office or environment, but it would make our day and yours easier if we were to discuss any problems with a positive attitude. I promise to pay attention to your concerns if you present them in a positive manner without insinuating that someone is at fault. Now tell me—what's bothering you?"

Terminating Mr. Trouble

Abandonment is a unilateral decision to terminate a patient without reasonable notice at a time when treatment is ongoing. Appropriate and legal termination, on the other hand, can still be a unilateral decision, but timing and adequate notice must be taken into consideration.

The first consideration for termination is this: will the patient's condition deteriorate in the time required to find alternative treatment and care? If the answer is "yes," then treatment must continue to a point where the patient's condition is at least stable.

Then the practitioner should give the patient *notice* of intent to terminate. In other areas of law, the notice requirement usually means that the affected person receives a warning of an impending, *but still undecided,* action against his or her interests. With notice, the individual can rectify the problem that forced the issue, or at least gather evidence as to why the decision should be reversed. This type of notice implies the possibility of rescinding the action.

In cases of terminating the stress-causing bad actors in a dental practice, however, "notice" *is* the announcement of a final, unappealable decision. In American constitutional and civil rights law, the aggrieved minority can rely on a series of legal cases requiring both *notice* and a *hearing* when an individual is about to lose a right. In this case, however, a hearing is not required. The terminated—and angry—patient will probably want a word with you, especially if he or she receives notice of termination in the mail.

The notice should be clear and cordial, businesslike and final. If the patient calls after receiving the letter, the same attitude should prevail throughout the conversation. Even if the patient argues that your decision is unfair and implores you to retract your decision, don't give in. You didn't write the termination notice on a whim. Don't be frivolous and change your mind under verbal attack. Listen to everything the patient has to say, the pleas and the requests for reinstatement. Before you say "no," make a "cushion statement," such as, "I wish I could do what you're asking." Then decline, politely, but firmly. This should be followed by an explanation of why you have to say "no." Finally, offer a suggestion that will be helpful, at least. Don't let the last thing on the former patient's mind be the fact that you would not reinstate him or her. If your "no" isn't accepted the first time, keep repeating it without losing control. Your objective is twofold: (1) to terminate the patient for the good of your emotional well-being, and (2) to keep the conversation (at least your end) firmly in control.

In a few cases in which the fine line between legal termination and abandonment has been at issue, the courts have said that the practitioner must make himself or herself available to the plaintiff for a reasonable period of time until the patient can find a new dentist. In this regard, it is common practice to make an effort to refer the patient to other sources of care. Local dental societies, health centers, or dental school clinics are good institutional referrals.

In addition to the obligation to stand by, the terminating dentist should make his or her records and/or X-rays available to the new practitioner. It would be unwise, however, to make this information available to the terminated patient.

10
Guarantees, Warranties, Contracts, and Fraud

Reassurance is something dentists offer nearly every patient, but spirited efforts at reassurance can unwittingly turn encouraging words into guarantees or warranties of specific results. Just when does a reassuring "discussion" of a proposed treatment plan turn into a verbal contract? Where do you draw the line?

Guarantees, Warranties, and Contracts

One of the first articulations of the principle of holding a practitioner to his promises occurred in a 1929 New Hampshire case, when a young man was taken to the offices of a physician. The palm of the boy's hand had been badly burned. The physician made an effort to answer the nervous parents' questions as to how long the boy would be in the hospital: "Three or four days, not over four; then the boy can go home and it will be just a few days until he will go back to work with a perfect hand."

The physician then set about removing scar tissue from the burned palm and grafting skin from the boy's chest onto the injured hand. When the procedure was finished, the graft "took" but, unfortunately, began to *sprout hair*.

The parents sued the doctor for failure to live up to his promises. They claimed that the boy was not able to return to work for months following the surgery. They also stated the hand was nowhere near "as good as new." If anything, the hand was worse, now that a tangled mat of hair grew in the palm.

The court was sympathetic to the surgeon's statement that the boy would be able to return to work in a short period of time. Such an estimate of healing time was permissible, said the court, because it was only an opinion as to the probable duration of the treatment. Noting that it is generally understood that people can heal at different rates for similar injuries or diseases, the court permitted the latitude necessary to make the "ballpark" estimate. The fact that the estimate was exceeded did not impose contractual liability.

Regarding the reassurances that the boy would have a perfect hand, however, the court said that those words amounted to a promise to perform. The hand would look and perform as a new hand; that is to say, with full function and no particular disfigurement. The defendant argued that no reasonable man could understand those words in that way. He stated further in his defense that the words were "an expression in strong language that he believed and expected that...he would give the patient a very good hand."

The practitioner has the full patient's trust. His or her promises are likely to encourage the patient to undergo the procedure: words significantly shape patients' understanding and decision making. Adding to the dilemma for this particular court's consideration was the testimony that the doctor had repeatedly solicited the patient and the family. The court found that if the defendant had spoken the words attributed to him, he did so with the intention that they should be accepted at face value, as an inducement for consenting to the operation.[1]

The "hairy hand" case is one of the first contract cases studied by students in law school. The promise of one party to do something, the acceptance by the second party, and the passing of consideration (service to one, fee to the other) are the basic elements of an enforceable contract.

Assertions by dentists that their treatments will "effect a speedy cure," "be painless," "improve appearance," "be better for you," or the like, can be the basis for suits in contract or warranty. These statements go beyond reassurance; they go beyond sales puffery. *They are promises of definitive, measurable results.* If the results achieved do not measure up to those expected, consumers (patients) may sue in precisely the same manner as they would sue the salesman who sold them faulty merchandise.

In a 1971 Michigan case, a physician assured his patient that a surgical procedure would "take care of all your troubles," and that "after the operation you can throw away your pillbox."[2] In a 1980 Illinois case, a dentist assured his patient that he would be able to eat corn on the cob after an implant operation.[3] Needless to say, the patients did not feel that the results measured up to the professionals' statements.

Trial lawyers like to add a special allegation of breach of contract or warranty where any sort of promise is either expressed by the defendant before the treatment or implied by the defendant's actions or by the public's general understanding.

For example, the patient may hear the dentist say something like this:

Dr. Trustee: "Mrs. V, your mouth and teeth are in perfect shape. I'll see you again in six months. Until then, don't worry about a thing. Everything is okay."

If such terms and words are admitted by Trustee, or if the jury tends to believe Mrs. V that such words were said, then there is an arguable case for breach of warranty. The assurances made by Trustee theoretically warranted that there was no periodontal disease in the patient's mouth. The patient can rely justifiably on the words, and need not seek a second opinion. Trustee examined her mouth and passed the information to her. She is permitted to go about her life free from the worry that she has a deteriorating condition, which dentists believe can be arrested if intercepted early enough.

In warranty claims, no expert testimony is necessary. The jury is allowed to consider, on the basis of the testimony of the two parties, whether or not a contract or warranty had been given.

Dr. Swifty: "When the bridges are cemented permanently, you won't have any further worry about cavities or the like."

Here the words do not match the exact problem (all prepared teeth eventually needed endodontic treatment), but a jury might interpret the words to mean that the teeth would be "problem-free." The fact pattern would lead the average person to believe that the teeth were never fixed to the patient's understanding. To the extent that these words led the patient to agree to the services, believing that the bridges would be "problem-free," the patient can raise the question of breach of warranty.

Dr. Swifty: "When it's all over, I promise you'll be satisfied."

Here the words establish a contingency that must be fulfilled before the contract is finished. In the ordinary course of business, if a custom-made service is provided under this kind of arrangement, especially if the words "personal satisfaction" are used, then the unsatisfied patient may avoid the contract (refuse to perform his part or pay for the services).

The courts will, however, make a distinction between a *retail business,* where the service or product may be retrieved from the unsatisfied buyer and resold to another, and a *custom service,* where the product cannot be reused or resold. In some cases of custom services, the buyer is under an obligation to pay for the "reasonable value for the effort," which could be well below the original contract price. In other cases, where *personal* satisfaction is guaranteed, the obligation disappears.

Bad Results

Unsatisfactory results often can lead to a breach-of-contract claim, but there are other causes as well which have been used to sue. They include (1) failure to perform in a specific manner, and (2) failure to render services according to a prior agreement.

Regarding the second of these causes, in a 1937 New York case a dentist was accused of failure to perform under a special contract.[4] The dentist was employed to extract four teeth, one of which contained a gold inlay. Apparently the inlay became detached and was swallowed.

The plaintiff claimed that the dentist had agreed to remove *every part of these teeth from every part of plaintiff's body.* Because the inlay was still in her body, however, the dentist had not completed his part of the contract; ergo, breach of contract. The dentist countered by saying he had done everything according to local standards. The plaintiff replied,

"So what? That doesn't matter." The evidence of standard care was immaterial to the plaintiff. The trial court, however, refused to submit the "special contract" claim to the jury.

The decision was reversed by a higher court on appeal. The lawyer drafting the legal answer to the complaint had failed to deny the existence of any "special contract." The higher court interpreted this failure to deny as an *admission* that the special contract did, in fact, exist. The court then found that since a special contract existed and since the inlay was still in the patient's body, there was no escaping the conclusion that the dentist had failed to perform, regardless of the degree of care exercised by him.

This time-honored case is now defended easily by standard answers to complaints. The words used by lawyers in stock replies are "Dr. X did not contract as alleged." This simple denial then requires the plaintiff to prove an agreement *other than* the usual dentist-patient contract.

In the normal course of events, dentists only agree to do their best, which means to use the skill and care practiced by reasonably prudent dentists in the community. That agreement, however, doesn't mean that a dentist and a patient can't make a special arrangement. It only means that *in the absence* of a special contract, the dentist implicitly agrees only to use reasonable care or his or her best judgment.

In cases where the plaintiff alleges *failure to perform in a specific manner,* the usual complication or breach leading to such complication is failing to use adequate anesthesia. The dental complication would arise in the context of such statements as "I'm going to use nitrous oxide and you won't feel a thing."

Naturally, the patient feels *everything,* and calls a lawyer. "Do I have a case? He told me I wouldn't feel anything and I cried all the way through it." The lawyer may or may not pick up on the contractual aspect of the incident. His or her first choice is to analyze the case on the question of negligence. In talking to proposed dentist experts about the facts, the lawyer will learn three things. First, there is no way to predict every patient's pain threshhold. Second, there is a limit to the amount of anesthesia that can be given safely to a patient at one time. Third, a procedure, once started, very often should be completed because of serious consequences attendant to incomplete treatment.

Without dental expert testimony to demonstrate professional negligence in causing excessive pain, the lawyer should decline the case or turn to the contract theory. The reason more lawyers don't automatically turn to the contract cause of action is that the potential damage award is not nearly as high as can be expected from a case of professional negligence.

Damages in Contract Cases

The measurement of injury in a contract case was an offshoot of the "hairy hand" case discussed earlier. The court, faced with the problem of evaluating a human injury in monetary terms, turned to commercial law for guidance.

In a business context, when a person buys a machine for a certain purpose, it is normally warranted to do that certain work. If the machine doesn't perform, the buyer can sue for damages, but the damages must be proven in order to recover. Typically the buyer can expect to recover the difference between the value of the machine if it had performed and its actual value (the weight of the scrap metal if it didn't work at all), together with any known incidental loss. Incidental losses, if anticipated by the buyer and known to the seller, include loss of business because the machine was faulty, or the cost of removal of the nonperforming machine.

In dentistry, the measure for monetary damages would be the difference between the value to the patient of a "perfect" result, such as the dentist may have promised, and the value of the mouth or teeth in their present condition, including incidentals.

The valuation of oral injury is the hard part for lawyers who are considering dental malpractice. If a special contract was made, however, and if the patient is a special person whose mouth and teeth are important to making a living, then the incidental damages can be extraordinary. Some examples of special patients include musicians, speech teachers, actors or actresses, and wine tasters (remember Totally Innocent in Case Study 3). For such patients, a higher level of informed consent is required in states using the "material risk" approach. The professional must be aware of how adverse results may affect this particular patient. Is the possibility of a complication apt to compel a change in the way the patient earns a living? If the answer is "yes," proceed with caution. Add a full explanation of the possible risks, and then *back off.* Let the patient decide whether or not to take the risk.

Typically, in a contract action, the injured party may not claim or collect damages for *ordinary* pain and suffering unless the dentist had induced the patient to undergo the procedure with promises of complete comfort. The pain that is necessarily incident to the procedure is the plaintiff's contribution to the agreement. The pain is the patient's legal detriment, which forms a part of his or her consideration for the contract. The other part of the patient's consideration is the payment of the fee.

Personal Satisfaction

When the plaintiff alleges that the agreement between the dentist and himself or herself provides that he or she need not pay for the dentist's work "until the patient is satisfied," the question arises whether the patient may escape liability even though the dissatisfaction is unreasonable. The court will look at the language used and the degree of objectivity required to obtain satisfaction.

If the language stipulated that the work would be done to the patient's "personal satisfaction," the court would apply a stricter standard than it would to an agreement to perform to the patient's "satisfaction."

The court will also look to the potential for "ill-gotten" gain on the part of the dissatisfied customer. For instance, in the case of a home furnace installed on a "satisfaction guaranteed" arrangement, the court frowns on an owner who claims dissatisfaction but continues to use the appliance. The seller-installer may be able to recoup all or part of the furnace's value if the court interprets the meaning of "satisfaction guaranteed" to mean a *reasonable man's* satisfaction. In that case, evidence must show that only an *un*reasonable man would find the product or service unsatisfactory.

In the case of a portrait artist, the dissatisfied buyer will not gain by his or her refusal to accept the finished portrait. Here neither party has any gain. The "loss" falls to the seller, who put time and energy into the project. Unfortunately, he or she has no claim to any costs if operating under a strict contract that calls for the buyer's personal satisfaction.

The typical situation in dentistry is more like the furnace example than the portrait. Dentists may place fine work, but if the patient is unhappy with the result, and if the dentist has been assuring the patient that he or she "will look better," or "look great," the possibility arises that a special contract had been entered into. This legal argument will normally surface just as or immediately after a dentist delivers a prosthetic case. If the patient does not like the shade, and has been led to believe that the dentist will "redo the shade until you are happy with it," then the dentist should not stop, terminate, or abandon the case until the patient has indicated satisfaction. (This is easier said than done.) Until that time, many state courts will not permit the dentist to sue the patient for the unpaid balance of the bill for the device. Why? Because the contract is not completed until the patient is satisfied. The dentist has not performed.

The courts, however, are more than likely to use a "reasonable man" rule. Was the patient's refusal to approve the shade reasonable? The court is permitted to substitute the reasonable man for the belligerent patient. The reasonable man may not like the color either, but it's a lot better trying to convince the fictional "reasonable man" than Fussy Florid. Everyone's dental practice has had a Mr. Florid: the gentleman who insists that he is not vain, but "don't you think the new cap is too yellowish?" or "too wide, too thick, too fat, short, skinny, depressed, expressed, impressed, digressed...?" Nothing convinces him that the new restoration is the very best modern dentistry can offer.

Historically, the courts have recognized the rights of parties to agree to "personal satisfaction" contracts. A 1916 Colorado case serves to make the point that the dissatisfied buyer had better have a pretty good reason to refuse delivery if the job is workmanlike in its presentation.[5] In that case a Mr. X sought the services of a private detective to investigate and discover who stole a certain jeweled necklace. The detective went about his business, eventually returned to the requesting party, and laid out a good case pointing the accusing finger at Mr. X's wife. Mr. X refused to believe that his own wife was a thief. He attempted to void the contract and refused to pay the detective. The agreement called for payment of $500 when Mr. X was satisfied. The court listened to the results of the detective's work, pronounced the work satisfactory by a "reasonable man" standard, and ordered Mr. X to pay the agreed-upon amount.

A number of cases have been litigated in connection with the fabrication of complete dentures. The patient will allege that the dentist failed to make and fit an acceptable set of dentures. They will further allege that the "plates" did not fulfill the reasonable functional requirements expected of such a device. Courts in a number of jurisdictions have found that if defects in the devices were not due to contributory negligence or lack of cooperation in the making and adjustment of the dentures, a judgment for plaintiff for the price of a satisfactory denture from another dentist is justified.

On the novel question of whether an expert witness is required to make a case, the court said that the claim was founded upon the denture's *functional* defects. Expert testimony was not necessary to determine whether or not the appliance was fit for the purpose for which it was intended. All the dentists in the world, swearing unanimously that the denture was made with all the skill and care ordinarily exercised by dentists, generally would not alter the fact that the denture did not fulfill the reasonable functional expectations expected of such an appliance.

Along a similar line, it can be and has been argued that a dentist can breach the implied guarantee that dental work would be satisfactory, and that the dentist performed the contract in a careless and negligent manner.

In a 1958 Washington State case, a patient was able to prevail on a theory of contract, and recovered the price paid for removable partial dentures.[6] Damages from pain and suffering, however, were not considered by the court to have been within the contemplation of the parties when the terms of the contract were established. If the recovery of monetary damages is not a part of the original understanding in a contract, the claim cannot be made to recover those kinds of damages in the event of a breach of the contract.

In a modern version of the same kind of claim, a 1984 South Carolina court ruled that a patient may recover for breach of an express pretreatment warranty given by a dentist to effect a particular result.[7] In that case, the plaintiff brought a lawsuit against the dentist and alleged, among other things, a breach of contract. The patient said that the dentist made statements amounting to an express warranty regarding the manufacture and fit of dentures to be supplied to the plaintiff. The plaintiff prevailed and was awarded $550.

The dentist appealed to the highest state court, which made two rulings of importance to dentists in South Carolina and elsewhere. First, the court found that there were no previous cases involving this question, but (ruling from the logic of the questions presented and from analogies in other areas of the law) said that a plaintiff could allege breach of warranty in dental cases.

To accomplish this result, the South Carolina court had to overrule some earlier cases that saw the situation differently. Several other states felt that in order to hold the dentist to a special contract, the patient had to pay extra consideration: that is, more than the normal consideration that a practitioner requires to exercise standard care and skill. The court said that if the warranty is given to induce the patient to consent to treatment, the recovery need not be based on the plaintiff's payment of a separate consideration.

Second, the court made an attempt to place some restriction on the action so as not to open the floodgates to allow any bad or poor result to be classified as a breach of contract. To do this, the court insisted on a slightly higher level of proof from the complaining party. The plaintiff must prove the existence of the alleged warranty by *clear and convincing evidence.*

In the case at hand, the court could accept a breach-of-warranty suit without the patient paying any special consideration in consideration for the warranty. The court sent the case back to the trial court, however, because it was not convinced that the plaintiff had carried the burden of proving by clear and convincing evidence the existence of the warranty in the first place.

Fraud and Dental Malpractice

Few fraud actions have been brought against dentists. Malpractice (professional negligence) claims provide plaintiffs with an overlapping basis for recovering a judgment. Moreover, plaintiffs alleging fraud against a dentist come up against some significant barriers to success. Even so, claims of fraud do occur from time to time, often enough to warrant a look at this potentially dangerous accusation.

In order to prove fraud, the plaintiff must show the following: (1) that the defendant made a material representation; (2) that it was false; (3) that the defendant knew or should have known of the falsity of the representation; (4) that he or she made the representation with the intention that it should be acted upon by the plaintiff; (5) that the plaintiff acted in reliance upon it; and (6) that the plaintiff suffered injury. For a plaintiff, that's a tough set of requirements.

It is nearly impossible to prove that a dentist knowingly made a false statement with the intention that the patient rely on it to his or her detriment. Dentists rarely make false assertions with the knowledge of their falsity or with such reckless disregard for the truth of the statement that an allegation in fraud could be sustained.

Fraud enters the picture in the determination of whether or not statements by the dentist prevented the patient from learning the truth of a matter. The statute of limitations restricts a patient to a certain amount of time following an incident to file such a case in court.

Assume that sometime during the running of that particular statutory time period and before the patient has filed a court case, an unscrupulous dentist knowingly reassures the patient that no negligence or malpractice was committed in the course of the incident in question. In such instances, the dentist is said to "step out" of his or her professional character. If the false statement delays the patient beyond the legal time limit, then the dentist is prevented from using the statute of limitations as a defense.

In a 1943 Wisconsin case, for example, a surgeon had left some needles in the plaintiff's abdomen.[8] Three years later, the patient was not feeling well and complained to the surgeon, indicating her desire to be examined by another physician. The defendant then falsely and deliberately assured her that the needles had been removed and there was no need to consult another practitioner. Relying on the representation, the plaintiff continued in the doctor's care until another surgeon removed the needles several years later.

In a subsequent lawsuit, the court held that the fraud complaint was applicable, and a longer statute of limitations for the actions was applied. The court found that when the plaintiff told the defendant about the second opinion and when the doctor forestalled this course of action by repeating the misrepresentations, the patient abandoned her quest for a second opinion. The defendant "stepped out" of his professional character and committed a new and substantive breach of the plaintiff's rights, constituting fraud.

The elements of fraud may be raised as an independent charge in the context of a dental malpractice suit, but for the most part, fraud charges are introduced to thwart the statute of limitations.

Fraud should and must be distinguished, however, from statements of opinion. In other words, a mild assurance that an operation "did not amount to much" will not rise to the level of misrepresentation and fraud. Fraud can be defined as an assertion or statement that is *not warranted by the facts* or by information available to the speaker.[9] The term "fraud" is often used in conjunction with a companion term, "deceit," which is defined as a statement made with knowledge of its falsity.

A few courts have said, however, that because of the health practitioner's superior knowledge in his or her area of specialty, some statements of "professional opinion" could be the basis for fraud and deceit. For instance, a representation by a physician that he could "cure" a patient rose to the level of misrepresentation and fraud because, in light of the source, the statement was more than a mere opinion.

As can be seen, it is not always clear where opinion leaves off and fraud and misrepresentation begin. In a 1981 California dental case, speculative statements on the dentist's part concerning what might happen to the plaintiff's teeth if certain treatment wasn't undertaken proved to be actionable fraud, and the plaintiff was permitted to recover.[10]

In another 1981 case, a physician knowingly and intentionally represented a method of treatment as safe to his patient.[11] The method required restrictions and controls which were not applied. The court held that a fraudulent cause of action could be maintained independent of malpractice, despite the lapsing of the one-year malpractice statute of limitations. Here again, the use of the longer statute of limitations in fraud was useful to a patient who did not discover the fraud until it was too late to file a normal malpractice action.

In a 1983 Georgia case, the same principle that evolved from the California case was used to extend the statute of limitations for malpractice.[12] This case involved the surgical removal of a prosthesis from the plaintiff's body and replacement with silicone implants. The Georgia physician, when questioned about potential leakage of the silicone, allegedly told the patient that the implants were self-sealing and would close around the punctures.

Several years later, and after the point when the plaintiff could have filed a legitimate malpractice action, the plaintiff was told by a second physician that the implants were perforated and silicone had leaked into the body. The plaintiff then filed an action, stating that the first physician had violated her trust and misrepresented the risk of silicone leakage. The misrepresentation amounted to fraud, and the Georgia court found that the action could survive the two-year statute of limitation because the patient had relied on the representation to her detriment. The court reasoned that since the parties were in a confidential relationship, even innocent reassurances could be construed against the maker of the statement because the patient would not be likely to distrust those statements and seek a second opinion.

In a dental context, it is easy to see that there are a number of situations in which patients request reassurance regarding the longevity of services performed by dentists. To avoid any problems related to fraud and extension of the malpractice statute of limitations, dentists should exercise care in communicating with patients.

In a 1985 Arizona case, a patient tried unsuccessfully to use the fraudulent concealment doctrine to overcome the statute of limitations.[13] The court determined, however, that there was insufficient evidence to support the charge. Generally, the courts require that the dentist have actual knowledge of the negligence and conceal it affirmatively from the patient.

In a 1985 Georgia case, however, the court found that silence on the part of the dentist when he should speak or failure to disclose what he ought to disclose is as much a fraud in law as an actual affirmative false representation.[14]

References: Guarantees, Warranties, Contracts, and Fraud

Guarantees, Warranties, and Contracts

1. Hawkins v. McGee 146 A. 641 (NH, 1929).
2. Guilmet v. Campbell 188 NW2d 601 (Mich, 1971).
3. Cirafici v. Goffen 407 NE2d 633 (Ill, 1980).
4. Keating v. Perkins 293 NY Supp 197 (NY, 1937).
5. McCartney v. Badovinac 190 P 190 (Co, 1916).
6. Carpenter v. Moore 322 P2d 125 (Wash, 1958).
7. Burns v. Wannamaker 315 SE2d 179 (SC, 1984).

Fraud

8. Krestich v. Stefanez 9NW2d 130 (Wis, 1943).
9. Jones v. U.S. 207 F2d 563 (Ca, 1953).
10. Helms v. Curry No NCC11713 Los Angeles, Ca, August 1980.
11. Nelson v. Gaunt 178 Cal Rptr 167 (1981).
12. Sutlive v. Hackney 297 SE2d 515 (Ga, 1982).
13. Trede v. Family Dental Centre 708 P2d 116 (Ariz, 1985).
14. Verre v. Allen 334 SE2d 350 (Ga, 1985).

11
Malpractice Insurance—
A Necessary Evil

Dental malpractice insurance rates are doubling, tripling, and, in some states, doing even worse. The premiums are a reflection of the insurer's costs or losses—or so it is said.

Each state regulates insurance separately. Companies are required to present their request for rate increases to the insurance commissioner or some similar body in the state government. In the case of a nationwide program, such as the one endorsed by the American Dental Association, the representative must go through fifty different bureaucracies.

Even though the dental malpractice insurer presents information to state regulators, the exact amount of premium income, liability payments, and profit remains secret. After all, the business of dental malpractice insurance is free enterprise and private business. Subject only to cursory review to guard against obvious abuse, the insurance industry can declare a "crisis" without producing the books for a real, old-fashioned audit.

In congressional hearings in early 1986, consumer advocate Ralph Nader said that the liability insurance industry was "a sacred cow feeding the public a line of bull" and was responsible for the increasing scarcity and skyrocketing cost of coverage.[1] Industry spokesmen, of course, saw it differently. They blamed the "crisis" on an unusually severe "cyclical downturn in the insurance market" and the enormous judgments being awarded by the courts.

Insurance carriers, however, are required to provide some loss information, and the figures they've made public do show a greater loss payout in almost every insurable endeavor. No activity is immune from higher liability risk and loss. From day care centers to bowling alleys, screams of agony can be heard. In early 1986, for instance, both the Baltimore and the Washington Bowling Proprietors Associations (BPAs) sent fee-raising announcements to all their league secretaries which began, "Because of the escalation of insurance costs..."[2] One insurance broker estimated that bowling center liability premiums, which had been in the $8,000 range, were expected to reach $25,000 or $35,000—if they were available at all.

At the same time, Schaghticoke, a small upstate New York township (pop. 7,090), was abandoned by its liability insurance carrier of many years.[3] The town boasted an un-blemished record, having never been sued. Yet the insurance company declared the town a bad insurance risk and pulled out of that and 229 other contracts in New York State alone.

The increased premiums force the insured to make some difficult choices. Either they drop the insurance protection or they pay for it and recover its costs through increased fees for the goods or services they provide.

In the dental profession, where competition and alternative delivery systems are squeezing the bottom line in many practices, the prospect of charging patients higher fees can be scary and frustrating. It's a great humanitarian—or poor businessman—who absorbs a giant insurance increase without passing on that increase to his or her patients.

Dentists can, of course, do without liability insurance or scramble for some sort of self-insurance or pooling arrangement. The least acceptable choice is to try to save money by dropping coverage completely. A look at some of the shortcomings of "going bare" reveals the fallacies of that approach.

How much can you save if you're extremely careful and have, let's say, only one frivolous suit to defend in the year when the coverage lapsed? Even a frivolous suit can soon cost *all* the premium money you saved, and quite a bit more. The cost comes from your own defense lawyer's time in simply

arranging for your defense. Your friendly counselor, whether
an in-law or a recognized trial specialist, can easily put in ten
hours doing an interview with you, conducting some superficial research in the claim, speaking with the claimant and the
claimant's lawyer, and drafting the answer to the claim for
filing in court. The ten-hour figure is used because it is
realistic and easy to multiply by currently applicable minimum lawyer's fees, which average about $100 per hour. That's
just for starters; you've become liable for $1,000 in attorney's
fees and you haven't even made a move. You've only "put up
your dukes," so to speak. Please note in this regard that
according to the A.D.A., liability insurance premiums for GPs
averaged $1,650 in 1985.

If your lawyer has to argue a preliminary matter in court,
you can kiss another $400 to $500 goodbye. The same holds
true if your attorney attends a deposition to defend your
interests or if he or she spends a few hours answering
interrogatories (questions) to or from the other side. Some
time between the filing of the suit and the actual trial, you
will have expended more in defense costs than you "saved" by
foregoing the insurance.

Fact #1.   Even on a simple case, the average defendant
dentist will incur attorney fees of $4000 to $5000 *before the
trial begins*. The actual trial is "heavy duty" expense; it may
take two to five days of lawyer time. I can't begin to imagine
the ultimate cost of *just defending* a dental malpractice case.
Conservatively, $10,000 to $15,000 isn't out of the question. At
current rates, that's almost ten years of premium payments.

At trial, the defendant needs to have one or more expert
witnesses to attest to the standard of care. As previously
noted, experts are entitled to reasonable fees. Finally, this
discussion does not even take into consideration the possibility
of losing and being required to pay a money judgment.

An insurance policy will pay for your defense. Insurance
companies command the services of some of the biggest and
most experienced law firms in the country. Could your broth-
er-in-law do as well?

Fact #2.   According to A.D.A. statistics, the average
award to a plaintiff in dental malpractice suits in 1982 was
$20,000 per claim. The Association also reports that on the

basis of 1982 experience, eight dentists out of every 100 will have a malpractice claim brought against them, a sharp increase over previous years. Those figures are only *averages;* even more important, they are already *out of date.* On the basis of the 8% per year figure, theoretically every dentist would be sued once every 12 years.

An insurance policy will pay for the judgment. If the case is lost, the policy will pay up to its limits less a deductible and/or defense fees, if applicable.

Conclusion. It's too great a risk to expose your practice and your estate to the monstrous costs of defending yourself in dental malpractice. As long as the premium for the average dentist is in the $1,000-to-$2,000 range, it is well worth the leverage the insurance buys. The protection and peace of mind of liability insurance are certainly preferable to the anxiety that accompanies opening correspondence from a strange law firm when you're "going bare."

Insurance Options

Now that we have discussed the positive economics of paying for professional liability insurance, let's consider the insurance options you might have. Since it's difficult to arrange for a custom-tailored insurance policy, there may be no real choices if you deal with one agent. The dentist may have to switch agents or companies to find any real options in liability coverage.

Insurers may withdraw selectively from geographic territories or from practitioners performing high-risk procedures, or they may price their product based on the practice profile of the dentist; that is, a 10% surcharge if endodontics forms more than 5% of the practice's gross income.

Some dentists who have been stung with a malpractice judgment are known in the trade as "risks with unacceptable loss histories." Those dentists may find liability coverage unavailable, for all practical purposes.

Where choices exist, however, the most significant choice is the difference between *occurrence* and *claims-made* policies. Traditionally, the *occurrence policy* has been used most frequently in dentistry. In this type of policy, a year's premium protects the insured dentist for acts or omissions committed during that year, *no matter when the claim is filed.* Since a claim can be filed years after the policy period, it's next to impossible to estimate the potential loss liability.

The *claims-made policy* gives the insured only *one year's protection.* Any claim filed even one day after the policy period ends would *not* be covered unless, of course, a new policy was issued for the second year. Insurance companies love claims-made policies because estimating losses or liability is much easier than under occurrence policies. The premiums, consequently, are somewhat lower. Presently, insurance companies and their agencies are pushing the changeover from occurrence to claims-made policies. The premiums for claims-made policies are stepped or staged to increase over a phase-in period until the companies reach the point where premium incomes are once again earning profits.

In this regard, special problems exist for practitioners about to retire. If you retire from practice and your last policy was claims-made, you have no automatic coverage for the early years after retirement, when a claim is *likely to occur.* To cover this "gap," the companies will sell an insurance policy known as a "tail" at a reduced premium that will guard against an uncovered claim in retirement. Also, if a dentist moves from a claims-made to an occurrence policy and a lawsuit arises based on acts or omissions during the claims-made year, the "occurrence" carrier will provide no protection. The occurrence policy will defend only against claims arising from the years *after* the policyholder starts with it. Therefore, as in the case of the retired dentist, the "switcher" must also obtain "tail" coverage for the period after the claims-made policy has lapsed.

Conclusion. Claims-made policies are slightly less expensive, but they can cost extra if you retire or want to change to an occurrence policy. Occurrence policies are more expensive and offer more protection, but are harder to find.

What Is and Isn't Covered

The standard insurance policy will cover a dentist and pay *judgments* or *settlements,* which the dentist is *legally required to pay* as damages due to *injuries* arising out of the *rendering* or *failure to render* professional services by the individual insured during the period. Each emphasized word has developed special meaning in insurance law. Recently the word "injuries" became the subject of court scrutiny. A 1983 Maryland jury awarded damages for both *physical* and *economic* injury in a malpractice case.[4] The case involved the birth of a child that was brain-damaged during delivery. The jury awarded $350,000 for physical injury to the child and $200,000 for "economic injury" to the child's father. The insurance company took a look at the policy and declared that it would pay only the $350,000 for the *physical* injury. After all, the company reasoned, the policy said "injury," and for years the term has been construed to mean "personal" injury or "bodily" injury. Therefore, only the judgment for the physical injury would be recognized.

The court felt otherwise, however, and defined the term "injury" to include economic or financial injury. The reasoning was that the term "personal injury" or "bodily injury" could have been used in the insurance document, but it wasn't.

The less specific term "injury" was then capable of a broader meaning consistent with public policy, said the court; thus the insurance company had to pay for the *economic* injuries as well. Hint: read the "insurance policy" to see if any of the emphasized words have been modified in favor of the insurer.

Punitive Damages

Disputes have also arisen over language in an insurance contract when the plaintiff declares that the defendant *willfully intended* to injure the patient. Such an allegation, if proved, could lead to the assessment of punitive damages. Policies may exclude payments for such damages, and careful dentists will read their policies carefully to look for this limitation.

In addition to negligence in diagnosis or treatment, this problem of punitive damages usually arises in the context of dental malpractice if the plaintiff can make a case of intentional infliction of emotional distress. The plaintiff must prove actual damages—not necessarily *physical* damages—using this additional accusation.

Punitive damages are awarded if the dentist's conduct was extreme and outrageous and "transcended all bounds of decency," such as holding a tearful patient up to ridicule in front of his or her family and friends; purposely making appointments for a patient in pain for a time following normal business hours when the dentist knew he would not be there; throwing a tearful patient out of the office after preparing a tooth but before placing a filling; placing a foreign body into a surgical incision as a joke to entertain the O.R. staff. The rules are especially protective of the sensibilities of certain groups, such as children, pregnant women, and elderly people.

How Much Is Enough?

How much liability insurance do you need? This question is easy to answer: *as much as you can get.* One could take the view that an amount two or three times as high as the current average dental award in a malpractice case would be appropriate. The American Dental Association has published figures showing that the average dental award was $20,000 in actions where plaintiffs prevailed. Using that figure as an index, you might imagine that $40,000 to $60,000 would be an appropriate lower limit of coverage. Nonsense! The primary reason dentists carry malpractice insurance is for protection in the one-in-a-million chance that a patient dies in the dental chair.

Monetary damages in a dental malpractice case are argued by plaintiff's counsel based on a number of factors. If the lawyer for the plaintiff convinces the jury that the economic loss reaches a certain level, the jury is permitted to award such an amount to the injured patient. The plaintiff's lawyer will present evidence to the jury demonstrating that the injury, when multiplied by the number of years that the patient will have to continue to suffer with the damages, is a significant amount of money. In other words, if a 28-year-old patient was administered a drug that interacted with other drugs already being taken to produce a period of anoxia and brain damage, the lawyer would demonstrate that the injured party has a reduced earning capacity for the year in which the damage occurred, and for *every year thereafter until the plaintiff reaches retirement age or older.*

If, for example, the injured party performed technical work before the injury, for which he was paid $50,000 per year, but after the injury was able to hold only a menial job that paid less than $10,000 a year, the plaintiff's lawyer is permitted to make the calculation that the injury cost the plaintiff the difference between his preinjury and postinjury incomes. The *difference* or *loss* in earnings capacity per year, in this example, would be $40,000.

If we presume that the injured party was 28 years old at the time of the injury, we are permitted to multiply that $40,000 difference by the number of years remaining in his active working life. Subtracting 28 from a presumed retirement age of 65 leaves 37 years. Multiplying the difference of $40,000 times the number of years of reduced earning capability (in this case 37) gives a total figure of $1,480,000. That's the kind of injury award a jury is likely to understand and apt to award to a bodily injured plaintiff. If you wonder why juries have been so generous lately, it's because this kind of reasoning has created the climate for high awards.

In dentistry, the injuries are seldom life-threatening and do not affect the way a person earns his or her livelihood. Most of the injuries are either aesthetic or functional in terms of comfort and ability to masticate properly. Even these kinds of injuries, however, can be presented in such a way as to alert juries to the value of the lost opportunity to enjoy good oral health into the later years. Cases that have received some of the highest dental malpractice awards involve problems associated with orthognathic surgery, problems associated with vestibular correction surgery for the placement of full dentures, and the injuries related to drug reactions, nitrous oxide, local anesthetic, and IV sedation techniques. In the cases just specified, it is not uncommon for juries to award damages over $100,000.

The typical dental malpractice insurance coverage will—if the limits are $100,000 per incident, per individual—cover that $100,000 judgment, pay it for the insured, and, in addition, pay the costs of defending the case through the jury award. Some insurance policies have the restriction that defense costs will be deducted from the policy limits. In other words, if the defense costs are $20,000 and the judgment was $100,000 (the policy limits), the insurance company makes a payment of $80,000 toward the judgment. The remaining $20,000 due the plaintiff is the responsibility of the insured. This contractual arrangement is placed prominently in the contract of insurance. Those who take the time to read through their policy will learn whether or not the costs of defense will be subtracted from policy limits, should a claim go to such limits.

Right to Settle

The insurer is inclined to settle a claim before a full hearing on the matter, and very often the insured dentist conflicts with the insurance carrier in this regard. In many insurance contracts, the insurance company has retained the right to make a settlement on behalf of the insured dentist. In other words, the dentist has no say about whether or not his or her insurance company settles a suit. The dentist may feel that his or her professional integrity and reputation would suffer if the insurance company makes even a nominal payment to a plaintiff in a case that the dentist knows had no foundation. Once again, however, a careful reading of the insurance contract will reveal whether or not the insurer has the power to settle without the written or express authority of the insured.

The possibility of injury to a young working or professional person is such that malpractice coverage in the million-dollar range is clearly indicated. Companies now offer million-dollar coverage for each incident, with a three-million-dollar maximum. Because of the realistic possibility of brain damage and death arising out of dental care, the prudent practitioner will purchase coverage with limits of one million to three million dollars.

Naturally, a minority of dentists take greater risks than usual in their office practice. Those dentists who are using a broad range of anesthetics, including nitrous oxide, IV sedation, and other methods, to provide some form and level of general anesthesia, should be carrying the higher limits of insurance. Yet even those dentists who restrict themselves to local anesthetics should be aware that an injury could occur in their office, which would merit a high jury award based on lost earning capacity or lost chance of survival.

Postoperative infections following extractions are examples of problems that can arise in a general practice office that uses only local anesthetics. Enough cases of rapidly developing cellulitis have been described in the dental literature to alert careful practitioners that situations can go out of control and patients can require prolonged periods of hospitalization.

Even in these high-damage cases, however, it must be proved that the dentist was somehow culpable in the initiation or the failure to recognize the impending rapidly developing, life-threatening infection. The dentist may feel that the procedures were performed according to the standard of care, and may have the moral support of the dentists in his or her community. Yet the plaintiff's attorneys may still find expert testimony that points an accusing finger at the dentist's techniques and procedures. Even if the evidence against the insured dentist is minimal compared to the supporting expert testimony provided by the insured dentist, the jury is permitted to decide on the evidence and can weigh the evidence independently. Juries can come to decisions which *may not reflect current standard treatment in the profession.*

In other words, even if a dentist is practicing according to standard procedures and standard treatment modalities, he or she may lose a malpractice case that appeared to be unlosable.

References: Malpractice Insurance—A Necessary Evil

1. "Nader calls insurance industry 'sacred cow,' " Leon. Daniel in *The Daily Record* (Baltimore, Md.), February 24, 1986.
2. "High insurance costs not sparing bowlers, proprietors," Henry Frankhauser in the *Montgomery Journal* (Rockville, Md.), Feb. 25, 1986.
3. "How a Good Town Became a Bad Risk," Kathy Sawyer in *The Washington Post* Feb. 25, 1986.
4. Interstate Fire v. Pacific Indemnity 586 F. Supp 633 (D.Md. 1983).

12
Infection Control and Liability

All dental offices are familiar with sterilizing techniques for infection control, but the dental workplace presents several problem areas that pose special perils to the attainment of asepsis.

Dental offices of the 1980s are often set up and decorated by lay persons who have no desire to replicate the "sterile" atmospheres of the offices of the past. Many readers will remember the black-and-white tile floors and the hospital-green walls that were common not so long ago.

Still, the ambition to create a "less threatening" environment can be a mistake. To the extent that a dental office contains features that are resistant to decontamination, such an office holds the possibility of transmission of infectious organisms. The major offenders are carpets, plants, and clutter on operatory work surfaces. Other possible sources of problems include failure to dispose of dental needles appropriately and the reuse of "disposable" items. To complicate the matter further, there is a general lack of consensus regarding the number and efficacy of barrier techniques.

If we start from the beginning and work toward the goal of optimum health and safety, we will see that the law demands that the dentist use every effort to protect his or her patients from acquiring infectious organisms in the dental office. All dentists will agree that practitioners must make their offices free of recognized hazards. If there is a known problem in an office and a reasonable solution exists, the dentist is required to take those steps best calculated to eliminate the hazard(s).

Dentists in private practice must protect both their employees and their patients.

At What Cost?

Will the courts entertain a defense that a proposed "solution" to an existing problem is too expensive? Probably not. Courts might consider as extravagant any solution that would threaten the business, but short of that dire prediction, dentists are obligated to make the expenditures. Those who choose to ignore this warning are taking a risk. The risk, clearly, is that dentists will not be able to defend themselves against charges of failure to provide safe and sanitary environments for their patients and employees.

Such a claim would or could arise from any person who developed a case of hepatitis or other readily transmitted disease subsequent to a dental visit. That person would have to be one who ordinarily does not come in contact with, and is not a member of, those population groups predisposed to the disease. If the victim visited a dentist before the onset of disease, however, and if an investigation isolated the dental office as a *potential* source, then the natural tendency would be to test that office against the standard of care.

If the dentist whose office is suspect had taken appropriate steps to minimize the risks of transmission and infection, his or her legal risk would be reduced appreciably. That dentist would have had to know of the existence of the hazard and the potential consequences of infection. A common mistake is to deny the existence of a problem. Taking the attitude, "I've been in practice for thirty years, and no one's died on me yet!" will only compound the problem when statistics catch up.

Dentists should routinely use and require employees to use rubber gloves, masks, eyewear, and other appropriate barriers. In addition, proper sterilization, disinfection, and aseptic procedures should be strictly enforced. In the case of hepatitis B, employers should make the availability of the vaccine known to all employees, and urge, *but not require*, that each employee seek the advice and guidance of the appropriate health professional concerning whether or not to receive the vaccine. Offering to pay for the vaccination serves to remove one hurdle to the acceptance of this recommendation.

Thus, if the dentist has taken all reasonable steps to make the office as free of potential problems as possible, the investigation of the source of the plaintiff's disease will not automatically point to the dentist. If one of the major barrier techniques has not been employed, however, or if the sterilization or disinfection routines do not stand the professional standards test, the dentist will be highly suspect as the source of the infection.

In this age of rapid dissemination of information, the problems of infectious disease and the techniques to combat those diseases are known to all. Ignorance is no excuse. The American Dental Association and the Public Health Service have both made repeated efforts to bring recommended procedures and products to the attention of the profession.

The courts will, in the end, make the final determination of what is appropriate care under the circumstances presented. Even if a procedure is not universally accepted by the profession, the court will be unmerciful if the omitted safety procedure was simple, safe, and effective. If we add to our hypothetical scenario that the dentist in question left out an *inexpensive* safeguard, the courts would be more than free to render a decision against the dentist even in the face of testimony that the procedure was not universally accepted by the profession.

All the commonly used barrier systems are relatively inexpensive to obtain and use. Such barrier systems include gloves, face masks, bracket table and counter top covers, headrest covers, disposable aprons, and other washable or disposable draping materials.

Face masks protect the dental team from splatter from the oral cavity. Splatter is generated by the use of air-driven handpieces and air-water spray syringes. Fitted paper masks should be changed often, as protection diminishes with the length of time in use.

Examination gloves made of latex rubber should be used by all personnel involved in treatment. Gloves should be discarded after use, as washing tends to leave outer surfaces sticky. Gloves for all treatment procedures will provide excellent barrier protection and, with time and practice, will not compromise tactile sense.

Covers should be provided for all surfaces that dentists touch in routine treatment procedures. Typically, the practitioners touch operating lights, syringes, one or more handpieces, and the chair controls. Tinfoil sheets can be prepared ahead of time and wrapped around light handles and adapted to chair switches. Syringes and handpieces may be partially sterilized and partially disinfected to block transmission of microorganisms. Hand instruments and treatment materials can be brought to the work area in packages that were put together in controlled sterilizing areas. All these precautions will greatly reduce the chance of cross-contamination.

Experts say that all mouths must be considered infectious. A good health history, completed *honestly* by every patient, will provide essential information about the patient's potential carrier status. Even so, there are many symptom-free disease carriers who do not actually know their status. Such health histories, obviously, are incomplete protection, but the effort must be made.

Practitioners may not abandon the practice of taking the health histories because some patients lie about their status in regard to certain disease states. Additional questions added to the standard health history can elicit warning signals, which then can be discussed by the practitioner in private consultation. Such consultation should be accomplished by the dentist, not a staff person, and should be conducted in private with assurances of confidentiality.

Herpes Simplex Virus

In a 1984 issue of the *Journal of the American Medical Association*, a group of investigators found a link between numerous patients and an infected dental hygienist who suffered an oral herpes outbreak.[1] A dentist had initiated the investigation when a number of his patients reported painful lip and intraoral ulcerations.

The subsequent study found the hygienist to be an active carrier of herpes simplex virus (HSV) Type I gingivostomatitis. The hygienist's active-stage period was determined to have been approximately two weeks long. During that time the hygienist exhibited herpetic whitlow, characterized by swelling, redness, tenderness, and pain in one or more of her fingers.

The investigators were able to find and interview 123 patients seen by the hygienist during the two weeks in question. When these patients reported developing fever, lip or intraoral ulcers, bleeding gums, sore throat, cervical adeno-pathy, or weight loss, their symptoms were considered to be directly related to their exposure by the hygienist. Of the 123 identified patients, 43% reported positive symptoms—a signif-icantly large number.

The *JAMA* article makes the point that HSV infection may be difficult to recognize. As hand lesions go, HSV may masquerade as simple dermatitis, bacterial infection, or post-traumatic tenderness.

The article repeated some common-sense guidelines for dentists and dental auxiliaries. Dental offices should postpone treatment of individuals who have active lesions. If treatment cannot be postponed, rubber gloves and rubber dams are an absolute necessity. After treatment, all disposable rubber and paper goods should be autoclaved before discarding. In addi-tion, all questionable hand lesions should be cultured for viral or bacterial infection.

Hepatitis

In a 1982 Tennessee case, a dentist was accused of transmitting serum hepatitis to a patient.[2] The complaint alleged that in October 1975 the defendant dentist was per-forming work on a "dental bridge" for the plaintiff. At some point during the visit, the dentist "lacerated his own finger and plaintiff's lip and ... their blood intermingled." One month later the plaintiff became ill, and in January 1976 was finally diagnosed as having serum hepatitis. At a subsequent visit to the dentist in July 1976, the dentist informed the patient that he had been infected with the disease at the time of the October 1975 visit.

In cases like this, liability would attach only if the dentist (1) failed to take precautions in contracting the disease (treatment of known carriers) or (2) failed to ensure that any infectious organisms could be transmitted in his or her office through inadequate sterilizing or barrier procedure.

The use of the word "serum hepatitis" dates the underlying medicine, and one has to be suspicious of the causal link. This case, however, is one of a limited number of cases addressing dentists' *potential* liability for cross-contamination of patients.

Hepatitis B

Of the forms of viral hepatitis, HBV (hepatitis B) is the most serious and the one most frequently identified with transmission from dentist to patient. The disease is transmittable via parenteral route during transfusions of blood and blood products, and is carried by a large number of asymptomatic victims. Asymptomatic carriers pose a serious threat to the dental environment. The use of sharp cutting instruments and high-speed drills exposes the dental staff to a mixture of blood and saliva. Dentists who sustain minor cuts or abrasions on their hands provide a potential point of entry for the infection.

In 1975 the ADA reported that general dentists had a 13.6% incidence rate of hepatitis B overall, and, surprisingly, that oral surgeons had an incidence rate of 21%. A second study by the U.S. Veterans Administration confirms the figures. The incidence rates of HBV among dentists is unusually high when you consider that the carrier rate in the general population is 2 to 3 percent. In 1983, the Center for Health Statistics ranked dental personnel in the highest risk category for acquiring hepatitis B.

There can be little doubt that the dental office has been identified correctly as the source of hepatitis B virus transmission. Research published in medical journals since 1976 has traced multiple cases of hepatitis B transmission to general dentists, oral surgeons, and dental hygienists.

The control of hepatitis B requires an effort at identifying high-risk patients. Good preventive technique begins with taking an accurate medical history before initiating diagnostic procedures or treating a new patient. The medical history is not an absolute protection, however, because many patients with a history of hepatitis do not know which type of hepatitis they suffered. In addition, many carriers of hepatitis B do not know they have the disease and have no symptoms to help them seek further testing.

Two other areas of prevention and identification will assist the dental staff in reducing exposure to HBV. Those areas are 1) identifying high-risk groups in order to take special precautions before beginning treatment, and 2) obtaining serological blood testing or medical referral for all patients with a recent history of hepatitis.

Of course, the barrier techniques previously described and the sterilization procedures used in dental offices will break the chain of transmission. It has been reported that oral surgeons incorporate the highest standard of barrier technique in their practices, including hand cleansing with antimicrobial soap, the employment of protective glasses, disposable masks, and rubber gloves, and the proper autoclaving of instruments. Yet in spite of these protections, oral surgeons still exhibit a much higher rate of disease than do general dentists or the public in general.

With that in mind, a protection available to dentists today, which has been shown to be both effective and safe, is the vaccine known as Heptavax. Health researchers believe that as more dentists become vaccinated, the incidence of hepatitis B in the profession will stabilize and drop off. The vaccine will not cure active disease, but it has been credited with 90% effectiveness in the prevention of HBV. Unfortunately, the profession has not taken to the vaccine in large numbers. Dentists who postpone this safe and effective health-care measure are taking a rather high risk of becoming infected.

In this same vein, consider a 1983 Connecticut case involving an oral surgeon.[3] The dentist was accused of transmitting hepatitis B to his patient, and through her to her husband and her *in-utero* infant. All three family members continued to show disease symptoms some three years postinfection, and the infant plaintiff developed liver dysfunction.

The claim against the dentist criticized the practitioner for negligently contracting the disease himself. Evidence was available to show that the oral surgeon contracted the disease while treating the institutionalized population of a mental hospital; apparently he carried out the treatments without wearing gloves. Evidence was also introduced to show that the dental community was on notice that such institutional groups are in a high-risk group for hepatitis B. In addition, the defendant dentist suffered a dermatitis condition which allegedly aided infection and transmission, although he remained asymptomatic at all times.

This case points out the danger in using unsafe barrier techniques. The wearing of rubber surgical gloves *at either end* of the transmission chain would have interrupted the flow of contamination.

Is the practicing dental profession really on notice that diseases are transmitted easily in the dental environment? The answer is yes. Dentistry has been an advocate of sterile field procedures and decontamination techniques since the time of Lister. There isn't a dental office in the country that doesn't have an autoclave and/or shelves of chemical disinfectant/sterilant liquids.

Recent research at the University of Maryland School of Dentistry illustrates the stubborn nature of some oral organisms.[4] The Maryland study demonstrated that certain bacteria survived out of the mouth for several hours. The study involved samples of blood and saliva smeared on dental records following treatment. The dentists involved in the study were apparently marking dental charts after treatment but before decontaminating themselves by discarding the gloves used in treatment. Cultures of the isolated smears were positive for a number of organisms.

Chemical Sterilizing

Chemical sterilizing and disinfecting agents are used by a large number of practitioners. Recent research has shown, however, that the quaternary ammonium compounds, although long established, are *not* effective against some dangerous microorganisms, including the hepatitis B virus. Yet as recently as 1985, dental supply companies reported at a major conference on office sterilization and asepsis procedures that the "quats" were still selling in large quantities.

Using outmoded sterilizing liquids or misusing appropriate products will render the whole procedure void. An ADA panel, considering the issue of sterilizing instruments, selected heat and steam systems as the best choice. At the ADA's

1985 meeting of the Council on Dental Therapeutics, these panelists were concerned that solutions are not being used in an informed way. Problems, they say, exist with the definition of "disinfecting" and "sterilizing."

In related findings, hospital research on infection control has revealed some interesting insights. British researchers found bacteria under the wedding rings of nurses—not the usual colonies, but 17 unexpected varieties, such as those linked to vaginal, intestinal, or respiratory infections.[5]

Litigation

Not all cases alleging cross-contamination are successful for the plaintiff. Two cases, one each from Louisiana and Texas, illustrate some difficulties in proving negligence or convincing a court of the merits of the case.

A 1980 Louisiana case involved a female patient who contracted "serum hepatitis and/or hepatic disease."[6] She claimed she contracted the disease because the defendant doctors and a hospital failed to employ sterile techniques when blood samples were drawn while she was undergoing medical tests in 1974. The patient died the next year of unrelated causes, but the case was brought nevertheless.

In defense, the hospital's expert witnesses all testified that the hospital used disposable sterile needles and syringes to draw blood. Furthermore, one treating doctor who saw the plaintiff testified that as of the dates in question, "she did not have hepatitis."

With such a strong defense, how could the plaintiff even think about filing such a case? The answer lies in one radiologist's report. A liver scan in October 1974 found an enlarged liver "suggestive of hepatocellular disease" or "hepatitis." That was all, but it was enough to spark a lawsuit. It wasn't enough to prevail, however; the case was thrown out after the three hospital experts submitted affidavits confirming their opinions.

The lesson for dentistry? The fact pattern is analogous to a dentist finding evidence of horizontal bone loss on one dental X-ray. Certainly a reduced bone level in relation to the cemento-enamel junction of the tooth is "suggestive of" periodontal disease, but few clinicians would base a diagnosis on radiographs alone.

The other unsuccessful case alleging transmission of infectious disease comes from a Texas court.[7] There the complaint alleged that a patient's leg was not washed before the application of a plaster cast. The leg became infected under the cast, and additional treatment was required. The plaintiff stated that when the cast was finally removed, she and five other witnesses found the presence of dirt and grass or "plant-like" substances.

The defendant doctor acknowledged that she herself did not wash the leg, but stated that the leg was clean. The nurse assisting on the case testified that she could not remember washing the leg, but that it was the usual procedure to do so.

On the basis of the evenly divided testimony, the jury chose to believe the doctor and the nurse because the plaintiff failed to prove that the leg was not washed. The whole matter might never have come to court if the notation "leg washed," or words to that effect, had been made in the record. The plaintiff's attorney might not have filed the action if such evidence had been available to their side in advance. It's one thing to go into court when the best you can do is say, "It's their word against mine." It's quite another when there is a record entry proving that the procedure in question was accomplished.

Washing hands in front of the patient has been a dental routine for years. Dental school teachers mention it on several occasions. "Convince your patient that you are careful about cleanliness. Wash your hands where they can see you."

With the advent of multioperatory clinical arrangements, the hand-washing ritual becomes even more important. When a dentist is seeing one patient for treatment and a dental hygienist is seeing one or more others, the potential can exist for forgetting to wash between patients. Since rubber gloves are now recommended for all intraoral treatment visits, it is simply a matter of stripping and disposing of many gloves per day.

Because a small cost factor is involved in the use of rubber gloves, there's a tendency to glove only for the major cases and simply to wash for the adjustments and hygiene patients. As mentioned previously in this chapter, however, the failure to use simple, effective, and inexpensive barrier systems will weigh strongly against a dentist whose office is charged with negligence in allowing cross-contamination to occur.

In a 1967 Oregon case, a hospitalized patient accused the institution of negligence.[8] During the hospital visit for neurosurgery, the patient developed a staphylococcus infection in the operative area. At trial, the patient tried to prove that the cause of the infection was the lack of proper antiseptic procedures. The patient said that nurses came in and out of her room *without washing their hands*.

One witness for the plaintiff, a clinical microbiologist, testified that the particular cause of the infection could not be determined. The microbiologist was able to say, however, that it was *more likely than not* that the infection was acquired from the hospital environment:

> ...the bacteria which the patient has on herself is not as dangerous to [the patient] as the bacteria she would pick up from a nurse who would walk into an infected room and out again without washing her hands.[9]

Two physicians testified to essentially the same thing: the infection *probably* came from the hospital environment.

Like the microbiologist, neither doctor was willing to trace the infection to a particular source. The court requires something more than a mere "possibility" of cause; experts must conclude that the negligence "probably" caused the injury. In this case they did, and the court ruled for the plaintiff.

Thus we see that failure to wash hands between patients can be used as an instance of negligence. Dentists and dental offices must take a careful look at their own system of infection control. If there are recurring breaches, changes can and should be made.

Sterilization, barrier control, and efficient medical history taking can provide a safe legal environment for dentists, staff, and patient. Failure in any of those areas presents both legal and clinical jeopardies.

AIDS

Available statistics show a deceptively low incidence of AIDS among health-care workers, but all sources agree that dentists, dental hygienists, and dental auxiliaries are a high-risk group.

The American Dental Association has gone on record stating that the glutaraldehyde sterilants will kill the virus, "provided it contacts the virus." The Center for Disease Control in Atlanta notes that heat treatment is "very effective" against AIDS. Still, when you consider all the potentially contaminated nonheat-treatable surfaces that a patient can spoil, or that dental personnel touch routinely during treatment, maintaining a germ-free environment becomes a less-than-certain proposition.

Whether to treat AIDS patients is an ethical dilemma for practitioners. If, for any good and sufficient reason, the practitioner feels that he or she cannot provide positive barrier protection for himself and his staff, he or she should think twice about accepting the medically compromised carrier of this particular disease.

This policy may not fit squarely with what some governmental agencies are saying about AIDS and transmissibility. In 1985 the Lost Angeles City Council passed an ordinance prohibiting discrimination against AIDS patients. Under the ordinance, medical professionals, including dentists, would be prohibited from denying treatment to AIDS victims. In Washington, D.C., a similar proposal was introduced in City Council that year. In editorially opposing the measure, the *Washington Post* granted that "given the inadequate state of medical knowledge about AIDS, nonvictims do have legitimate concerns about the spread of any deadly virus." The nonvictims are the dentist's staff and the healthy patients who follow the AIDS victim.

The first line of protection against treating a known carrier or infected individual is in the medical history. Two additional questions could be added to many of the present long forms now widely available: "Have you ever had your blood tested for the presence of an infectious disease?" If the answer is yes, a follow-up question should be: "Were you told that you are a carrier of any infectious or transmissible disease?"

If you assume that the carrier of AIDS tells the truth in the form, treatment *is* possible, but only under strict sterilizing control. University researchers have published systems for providing dental care for infected patients.[10] The plans call for a circulating assistant to act as a clean intermediary between the operator and his or her cabinets and equipment. Disposal of contaminated nonreusable items requires double bagging and warning labels. The prospect of treating an AIDS victim need not frighten or confuse the profession, but the dentist must not become a link in the chain of transmission of this deadly disease.

References: Infection Control and Liability

1. Manzella et al., An Outbreak of Herpes Simplex Virus in a Dental Hygiene Practice, JAMA 252:2019, 1984.
2. Foster v. Harris 633 Sw2d 304 (Tenn., 1982).
3. _____ v. Harris, New London Sup Ct. No. 8000627835 (Conn., 1983).
4. Thomas, L, et al., Survival of Herpes Simplex on Patient Charts, JADA 111(9):461 1985.
5. McCarthy, P. Wedded Blues, American Health 4(7):34, 1985.
6. Vanderdoes v. Ochsner 377 So2d 1368 (La., 1979).
7. Carrasco v. Goatcher 623 SW2d 769 (Tex., 1981).
8. Sneath v. P&S Hospital 431 P2d 835 (Or., 1967).
9. Ibid.
10. Heuer et al., A Protocol for the Treatment of Hepatitis Patients, J Dent Educ 49(8): 596, 1985.

Appendix A

Pattern Interrogatories

These questions, called *interrogatories*, are routine requests for information in a dental malpractice case. The law varies from state to state regarding how many questions may be asked and other procedural and substantive issues. Concerning the actual phrasing of the questions and the requirements for prompt and complete answers, your defense counsel will assist and advise you as to which questions violate state law and need not be answered.

1. What is the address of each office maintained by you for the purpose of practicing dentistry, and the inclusive dates you maintained each such office?
2. Were you associated, or in a partnership, with any other practitioner of dentistry at the time of the occurrences complained of in this action?
3. If the answer to the previous question was yes, state the name, present address, specialty, and qualifications of each person with whom you were associated or in partnership, the nature of the business relationship, and the inclusive dates of the relationship.
4. State the names and addresses of all persons who have knowledge of any relevant facts relating to the case.
5. State the names and addresses of any and all proposed expert witnesses, and annex true copies of all written reports rendered to you by any such expert witnesses.
6. As to any person you expect to call at trial as an expert witness and as to any person who has conducted a physical examination of the plaintiff, whether or not you expect such person to testify, state the name and

address of such person and all his/her qualifications, the subject matter on which the expert is expected to testify, the substance of the facts to which said expert is expected to testify, the substance of the opinions to which the expert is expected to testify, a summary of the grounds for each opinion to which said expert is expected to testify.

7. Has any expert rendered an opinion, either oral or written, to you whom you do not intend to call as a proposed expert witness?

8. If you answered the above interrogatory in the affirmative, state the name and address of the expert and the topic or subject matter of his report.

9. Has any expert rendered a report to anyone, other than yourself, such as the insurance company that represents you, pertaining to this matter in any way?

10. If you answered the preceding interrogatory in the affirmative, state the name and address of such person and the subject matter or topic of said report.

11. In regard to the reports rendered by experts whom you do not intend to call upon as expert witnesses but who have rendered reports, either oral or written, to you or anyone who represents you, attach copies of those reports, if written or oral, hereto.

12. What is the name and address of each accredited dental school of which you are a graduate and the inclusive dates you attended each school?

13. What is the name and address of each undergraduate and postgraduate college which you have attended and the inclusive dates you attended each?

14. In what states are you now, or have you ever been, licensed to practice dentistry, and in what year did you receive your license to practice in each state?

15. Have you ever been licensed to practice dentistry in any country other than the United States? If so, state the name of each such country and the inclusive dates you were licensed.

16. Have you ever had a dental license suspended, revoked, or terminated in any state or country? If so, for each such license, indicate specifically whether re-

voked, suspended, terminated, or other final or probationary action taken by the state and the reason for same.

17. Have you ever had any training in a specialty of dentistry or medicine? If so, for each such training, state the name of the specialty, the institution where you trained, and the inclusive dates of such training.

18. Have you ever limited your practice to any recognized specialty of dentistry or any subspecialty? If so, for each such specialty or subspecialty state the name of each and the inclusive dates you limited your practice to same.

19. Are you now, or have you ever been, a member or diplomate of any specialty board? If so, for each such specialty board, state the name and address of the specialty board, the inclusive dates of membership, and the qualifications for membership.

20. Are you, or have you ever been, a member of any dental association, society, or organization?

21. If so, for each association, society, or organization, state the identity of the organization, the aims and purposes of the organization, whether you have held any office in the organization, and, if so, identify the office and the inclusive dates you held such office.

22. Do you or have you ever had any staff privilege at, or in association with, any hospital?

23. If so, identify each such hospital and state its name and address, the nature of your relationship to it, a description of each staff privilege, and inclusive dates you held each privilege.

24. Have you ever had any staff privilege revoked or curtailed at any hospital?

25. If so, for each such privilege, state a description of the privilege, specify whether revoked or curtailed, and explain. Give the date of revocation or curtailment, the reason for revocation or curtailment, and the name of the disciplinary body involved.

26. Have you ever held a position or office in any hospital?

27. If so, for each position or office, state its name and designation, the duties and privileges attached to it,

the name and address of the hospital at which it was
held, and the inclusive dates it was held.

28. Have you ever been associated in a teaching capacity
with any dental institution?

29. If so, for each institution, state its name and address,
give a description of each position you held and the
inclusive dates thereof, and name each subject taught
by you.

30. Have you ever written, or contributed to, a dental
textbook?

31. If so, for each textbook, state the title, the name and
present address of any co-authors, the name and
address of the publisher, and the date of publication.

32. Have you ever written, or contributed to, a dental
paper or article?

33. If so, for each paper or article, state the title, the
subject matter on which you wrote, the title, edition,
and date of each publication, the name and address of
the publisher, and the name and address of any co-
authors.

34. At any time in your dental career have you received
any award or honor?

35. If so, for each award or honor, state the identity of the
award, the name and address of the institution from
which it came, the achievement for which it was given,
and the date you received it.

36. State the name, author, subject matter, date, and
publisher of each dental textbook or journal in your
possession.

37. At the time of the occurrences complained of in this
action, was there a policy of professional insurance
covering you?

38. If so, for each policy, state the name and address of the
insurer, the number of the policy, the effective dates of
the policy, and the limits of liability.

39. Did the defendant ever treat the plaintiff or perform
any surgery upon the plaintiff for any dental condition?

40. If the answer to the previous question is in the
affirmative, state the date or dates on which such

treatment or surgery was rendered, a description of the treatment or surgery rendered, and the names and addresses of all persons who assisted the defendant in the performance of such surgery, and attach all office records related to such treatment or surgery.

41. Did the defendant have any discussions with the plaintiff concerning surgery referred to in the previous question?

42. If the answer to the previous question is in the affirmative, state the date or dates on which the discussions were held, where such discussions were held, the names and addresses of all persons present during such discussions, and the contents of such discussions, and if such discussions were reduced to writing, attach copies hereto.

43. Did the defendant have any discussions with the plaintiff's spouse concerning the treatment referred to in the previous question?

44. If the answer to the previous question is in the affirmative, state the date or dates of such discussions, where such discussions were held, the names and addresses of all persons present when such discussions were held, and the contents of such discussions, and if such discussions were reduced to writing, attach copies hereto.

45. Did the defendant ever procure the consent of the plaintiff concerning the treatment or surgery referred to in the complaint?

46. If the answer to the previous question is in the affirmative, state the date on which such consent was procured, and how such consent was procured, and if such consent was reduced to writing, attach a copy hereto.

47. Did the defendant ever procure the consent of the plaintiff's spouse with respect to the treatment referred to in the complaint?

48. If the answer to the previous question is in the affirmative, state the date on which such consent was procured, and how such consent was procured, and if such consent was reduced to writing, attach a copy hereto.

49. Did the defendant ever disclose to the plaintiff or the plaintiff's spouse any known dangers of the proposed treatment or surgery?

50. If the answer to the previous question is in the affirmative, state the date or dates on which such disclosure was made, where such disclosures were made, the names and addresses of all persons present during such disclosure, and the contents of such disclosure, and if such disclosure was reduced to writing, attach a copy hereto.

51. Did the defendant ever prepare any dental records regarding the treatment rendered to or the surgery performed upon the plaintiff?

52. If the answer to the previous question is in the affirmative, state the date or dates on which such records were prepared, the location of such records, the name and address of the custodian of such dental records, and the contents of such dental records, and if such dental records were reduced to writing, attach a copy hereto.

53. Did any complications arise concerning the treatment or surgery performed upon the plaintiff by the defendant?

54. If the answer to the previous question is in the affirmative, state the date on which the complication arose, the description of the complications that arose, the reason for the complications, and the steps taken to ameliorate such complications.

55. Did the defendant have any discussions with any other persons concerning the complications referred to in the previous question?

56. If the answer to the previous question is in the affirmative, state the date or dates on which such discussions took place, where such discussions took place, the names and addresses of all persons present during such discussion, and the contents of such discussion, and if such discussions were reduced to writing, attach a copy hereto.

57. State the factual basis upon which the defendant asserts that the allegations contained in the complaint

fail to state a claim upon which relief can be granted.

58. State the factual basis upon which the defendant asserts that any and all injuries and damages sustained by the injured plaintiff were the result of the actual omissions of a third party over whom the defendant had no control.

59. State the factual basis upon which the defendant asserts that the recovery on the claim set forth in the complaint is diminished or barred by the failure of the injured plaintiff to mitigate damages.

60. State the factual basis upon which the defendant asserts that recovery on the claim set forth in the complaint is diminished or barred by the negligence of the injured plaintiff.

61. Please state in detail the dental history the plaintiff related to you the first time you were in contact with the plaintiff with regard to the problem for which you were attending to the plaintiff, including in your answer the plaintiff's chief complaint, history of present illness, past history, family history, and review of systems.

62. Please describe in complete detail the dental examination which you performed on the plaintiff the first time you saw the plaintiff for the problem for which you were attending the plaintiff, and submit a comprehensive list of your findings.

63. Please set forth in complete detail the substance of all conversations between you and the plaintiff at the time you agreed to care for the plaintiff for the injury, illness, or disability for which you were treating plaintiff.

64. From the time you first undertook the plaintiff's care for the problem for which you were attending to the plaintiff, did you ask any other member of the dental profession for an opinion or for assistance with the plaintiff's case?

65. If your answer to the previous question is in the affirmative, please indicate as to each such dental professional the name, occupation, title, address, area of specialization and professional relationship to you,

the date, time of day, nature, and scope of your request, the nature and scope of the opinion or assistance, and the date and time of day it was first rendered.

66. Please state the initial differential diagnosis you made on the problem for which you were attending to the plaintiff.

67. Indicate your impression at the time you first examined the plaintiff for the problem for which you were attending to the plaintiff of the relative likelihood of each diagnosis in the differential, and specify the data on which you base your opinion.

68. Did you at any time order X-rays to be taken of the plaintiff?

69. If your answer to the preceding interrogatory is in the affirmative, please state the date and time of day of each such X-ray or series of X-rays, the name, address, and professional title of the person who took the X-rays, the name, address, and professional title of the person who checked the results of each such X-ray or X-rays, what decisions were made as a result of such X-rays, and the name and address of the person or persons who currently have custody of each such set of X-rays.

Appendix B

Case Study Interrogatories

The following are sample questions that the fictional dentists in the case studies might be asked to answer. These formal questions would be sent to the defendant by the plaintiff's lawyer. They are best answered with the assistance of defense counsel. Unlike the "pattern interrogatories" in Appendix A, these questions are custom-made and designed specifically for the case at hand.

Many of the questions deal with the clinical aspects of the treatment or misdiagnosis that is central to the case. Lawyers obtain help with these kinds of technical questions from consultations with their own proposed expert witness or from general texts available to lay persons on the subject of dentistry. Naturally, the questions must be answered truthfully and under oath.

Case Study 1.
Undiagnosed Periodontal Disease:
Interrogatories

This is the case where Mrs. V (for victim) discovers that a periodontal condition has left her with few healthy teeth, even though she has been visiting her dentist for a number of years without his having made mention of the disease. Dr. Trustee is now faced with the uncomfortable task of truthfully answering questions on various aspects of his care and treatment of the plaintiff.

1. When did you first examine the plaintiff? List all your clinical and radiographic findings from that particular examination.

1a. On the dental records or charts that you maintained on the plaintiff, please identify the exact location where these findings are recorded.

2. As a result of your first examination, state precisely the periodontal condition of the plaintiff's mouth as of the date of that first examination.

2a. On the dental records or charts that you maintained on the plaintiff, please identify the location where the periodontal diagnosis from the first examination was recorded.

3. As a result of your first examination, did you have an occasion to discuss your findings with the patient? If so, describe the information given and the patient's response.

4. As a result of your first examination, did you have an occasion to provide the patient with detailed home care instructions? If so, describe the methods and materials you selected for this patient and the rationale for the particular methods and materials.

4a. On the dental records or charts you maintained on the plaintiff, please identify the exact location where these recommended methods or recommended/dispensed materials are recorded.

5. (Repeat questions 1-4a for the last examination performed on plaintiff before the patient left the practice.)

6. Do you own as part of your dental professional equipment an item known as a "periodontal probe," one that is calibrated in millimeters (mm) and commonly used to measure the depth of periodontal pockets?

6a. If your answer to question 6 is in the affirmative, exactly how many such instruments do you own or have available to you in your dental office for regular and routine use in the diagnosis and treatment of dental patients such as the plaintiff in this case?

6b. Is the use of the periodontal probe involved in all examinations of patients such as the plaintiff in this action? If not, with what percentage of your patients would you say you regularly employed the periodontal probe?

7. Would you consider any patient's report of symptoms of irregular spontaneous bleeding from the gum tissues a significant event? If so, is it your practice to record such information on your dental records?

7a. Did the plaintiff in this action ever report a symptom of spontaneous bleeding from the gum tissues to you at any appointment? If so, did you record the reported finding on your records or charts?

8. What is your routine practice in recommending and/or taking periodic dental X-rays for the majority of your patients?

8a. How often and why were dental X-rays taken of the plaintiff in this action?

8b. Did plaintiff ever refuse to have dental radiographs? If so, on what occasions, and what were the reasons for the refusal?

8c. Did you ever provide the patient with detailed information on how the refusal to have X-rays taken would limit your diagnosis? If so, on how many occasions? When were the occasions? Were the discussions of refusal of dental X-rays ever recorded on your dental charts or records?

9. Have you attended a continuing dental education course in the last five years where the sole topic was the diagnosis and/or treatment of periodontal disease? If so, state when such course was given, the name and address of the course sponsor or the instructor, and whether or not such course was eligible for continuing-education credit.

Case Study 2.
Premature Crown and Bridge Failure: Interrogatories

Dr. Swifty performs a large number of full-coverage C & B units in a short period of time to a patient by the name of Mr. Newvo. Shortly after cementation, the units require repeated adjustment, the porcelain peels off, and multiple individual root canal procedures are required (Murphy's Law Accelerated). Dr. Secondhand is faced with a dilemma. He sees gross error in the work and feels that the units cannot be adjusted and repaired. The entire case needs to be redone, even though the work is less than two years old.

1. How long, on the average, does it take to prepare a single posterior tooth for the eventual placement of a porcelain-fused-to-metal crown? If an average time cannot be given, what is the range of time necessary to complete one such preparation on a patient like the plaintiff?
2. How many teeth were prepared on the plaintiff on the date in question?
3. How much time was allotted on the appointment book for the procedures completed that day on the plaintiff?
4. Compute the average time per tooth actually spent for the preparation of the abutment teeth for the crownwork eventually placed in the mouth of the plaintiff on the date in question.
5. How much anesthesia was administered to the plaintiff on the day in question, and where was that information recorded on the dental records maintained on the plaintiff?
6. Did the patient ever complain of any sensitivity or pain during the procedure to prepare his teeth for the crownwork eventually placed in his mouth?
7. Did the plaintiff ever complain of pain or sensitivity in any of the teeth prepared for crownwork that was eventually placed in his mouth *before* the preparation appointment?
8. When and how did the patient bring the symptoms of pain and sensitivity to your attention *after* the preparation appointment? Were all such reported incidences recorded on the dental record you maintain on the plaintiff? If not, why not?
9. Did you have any advance indication that the preparation of the abutment teeth on the plaintiff would lead to the need for endodontic procedures in the future? If so, what were the indications and circumstances surrounding the identification of same?

10. Did you have any discussions with plaintiff *before* you began the preparation of the plaintiff's teeth for the crownwork concerning the possibility or likelihood that one or more of the prepared teeth might or would require endodontic treatment in the future? If so, when were the adverse risks of treatment discussed? Were the discussions recorded on the dental records or chart that you maintained on the plaintiff?

11. Would you say that the average patient with no specific dental training would be aware that tooth preparation for crownwork could lead to nerve damage in that tooth and the possibility of needing root canal therapy in the future?

12. What was the exact composition of the underlying metal used in the crownwork provided to the plaintiff? Identify the brand name of the porcelain system used to finish the case.

13. Name the dental laboratory used to fabricate the crownwork provided to plaintiff and state how many years the lab has been providing custom lab work for your dental office.

14. During the period of time you have been using the dental laboratory identified above, have you ever had occasion to return custom-made fixed work of the kind provided to plaintiff because of defects discovered by you before placing the work in your patient's mouth? If so, on how many occasions?

15. During the period of time you have been in practice, approximately how many different dental prosthetic laboratories have you used for fabricating the kind of crownwork used on plaintiff? Of that group of formerly used dental laboratories, how many did you stop using because of inadequate or poor-quality work?

16. What is the meaning of an "open margin" on a crown of the type and kind used for the plaintiff's crownwork?

17. Did any such open margins exist on the dental work you provided to plaintiff on the dates in question?

18. What is the meaning of the term "overcontoured" when used to describe the shape of crownwork of the type and kind that you supplied to the plaintiff?

19. Did any such overcontouring occur on the crownwork you supplied to the plaintiff on the dates in question?
20. What does the term "inadequate embrasure space" mean to you when used to describe the kind and type of fixed bridgework used on the plaintiff's completed case?
21. Did any such inadequacy occur in the bridgework you supplied to the plaintiff on the dates in question?
22. What does the term "tepee" mean to a dentist when used to describe the final shape of a tooth prepared to receive the kind of dental crown and bridgework that you used on the plaintiff?
23. Did any of your preparations of plaintiff's teeth look like a tepee?
24. How long does the kind and type of bridgework you placed in plaintiff's mouth on the dates in question last, on the average, before needing replacement?

Case Study 3.
Oral Surgery Mishap:
Interrogatories

In this case, assume that Dr. Newon Block performs surgical procedures on both lower third molars. Preoperatively, only the left side is swollen and painful; the right is totally asymptomatic. Assume that shortly after the session, Dr. Block leaves town for the weekend. Upon his return, the patient is in the hospital for airway management and intensive antibiotic care following a facial cellulitis. In addition, the patient suffers lip and tongue paresthesia on the side of the elective surgery.

1. How many fully impacted lower third molar surgical removals have you accomplished in your career?
2. Of the number used in response to question 1 above, how many had a postoperative complication?
3. Name the types and kinds of postoperative complications you have seen and experienced in the provision of oral surgery services in your office during your career.

4. Estimate the number of postoperative infections that have caused additional treatment as the result of surgical removal of lower third molar teeth by you in your office.

5. Do you routinely provide all patients going through the procedures you provided for plaintiff with antibiotics following treatment? If so, how much and how many do you prescribe, how often are patients required to take the medication, and what is the strength of the antibiotic?

6. Did you have a discussion of the possible adverse outcomes of the proposed surgery? If so, when was the discussion held?

7. Did you enter on the records or dental charts that you maintained on the plaintiff the outcome of the discussion of adverse consequences with the plaintiff?

8. Were you aware that the plaintiff was employed full time as a wine taster at the XYZ Winery before the surgical operation that you performed on the date in question?

9. Does the fact that plaintiff relied heavily on taste sensation in her work require any special consideration in terms of the information supplied to obtain the patient's consent to this particular surgical procedure?

10. Have you ever seen or treated a patient with a numb lip or tongue following lower third molar surgery?

11. Did the plaintiff ever complain of pain or swelling in or about the lower left tooth? Did the plaintiff ever complain or report any symptoms of any kind to you concerning the lower right third molar tooth or third molar area?

12. Would you consider the removal of the asymptomatic tooth (lower right third molar) an "elective" procedure?

13. What does the term "elective procedure" mean to you in terms of dental surgical procedures?

14. What are the kinds and types of instructions that you provide to your patients following the extraction of

teeth similar to the procedures you provided to plaintiff on the dates in question?

15. How are such instructions communicated to the patient, and by whom are they usually given?

16. Do you have a recollection, independent of the information that may or may not be on your dental records, that you or someone on your staff gave the plaintiff the postoperative instructions? If so, who gave the instructions and when were they given? What were the contents of the exact instructions?

17. If you have no independent recollection of the exact postoperative instructions given to the plaintiff on the date in question, do your records have an entry describing the postoperative instructions given? If so, exactly where are such instructions recorded?

18. Was any dental radiograph taken of the lower third molar teeth? If so, was there any indication in the dental radiograph that a possibility of postoperative nerve damage existed?

19. While in your care, did the plaintiff ever refuse to have any tests or radiographs done or refuse to follow instructions?

20. While in your care, did plaintiff's behavior force you to compromise treatment, elect a substitute treatment alternative, or alter the agreed-upon treatment plan?

21. Would you describe the plaintiff's behavior as cooperative and compliant?

22. Did plaintiff pay her bill in an expeditious manner?

23. What is your usual policy on patient contact over the evenings, weekends, and holidays?

24. During the weekend in question, were the usual procedures in place to allow for patient contact?

25. Do you have a recollection, independent of the dental records, that you told plaintiff that you would not be available for consultation on the weekend in question?

26. What, if any, system for taking emergency calls from your patients did you have in place over the weekend in question?

Appendix C

Practical Risk Management

To "manage" risk is to bring it under some control. Management techniques differ among dentists, but the objective is the same: bringing order out of chaos.

The "chaos" in this case is the specter of a dental malpractice claim. The best way to control or reduce exposure to these claims is to review all procedures and systems for indications of susceptibility.

The purpose of this appendix is to highlight, in summary form, the areas of dental practice most often attacked successfully by plaintiffs. The information is presented in "update" listings. The dentist is urged and encouraged to take a particular look at two specialty areas, *periodontics* and *oral surgery*, and two procedural areas, *record keeping* and *informed consent*.

If the practitioner can truthfully say that he or she is up to date in each of these areas, the chance of being sued, let alone being sued *successfully*, drops significantly. No accurate improvement figures can be claimed, but removing the listed problems from your practice will stand you in good stead.

Dentists who are on the receiving end of a summons for malpractice are always shocked into retroactive efforts to repair a damaged system or procedure. One can't, of course, go back and change all previous encounters and records, but improving procedures with the next patient is a good start. It's wise to update systems without the prompting of a civil lawsuit.

Update All Patients Periodontally

1. Take and *record findings* of periodontal significance, including pocket depths, on a predetermined survey group of teeth or on all teeth as required.

2. Measure mobility, gingival recession levels, and other signs of disease on suspected teeth, and *record findings*.
3. Update dental X-rays where indicated. Ask patients who have refused in the past to reconsider having them taken. *Record findings* on chart.
4. Make a diagnosis; *record prominently on chart* next to the date.
5. Draft a treatment plan *in writing* on chart.
6. Discuss diagnosis and treatment plan with patient and *record* patient acceptance or rejection (with reasons) *on chart.*
7. Discuss home care instructions and *list elements* presented and/or dispensed *on the record.*

Do the above with all new patients at the initial visit. Do the above with all patients who return on recall and do not have such information in their charts. Update all areas on recall patients who have such information from an earlier time.

If it is your routine to do all or most of the above, but if you do not *record* all the details, form a new habit of spending another two or three minutes on chart management. If it isn't in the chart, the assumption is that it wasn't done!

Update Record Keeping for All Patients

1. Obtain record-keeping forms that allow detailed entry of findings and patient discussions. Use an 8½ × 11 page.
2. Obtain a comprehensive, patient-completed medical history form and update at each appointment.
3. Routinely record *all procedures in detail*. For example, list the brand, strength, and amount of local anesthetic along with the strength of the vasoconstrictor, if any.
4. If you are not already doing so, switch to the ADA-endorsed universal tooth-numbering system.
5. Write or print legibly.
6. Update dental X-ray processing facilities so you can produce consistent, archival-quality X-rays.

The litigation system dotes on dental records. In any malpractice action, the defendant's records are copied and distributed to the plaintiff's lawyer and then to proposed dental experts. The insurance company will receive a copy to distribute to its proposed experts for review. The judge and jury will want to see whether your records substantiate what you say you did.

To stand up to this rigid scrutiny, dental records must be complete and legible. If you want to convey the impression that you are well organized and precise, your records must show it. Well-documented and easy-to-decipher findings, diagnoses, treatment plans, and treatment visits and high-quality X-rays form the basis of a solid malpractice defense.

Update Informed Consent

1. During the discussion of asymptomatic lower third-molar surgery, the practitioner should mention the small chance of lingual or inferior alveolar nerve damage and test the patient's willingness to risk residual numbness (short- and long-term). Either the patient is willing to take the small chance, or he or she is not.

   After the patient has been informed, let him or her consent. Don't be in such a rush that it appears you must have a decision instantly. Try to remember how you feel when you are in an auto showroom and a salesman is pressing for a decision on the deal he has just offered. No one likes to be pressured into accepting a major commitment of money or jeopardy to future comfort, especially in exchange for the removal of an asymptomatic tooth.

   If you use this approach, the patient may ask more questions, such as, "Does the tooth really have to come out?" A complete answer will take a few moments, but it's well worth the time required.

   All third-molar surgical patients should know that a small number of cases end up with a residual numbness of the side of the tongue or a portion of the lip and chin. Dentists can eliminate the most troublesome postoperative surgical complaint by making sure the patient has freely chosen to have the tooth removed and to risk the possibility of paresthesia or anesthesia of the tongue or lip.

2. Add the "alternative" of no treatment to your discussion. When informing patients on treatment needs, be sure to mention as a final point that no treatment is a choice, but that certain risks and consequences may follow.
3. Add the possibility of failure of treatment to your discussion, especially in all complicated treatment areas of endodontics, periodontics, and prosthodontics.

Update Postoperative Instructions

1. Post-op instructions. Dental offices should provide a pattern of instructions for postoperative care. Assume that all patients will have a breakdown or complication, and be prepared for it. Never be out of touch with your patients. Even a few hours in the evening can mean the difference. Make sure patients can contact you or that you have a competent and available standby practitioner available.

2. Complications. When alerted to a postoperative problem, put other cases or commitments aside and deal positively and aggressively with the problem. In cases of post-op infections, don't be afraid to consult an oral surgeon or an infectious-disease physician if standard routines do not produce immediate results. Assume that the antibiotic is ineffective in terms of strength or type if as few as 24 hours have passed with no relief. Be aggressive in this situation; call the patient back into the office to obtain clinical readings (body temperature, observation of surgical site, palpation of associated tissue areas). Then make alterations in treatment and make positive arrangements to call or be called (by the patient) with any changes in condition. Don't send a patient out into the night with a casual remark like, "Well, that ought to do it!"

Even if you practice in a large metropolitan community and you know that the patient could easily contact one of a hundred or so emergency specialists in a minute, don't forget the patient has put his or her confidence and trust in you. Patients are notoriously loyal, and will allow conditions to grow worse because they don't want to bother you or because they trust that your regimen will eventually overcome the problem.

3. *Breakage.* If the tooth or the jaw breaks during a surgical procedure, the standard of care is to inform the patient and then either provide the treatment necessary to correct the problem or refer the patient to an oral surgeon for care. Sooner or later, you will have to deal with the question of who is responsible for such follow-up care. Who should pay for the extra treatment? In the case where the possibility of breakage was explained to the patient *in advance*, there is no question that the patient must stand the financial responsibility.

Sometimes incomplete information is given at the outset, either because of negligence or with studied attention to the extremely small number of times such events have occurred in the past. Either approach is dangerous. It is safer either to mention the possibilities of real injury or to take the responsibility for the cost of follow-up care.

4. *Payment not an admission.* The act of paying for the services of an oral surgeon to treat a complication should not be taken as an admission of guilt. Most jurisdictions will not allow a jury to hear that you paid for follow-up care after an accident. The American system of law encourages parties to settle disputes among themselves, and a payment for follow-up care is a form of settlement. The court will not permit a plaintiff to sue and use your payment as an admission against your best interest, unless you made separate statements admitting negligence.

Glossary

This glossary presents definitions of a few of the more common legal terms used in dental malpractice cases.

Abandonment: giving up one's right or claim to property without any future intent to regain title or possession. In malpractice claims, failure by a practitioner to provide needed treatment to a patient. A dentist who refuses to see a patient in midtreatment may be charged with *abandonment*.

Action: a proceeding in a court of law where one party prosecutes another for the enforcement or protection of a right and/or the redress or prevention of a wrong. Any patient who feels that he or she has suffered an injury caused by the conduct of the dentist is said to have a *cause of action* against the dentist.

Admissions against interest: voluntary statements by a party or someone identified with him or her in legal interest, of the existence of a fact which is relevant to the opponent's cause. If an accident occurs in a dental office and the dentist or an employee states that the incident happened because of the fault of the dentist or an employee, such a statement is an *admission against interest*, which may be used against the party in court.

Assault: any unjustifiable act causing a well-founded apprehension of immediate peril from a force already partially or fully set in motion.

Battery: any unlawful touching or other wrongful physical force or constraint inflicted on a human being without his or her consent. The extraction of a tooth other than one already discussed with the patient constitutes a *battery* against the patient.

Breach of contract: the failure, without legal excuse, to perform any promise which forms part or all of a contract. The dentist-patient relationship is contractual. Failure of the patient to pay a reasonable fee for services provided is a *breach of contract.*

Breach of duty: in a general sense, any violation or omission of a legal or moral duty. When a dentist fails to live up to the standard of care of the profession, a claim for *breach of duty* may be brought.

Claims made: a professional liability insurance contract whereby the insurer agrees to protect the policyholder from all claims presented during the premium year only. A separate policy (tail) must be purchased to protect the policyholder from claims for acts or omissions of the premium year that are presented in future years.

Complaint: a formal written request for a certain thing to be done. The *complaint* is the first document to be transmitted to the court and the defendant in a dental malpractice litigation. (*See also* **petition**.)

Consent: voluntary agreement by a person in the possession and exercise of sufficient mentality to make an intelligent choice to do something proposed by another. A patient who *consents* to a particular action may not later assert that such action was negligent.

Contract: deliberate agreement between two or more persons to do or refrain from doing a particular lawful thing. The only thing a dentist contracts to do for the patient is to use the skill and learning of a reasonably prudent dentist in return for a reasonable fee for the service.

Contribution: the sharing of a loss or payment among several parties. The act of any one or several of a number of co-debtors in reimbursing one of their number who has paid the whole debt or suffered the whole liability. After a dental malpractice judgment has been awarded to a plaintiff, the insurance company for one of several dentists adjudged negligent will pay the total amount and then collect *contributions* from the carriers for the other defendants.

Contributory negligence: an act or omission on the part of a person, amounting to failure to observe principles of ordinary care. In dentistry, the patient who fails to return to the dentist for requested postoperative care is demonstrating *contributory negligence.*

Damages: a sum of money assessed by a jury on finding for the plaintiff or successful party in an action as a compensation for the injury done him or her by the opposite party. Every person who suffers detriment from the unlawful act or omission of another may recover from the person in fault a compensation in monetary terms. The plaintiff must translate his or her injury into monetary *damages.*

Defendant: the party being sued. The typical dental malpractice action is brought by the plaintiff (former patient) against the *defendant* (dentist).

Deposition: a method of pretrial discovery which consists of a statement of a witness under oath, taken in question-and-answer form as it would be in court, with the adversary present. The entire session is transcribed for later use. Lawyers like to have a *deposition* transcript from each witness before going to trial.

Duty of care: (*also* **standard of care**) The legal duty of the dentist who must possess and exercise that degree of skill and care which would be exhibited by the other prudent dentists in the community. A plaintiff in a dental malpractice case must assert that the dentist failed to provide a *duty of care* and that the failure to do so caused an injury to the plaintiff.

Expert witness: a person possessing special or peculiar training or knowledge acquired from practical experience, who is qualified to testify in court as to the standard of care in the professional field he or she represents. An *expert witness* in a dental malpractice case will explain to the judge and/or jury the standard dental procedures as they relate to the allegations in the case. Experts, but not fact witnesses, may offer opinions on the ultimate issue of negligence.

Indemnity: a collateral contract or assurance by which one person agrees to hold harmless another person for any anticipated loss or to prevent him or her from being damaged by the legal consequences of an act or forbearance on the part of one of the parties or some third person. Thus, dental malpractice insurance is a contract of *indemnity*. The term is also used to denote a compensation given to make the person whole from a loss already sustained.

Injury: a legal loss which a person suffers and alleges to have been caused by the negligence of another. A plaintiff must demonstrate an *injury* caused by the negligence of the dentist.

Interrogatories: formal questions concerning the lawsuit, which must be answered truthfully and under oath.

Joint and several liability: a condition in which liability is shared among a group of defendants collectively and individually. Partners are *jointly and severally* liable for the negligence of either partner in the course of doing business.

Judgment: the final determination by a court of competent jurisdiction, of the rights of the parties in an action or proceeding. When a judge or jury reaches a final verdict in a dental malpractice case, a *judgment* is rendered.

Malpractice: any professional misconduct or unreasonable lack of skill in professional duties. The public recognizes the term *malpractice* when an action for professional negligence is brought against a member of the health-care professions.

Master-servant: *See* **principal and agent**

Mitigation of damages: a duty to minimize damages even though the injury was caused by the negligence of another. A patient must *mitigate* his or her damages by immediately seeking further dental care to prevent further deterioration of the dental condition.

Negligence: the failure to do something which a reasonable man, guided by those conditions or considerations which ordinarily regulate human affairs, would do; the doing of something which a reasonable and prudent man would not do. Many dental incidents can give rise to a claim of professional *negligence*.

Occurrence: a professional liability insurance contract whereby the insurer agrees to protect the policyholder from claims arising from acts or omissions committed in the premium year, no matter when the claim is eventually presented.

Petition: *See* **Complaint**

Plaintiff or claimant: the person asserting a cause of action and instituting a lawsuit. The patient may file a suit in which he or she is identified as the *plaintiff*.

Precedent: a previously decided case which is recognized as authority for the disposition of future cases. (*See* **stare decisis.**)

Principal and agent: a relationship in which one person performs services for another. The performing person (agent) works under the direct control of the other (principal). The dental hygienist is the *agent* of the dentist while performing duties related to employment.

Proximate cause: a cause which in natural and continuous sequence, unbroken by any new independent cause, produces an event, and without which the injury would not have occurred. In a dental malpractice case, personal and professional liability is generally limited to results *proximately caused* by the dentist's conduct.

Reasonable care: the degree of care which the reasonable dentist would exercise under the circumstances. The dentist's defense in a malpractice case is that the dentist acted with *reasonable care.*

Res Ipsa Loquitur: literally, "the thing speaks for itself." A legal doctrine applied when the injury was caused by an instrument under the exclusive control of one person and which would not cause injury unless the person was negligent. No expert need testify, as the jury can see the obvious injury; for example, when a patient awakens from an appendectomy and discovers a broken arm. The injured plaintiff would argue that the staff injured the patient under anesthesia, invoking *res ipsa loquitur* without the aid of a surgeon testifying to the standard of care for appendectomies.

Res judicata: a matter that is finally determined by a court, and which therefore may not be retried by that court or any other court on the same facts arising out of the same events. Once a judgment has been rendered in a dental malpractice action for the defendant dentist, the plaintiff may not file another malpractice suit arising out of the dentist's care, as he or she is foreclosed by *res judicata.*

Respondeat Superior: literally, "let the superior reply." The legal doctrine that holds the employer liable for the acts of the employee while the employee is carrying out the business of the employer. If the dental assistant is running an errand for the dentist during lunch hour and causes an automobile accident, the dentist may be held liable for the injuries under the theory of *respondeat superior.*

Standard of Care: (See **Duty of care***).*

Stare Decisis: literally, "to stand by that which was decided." Courts will not interfere with established principles from earlier legal decisions unless good cause is shown. (*See* **precedent.**)

Statute of Limitations: the state law that sets forth a time limit in which a legal action must be commenced before the right to bring the action is lost. Filing a dental malpractice case after a set number of years may be a violation of the *statute of limitations*.

Subpoena: a writ issued under authority of court to compel the appearance of a witness. A dentist may receive a *subpoena* to appear in a dental malpractice case involving one of his or her patients. (A subpoena *duces tecum* means that the dentist witness must appear and bring all papers and records pertaining to that patient.)

Summons: a document requiring the defendant to answer the pleadings and to appear in court under penalty of having a judgment entered against him or her. The complaint in a dental malpractice case will be accompanied by a *summons*.

Tort: the legal wrong committed upon the person or property of another, independent of any contract between the two parties. The subject matter of professional negligence (malpractice) can be found in the law of *torts*.

Index

Index to Legal Cases Cited

Index to Legal Cases Cited by Dental Specialty

Endodontics
_____ v. _____, Fredricksburg Circuit Ct. Va., August 22, 1985.

La Roche v. U.S., 730 F2d 538 (S.D., March 23, 1984).

Battcher v. Anton, New York, Nassau County Supreme Court, Index No. 22236-80, Oct. 29, 1982.

Kline v. Bromboz, U.S. District Ct., N.D. Cal., No. C83 3369 TEH, June 1, 1984.

Pierce v. Long, Colorado, Denver County District Court, No. 83CV2023, Nov. 3, 1983.

Schwartz v. Robson, Idaho, Kootenai County District Court, No. 40320, Mar. 1, 1985.

Simpson v. Davis, 549 P2d 950 (Kan. 1976).

Sprowl v. Ward 441 So.2d 898 (Ala., 1983).

LaRouche v. U.S. 730 F2d 538 (8th Cir. 1984).

Fixed Prosthodontics
Goodman v. Tesher, 17 ATLA News L. (Fla. 1974).

General Anesthesia
O'Keefe v. Boca Raton Community Hospital, 16 ATLA News L. 170 (Fla., 1973).

Lake v. St. Lukes Hospital, St. Louis City Cir., Ct., No 792-3656, Jan. 22, 1982.

McKinley v. Vize, 563 SW2d 505 (Mo., 1978).

Goodman v. Howard University Hospital, D.C. Superior Ct., No 11285-76, May 22, 1978.

Pittman V. Beauchamp, Cal., Los Angeles County Superior Court, No. SOC 35227, March 28, 1978.

Lord v. Harcon, 133 d District Court 987, 929 Harrison County, Texas, June 29, 1977.

Colter v. _____ , Phoenix, Arizona, 20 ATLA L. Rep. 274 August, 1977.

General Practice

Bryan v. Griffith, Mont. Cty. Cir. Ct. Law #65633 (Md., 1984).

Foster v. Harris, 633 SW2nd 304 (Tenn., 1982).

Verre v. Allen, 334 SE2d 350 (Ga., 1985).

Helms v. Curry, No NCC11713 Los Angeles, Ca., Aug., 1980.

Baker v. Titus 458 A2d 1125, (Vt., 1983).

General Practice/Occlusion

Coleman v. Middlestaff, 305 P2d 1020 (Calif., 1957).

Sullivan v. Russell 417 Mich., 398, 338 N.W.2nd 181, (Mich., 1983).

General Practice/Operative

Wellman v. Drake 43 SW2d 777 (W.V., 1947).

Vincent v. Vanker, No. 80-199-458 Oakland City, Michigan, June 1982.

Petrizzo v. Olsen, No 78 Civ 3625 US Dist Ct., S.D.N.Y., June 1979.

Implant

Cirafici v. Goffen 407 NE2d 633 (Ill., 1980).

Local Anesthesia

Barreto v. Justen, Cal., Santa Barbara Superior Court, No. SM 15783, Oct. 27, 1978.

LeBeuf v. Atkins 594 P2d 923 (Wash., 1979)

Stanton v. Astra Pharmaceutical, 718 F2d 553 (C.A. 3, Pa., 1983).

LaRocque v. LaMarche, 292 A2d 259, (Vt. 1972).

Operative Dentistry

Alonzo v. Rogers 283 P 709 (Wash., 1930).

Ellering v. Gross 248 NW 330 (Minn., 1933).

Oral Surgery

_____ v. Harris, New London Sup. Ct. No. 8000627835 (Conn., 1983).

Keating v. Perkins 293 NY Supp 197 (NY, 1937).

McClarry v. Group Health Hospital, Wash., King County Superior Ct., No. 82-2-12516-4, Mar., 1985.

Engstrom v. Friedman, N.Y., Nassau County Supreme Ct. No. 4725/81, May, 1984.

Rajewsky v. Thomson, Cal., Los Angeles Superior Ct., No. C-324, 047, Oct. 9, 1984.

Lorrumbide v. Doctors Hospital, Tex., Dallas County, 191st Judicial Circuit No. 81-5216-J, Nov., 1984.

Nickels v. Lewis, Cal., Napa Valley Superior Ct., Npo. 41267, Oct. 13, 1983.

Pascarella v. Wagner, New York, Erie County Supreme Ct., No. 83-812, Nov. 30, 1983.

Haeri v. Foote, Cal., Orange County Supreme Ct., No. 34-85-68, Dec., 1983.

Brian v. Kopecky, Tex., Dallas County 14th Judicial District Ct., N. 79-10851-A, June 11, 1982.

Lloyd v. Wood-Smith, US District Ct., SDNY No. 80 CIV 3896, Nov., 1981.

Varner v. Hall, Cal., Sacramento County Superior Ct. No. 278756, Mar. 30, 1981.

Snow v. Yavner, Mass., Middlesex Cty Sup. Ct., No. 75-1863, October 6, 1981.

Speed v. State of Iowa, 240 NW2d 901 (Iowa, 1976).

Butts v. Watts 290 SW2d 57 (Ky., 1956).

Pederson v. Dumouchel 431 P2d 973 (Wash., 1967).

Berardi v. Menicks 164 NE2d 544 (Mass., 1960).

Bulman v. Myers 467 A2d 1353 (Pa., 1983).

Gemme v. Tomlin 455 NE2d 294 (Ill., 1983).

Pittman v. Hodges 462 So2d 330 (Miss., 1980).

Tanner v. Sanders 56 SW2d 718 (Ky., 1933).

Chubb v. Holmes 150 A 516 (Conn., 1930).

Welch v. Page 154 NE 24 (Ind., 1926).

Orthodontics/Oral Surgery
Llera v. Wisner, et al., 557 P2d 805 (Mont., 1976).

Orthodontics
Gurdin v. Dongieux 468 So.2d 1241 (La App. 4 Cir. 1985).

Periodontics
Costa v. Storm 682 SW2d 599 (Tex. Ct of App., Oct. 18, 1984).

Costillo v. Domenech, Fla., Dade County Circuit Ct. No. 83-24116, Jan. 26, 1884.

Brantley v. Hall, N.C., Wake County Superior Court, No. 80CVS 2915, May 15, 1981.

Helms v. Curry, Cal., Los Angeles County Superior Court, No. Nc-C-11713, Aug. 20, 1980.

McSheffrey v. Stage, Fla., Duval County Court No. 78-6611-CA, Feb. 23, 1979.

Zaryczny v. Brimker 77 Civ 3963 (WCC) USDC SDNY, 1979.

Masi v. Seale 682 P2d 102 (Idaho, 1984).

Schneider v. Brunk 324 SE2d 922 (NS App. 1985).

Prosthodontics
Burns v. Wannamaker, 315 SE2d 179 (SC, 1984).

Carpenter v. Moore, 322 P2d 125 (Wash., 1958).

_____ v. Sterling Dental Centers, Md. Health Claims Arbitration, 1985.

Dimoff v. Maitre 432 So.2d 1225 (Ala. 1983).

Baker v. Scott 447 So. 2d 529 (La. 1984).

TMJ
White v. Dan, St. Louis, Missouri, 1984.

Weisshaar v. Whiston, 31st Judicial Court of Virginia Review Panel, August 1984.

Boknecht v. Ladd, Allen Superior Court (IN) No. 5-84-1175, 1984.

Pesavento v. Golden, Mich., Oakland Cty Cir. Ct. No. 83 270107 NM, Jan 17, 1985.

Schlesinger v. Maza, Mich., Oakland County Cir. Ct., No. 82 240231 NM, June 6, 1983.

Short v. Kincaid, Colo. App. 685 P2d 210 1983.

Unknown or Medical Negligence

Sneath v. P&S Hospital 431 P2d 835 (Or., 1967).

Carrasco v. Goatcher 623 SW2d 769 (Tex., 1981).

Vanderdoes v. Ochsner, 377 So2d 1368 (La., 1979).

Interstate Fire v. Pacific Indemnity, 586 F. Supp 633 (D.Md. 1983).

Trede v. Family Dental Centre 708 P2d 116 (Ariz., 1985).

Sutlive v. Hackney, 297 SE2d 515 (Ga., 1982).

Nelson v. Gaunt, 178 Cal Rptr 167 (1981).

Jones v. U.S., 207 F2d 563 (Ca., 1953).

Krestich v. Stefanez 9 NW2d 130 (Wis., 1943).

McCartney v. Badovinac, 190 P 190 (Co., 1916).

Guilmet v. Campbell, 188 NW2d 601 (Mich., 1971).

Hawkins v. McGee, 146 S2d 641 (N.H., 1929).

Fla., Patient's Compensation Fund v. Tillman 435 So2d 1316, (Fla., 1984).

Francis v. Hopper Newport County Superior Court, No. C.A. 75-154, Oct. 13, 1978 (R.I.).

Barnes v. Bovenmeyer 122 NW2d 312 (Iowa, 1963).

Ketsetos v. Nolan 368 A2d 172 (Conn., 1976).

O'Neill v. Montefiore Hospital 202 NYS2d 436 (N.Y., 1960).

Gates v. Jensen 594 P2d 919 (Wash., 1979).

Canterbury v. Spence 464 F2d 354 (D.C., Cir., 1972).

Haley v. U.S., 739 F2d 1502 (1984).

Rehill v. Goodman, Norfolk Cty Superior Ct. No 115125 (Mass., 1978).

May v. Moore, 424 So2d 596 (Ala., 1982).

Application of Polly P., 399 NYS2d 584 (N.Y., 1977).

In re Culbertson's Will, 292 NYS2d 806 (N.Y., 1968).

McGarry v. Mercier, 262 NW 296 (Mich., 1935).

Foster v. Harris 633 SW 2d 304 (Tenn., 1982).

Strong v. Pontiac Hospital 323 NW2d 629 (Mich., 1982)

Shane v. Mouw 323 N.W. 2d 537 (Mich., 1982).

Index to Legal Cases Cited by State

Alabama

Dimoff v. Maitre 432 So. 2d 1225 (Ala., 1983).

Sprowl v. Ward 441 So. 2d 898 (Ala., 1983).

May v. Moore, 424 So2d 596 (Ala., 1982).

Trede v. Family Dental Centre 708 P2d 116 (Ariz., 1985).

Colter v. _____, Phoenix, Arizona, 20 ATLA L. Rep. 274 August, 1977.

California

Nelson v. Gaunt, 178 Cal Rptr 167 (1981).

Helms v. Curry, No NCC11713 Los Angeles (Ca. Aug., 1980).

Jones v. U.S., 207 F2d 563 (Ca., 1953).

Rajewsky v. Thomson, Cal., Los Angeles Superior Ct., No. C-324, 047, Oct. 9, 1984.

Nickels v. Lewis, Cal., Napa Valley Superior Ct., Npo. 41267, Oct. 13, 1983.

Haeri v. Foote, Cal., Orange County Supreme Ct., No. 34-85-68, Dec., 1983.

Varner v. Hall, Cal., Sacramento County Superior Ct. No. 278756, Mar. 30, 1981.

Pittman v. Beauchamp, Cal., Los Angeles County Superior Court, No. SOC 35227, March 28, 1978.

Barreto v. Justen, Cal., Santa Barbara Superior Court, No. SM 15783, Oct. 27, 1978.

Kline v. Bromboz, U.S. District Ct., N.D. Cal., No. C83 3369 TEH, June 1, 1984.

Helms v. Curry, Cal., Los Angeles County Superior Court, No. Nc-C-11713, Aug. 20, 1980.

Coleman v. Middlestaff 305 P2d 1020 (Calif., 1957).

Colorado

McCartney v. Badovinac, 190 P 190 (Co., 1916).

Short v. Kincaid, Colo. App. 685 P2d 210 1983.

Pierce v. Long, Colorado, Denver County District Court, No. 83CV2023, Nov. 3, 1983.

Connecticut

_____ v. Harris, New London Sup Ct. No. 8000627835 (Conn., 1983).

Ketsetos v. Nolan 368 A2d 172 (Conn., 1976).

Chubb v. Holmes 150 A 516 (Conn., 1930).

District of Columbia

Goodman v. Howard University Hospital, D.C. Superior Ct., No 11285-76, May 22, 1978

Canterbury v. Spence 464 F2d 354 (D.C., Cir., 1972).

Florida

Goodman v. Tesher, 17 ATLA News L. (Fla., 1974).

O'Keefe v. Boca Raton Community Hospital, 16 ATLA News L. 170 (Fla., 1973).

Costillo v. Domenech, Fla., Dade County Circuit Ct. No. 83-24116, Jan. 26, 1884.

McSheffrey v. Stage, Fla., Duval County Court No. 78-6611-CA, Feb., 23, 1979.

Fla., Patient's Compensation Fund v. Tillman 435 So2d 1316, (Fla., 1984).

Georgia

Verre v. Allen, 334 Se2d 350 (Ga., 1985).

Sutlive v. Hackney, 297 Se2d 515 (Ga., 1982).

Idaho

Schwartz v. Robson, Idaho, Kootenai County District Court, No. 40320, Mar. 1, 1985.

Masi v. Seale 682 P2d 102 (Idaho, 1984).

Illinois

Cirafici v. Goffen 407 NE2d 633 (Ill., 1980).

Gemme v. Tomlin 455 NE2d 294 (Ill., 1983).

Indiana

Boknecht v. Ladd, Allen Superior Court (IN) No. 5-84-1175, 1984.

Welch v. Page 154 NE 24 (Ind., 1926).

Iowa

Speed v. State of Iowa, 240 NW2d 901 (Iowa, 1976).

Barnes v. Bovenmeyer 122 NW2d 312 (Iowa, 1963).

Kansas

Simpson v. Davis, 549 P2d 950 (Kan., 1976).

Kentucky

Butts v. Watts 290 SW2d 57 (Ky., 1956).

Tanner v. Sanders 56 SW2d 718 (Ky., 1933).

Louisiana

Vanderdoes v. Ochsner, 377 So2d 1368, (La., 1979).

Baker v. Scott 447 So.2d 529 (La., 1984).

Gurdin v. Dongieux 468 So.2d 1241 (La App. 4 Cir. 1985).

Maryland

Interstate Fire v. Pacific Indemnity, 586 F. Supp 633 (D. Md., 1983).

_____ v. Sterling Dental Centers, Md. Health Claims Arbitration, 1985.

Bryan v. Griffith, Mont. Cty. Cir. Ct. Law #65633 (Md., 1984).

Massachusetts

Snow v. Yavner, Mass., Middlesex Cty Sup. Ct., No. 75-1863, October, 6, 1981.

Berardi v. Menicks 164 NE2d 544 (Mass., 1960).

Rehill v. Goodman, Norfolk Cty Superior Ct. No 115125 (Mass., 1978).

Michigan

Guilmet v. Campbell, 188 NW2d 601 (Mich., 1971).

Pesavento v. Golden, Mich., Oakland Cty Cir. Ct. No. 83 270107 NM, Jan 17, 1985.

Schlesinger v. Maza, Mich., Oakland County Cir. Ct., No. 82 240231 NM, June 6, 1983.

Sullivan v. Russell 417 Mich., 398, 338 N.W.2d 181, (Mich., 1983).

Vincent v. Vanker, No 80-199-458 Oakland City, Michigan, June 1982.

McGarry v. Mercier, 262 NW 296 (Mich., 1935).

Strong v. Pontiac Hospital 323 NW2d 629 (Mich., 1982).

Shane v. Mouw 323 N.W.2d 537 (Mich., 1982).

Minnesota

Ellering v. Gross 248 NW 330 (Minn., 1933).

Mississippi

Pittman v. Hodges 462 So2d 330 (Miss., 1980).

Missouri

Lake v. St. Lukes Hospital, St. Louis City Cir., Ct., No 792-3656, Jan. 22, 1982.

McKinley v. Vize, 563 SW2d 505 (Mo., 1978).

White v. Dan, St. Louis, Missouri, 1984.

Montana

Llera v. Wisner, et al., 557 P2d 805 (Mont., 1976).

New Hampshire

Hawkins v. McGee, 146 A2d 641 (N.H., 1929).

New York

Keating v. Perkins 293 NY Supp 197 (NY, 1937).

Engstrom v. Friedman, N.Y., Nassau County Supreme Ct. No. 4725/81, May, 1984.

Pascarella v. Wagner, New York, Erie County Supreme Ct., No. 83-812, Nov. 30, 1983.

Lloyd v. Wood-Smith, US District Ct., SDNY Co. 80 CIV 3896, Nov., 1981.

Battcher v. Anton, New York, Nassau County Supreme Court, Index No. 22236-80, Oct. 29, 1982.

Zaryczny v. Brimker 77 Civ 3963 (WCC) USDC SDNY, 1979.

O'Neill v. Montefiore Hospital 202 NYS2d 436 (NY, 1960).

Lord v. Harcon, 133 d District Court 987, 929 Harrison County, Texas, June 29, 1977.

Costa v. Storm 682 SW2d 599 (Tex. Ct of App., Oct. 18, 1984).

United States

LaRouche v. U.S. 730 F2d 538 (8th Cir. 1984).

Unknown

Haley v. U.S., 739 F2d 1502 (1984).

Vermont

LaRocque v. LaMarche, 292 A2d 259, (Vt., 1972).

Baker v. Titus 458 A2d 1125, (Vt., 1983).

Virginia

Weisshaar v. Whiston, 31st Judicial Court of Virginia Review Panel, August 1984.

_____ v. _____, Fredricksburg Circuit Ct. Va., August 22, 1985.

Washington

Carpenter v. Moore, 322 P2d 125 (Wash., 1958).

McClarry v. Group Health Hospital, Wash., King County Superior Ct., No. 82-2-12516-4, Mar., 1985.

LeBeuf v. Atkins 594 P2d 923 (Wash., 1979).

Pederson v. Dumouchel 431 P2d 973 (Wash., 1967).

Gates v. Jensen 594 P2d 919 (Wash., 1979).

Alonzo v. Rogers 283 P 709 (Wash., 1930).

West Virginia

Wellman v. Drake 43 SE2d 777 (W. Va., 1947).

Wisconsin

Krestich v. Stefanez 9 NW2d 130 (Wis., 1943).

Index to Legal Cases Cited by Year

Simpson v. Davis, 549 P2d 950 (Kan., 1976).

Llera v. Wisner, et al., 557 P2d 805 (Mont., 1976).

Ketsetos v. Nolan 368 A2d 172 (Conn., 1976).

Lord v. Harcon, 133 d District Court 987, 929 Harrison County, Texas, June 29, 1977.

Colter v. _____, Phoenix, Arizona, 20 ATLA L. Rep. 274 August, 1977.

Application of Polly P., 399 NYS2d 584 (NY, 1977).

McKinley v. Vize, 563 SW2d 505 (Mo., 1978).

Goodman v. Howard University Hospital, D.C. Superior Ct., No 11285-76, May 22, 1978.

Pittman v. Beauchamp, Cal., Los Angeles County Superior Court, No. SOC 35227, March 28, 1978.

Barreto v. Justen, Cal., Santa Barbara Superior Court, No. SM 15783, Oct. 27, 1978.

Francis v. Hopper Newport County Superior Court, No. C.A. 75-154, Oct. 13, 1978 (R.I.)

Rehill v. Goodman, Norfolk Cty Superior Ct. No 115125 (Mass., 1978).

Vanderdoes v. Ochsner, 377 So2d 1368 (La., 1979).

LeBeuf v. Atkins 594 P2d 923 (Wash., 1979).

McSheffrey v. Stage, Fla., Duval County Court No. 78-6611-CA, Feb., 23, 1979.

Zaryczny v. Brimker 77 Civ 3963 (WCC) USDC SDNY, 1979.

Gates v. Jensen 594 P2d 919 (Wash., 1979).

Petrizzo v. Olsen, No 78 Civ 3625 US Dist Ct., S.D.N.Y., June, 1979.

Helms v. Curry, No NCC11713 Los Angeles, Ca., Aug., 1980.

Cirafici v. Goffen 407 NE2d 633 (Ill., 1980).

Helms v. Curry, Cal., Los Angeles County Superior Court, No. Nc-C-11713, Aug. 20, 1980.

Pittman v. Hodges 462 So2d 330 (Miss., 1980).

Carrasco v. Goatcher 623 SW2d 769 (Tex., 1981).

Nelson v. Gaunt, 178 Cal Rptr 167 (1981).

Lloyd v. Wood-Smith, US District Ct., SDNY No. 80 CIV 3896, Nov., 1981.

Varner v. Hall, Cal., Sacramento County Superior Ct. No. 278756, Mar. 30, 1981.

Snow v. Yavner, Mass., Middlesex Cty Sup. Ct., No. 75-1863, October 6, 1981.

Burns v. Wannamaker, 315 SE2d179 (SC, 1984).

Engstrom v. Friedman, N.Y., Nassau County Supreme Ct. No. 4725/81, May, 1984.

Rajewsky v. Thomson, Cal., Los Angeles Superior Ct., No. C-324, 047, Oct. 9, 1984.

Lorrumbide v. Doctors Hospital, Tex., Dallas County, 191st Judicial Circuit No. 81-5216-J, Nov., 1984.

White v. Dan, St. Louis, Missouri, 1984.

Weisshaar v. Whiston, 31st Judicial Court of Virginia Review Panel, August, 1984.

Boknecht v. Ladd, Allen Superior Court (IN) No. 5-84-1175, 1984.

La Roche v. U.S., 730 F2d 538 (S.D., March 23, 1984).

Kline v. Bromboz, U.S. District Ct., N.D. Cal., No. C83 3369 TEH, June 1, 1984.

Baker v. Scott 447 So.2d 529 (La., 1984).

Costa v. Storm 682 SW2d 599 (Tex., Ct of App., Oct. 18, 1984).

Costillo v. Domenech, Fla., Dade County Circuit Ct. No. 83-24116, Jan. 26, 1884.

Fla., Patient's Compensation Fund v. Tillman 435 So2d 1316, (Fla., 1984).

Bryan v. Griffith, Mont. Cty. Cir. Ct. Law #65633 (Md., 1984).

Haley v. U.S., 739 F2d 1502 (1984).

Masi v. Seale 682 P2d 102 (Idaho 1984).

LaRouche v. U.S. 730 F2d 538 (8th Cir. 1984).

Verre v. Allen, 334 SE2d 350 (Ga., 1985).

Trede v. Family Dental Centre 708 P2d 116 (Ariz., 1985).

McClarry v. Group Health Hospital, Wash., King County Superior Ct., No. 82-2-12516-4, Mar., 1985.

Pesavento v. Golden, Mich., Oakland Cty Cir. Ct. No. 83 270107 NM, Jan 17, 1985.

_____ v. _____, Fredricksburg Circuit Ct. Va., August 22, 1985.

Schwartz v. Robson, Idaho, Kootenai County District Court, No. 40320, Mar. 1, 1985.

_____ v. Sterling Dental Centers, Md. Health Claims Arbitration, 1985.

Schneider v Brunk 324 SE2d 922 (NC App., 1985).

Gurdin v. Dongieux 468 So.2d 1241 (La App. 4 Cir., 1985).